The Journey
from the Center
to the Page

The Journey from the Center to the Page

Yoga Philosophies & Practices as Muse for Authentic Writing

Jeff Davis

GOTHAM BOOKS

PUBLISHERS NOTE: This book is not an instructional yoga book, but a series of suggestions concerning how yoga philosophies, principles, and practices can deepen writers' understanding of and experience of their writing process, writing style, and writing life. Any questions as to whether or not to proceed with particular poses or practices as well as any medical questions regarding contraindications should be referred either to a holistic health professional or to a qualified yoga teacher.

GOTHAM BOOKS
Published by Penguin Group (USA) Inc.
375 Hudson Street, New York, New York 10014, U.S.A.
Penguin Books Ltd, Registered Offices: 80 Strand, London WC2R 0RL, England
Penguin Books Australia Ltd, 250 Camberwell Road, Camberwell,
Victoria 3124, Australia
Penguin Books Canada Ltd, 10 Alcorn Avenue, Toronto, Ontario, Canada M4V 3B2
Penguin Books (NZ) Ltd, Cnr Rosedale and Airborne Roads, Albany,
Auckland 1310, New Zealand

Published by Gotham Books, a division of Penguin Group (USA) Inc.

First printing, June 2004
10   9   8   7   6   5   4   3   2   1

Grateful acknowledgment is made for permission to reprint the following:

Excerpt from "That Lean and Hungry Look" by Suzanne Britt, *Newsweek*,
October 9, 1978, reprinted by permission of the author

Excerpt from "Morning Swim" by Maxine Kumin, copyright © 1965 by Maxine Kumin,
from *Selected Poems 1960–1990* by Maxine Kumin. Used by permission of
W. W. Norton & Company, Inc.

Gotham Books and the skyscraper logo are trademarks of Penguin Group (USA) Inc.

LIBRARY OF CONGRESS CATALOGING-IN-PUBLICATION DATA
has been applied for.

ISBN: 1-592-40068-X

Printed in the United States of America
Set in Goudy • Designed by Sabrina Bowers

This book is printed on acid-free paper. ∞

for my mother and father, Sharlette and Jimmy;
for my generous yoga teachers, most notably
Michele Andrie and the teachers of Krishnamacharya
Yoga Mandiram; for my generous writing teachers,
Charles Bambach and David Wevill;
and
for Cory,
my first yoga teacher and
my beloved muse

Contents

Contents

Introduction:
Remember Your Body

This book takes as its premise something simple yet potentially transformational: Yoga's philosophical principles and myriad skillful tools (*upaya*) can help you as a creative writer deepen your writing practice, become more versatile in your writing process, and enrich your writing style. My journey as a writer, as well as my ongoing work with thousands of writers and students, have led me to discover that a wellspring for our creative writing is as close as our nose. Our breath and body—these in part can be the muses that help us learn to navigate our fluttering minds, our tricky imagination, and our unpredictable hearts as we write (and rewrite).

For the nonyogis reading this book, keep reading. If the focus on yoga intimidates as much as intrigues you, maybe it's because you imagine svelte yogis sweating and twisting their bodies into impossible shapes. You need not worry, though, if your day's most physical act has been to walk to the corner shop for coffee and a bagel. Don't sweat. Really. Although sweating does loosen ligaments and prepare muscles for physically intense yoga sessions, your torso need not drop buckets of water to derive yoga's benefits for authentic writing. As this book will show you, being able to twist your imagination with a flexible spirit is more important for authentic writing than being able to secure your foot behind your head.

"Don't accept anything the speaker is saying. Test it out for yourself," the twentieth-century Indian philosopher J. Krishnamurti frequently said. This skeptical inquiry and this thrust of testing out things define the essential mindset for practicing yoga. Part of what distinguishes yoga from forms of exercise as well as from many other spiritual disciplines is its all-encompassing tools to understand *through the body's experience* how body, mind, and other faculties relate. For had someone approached me fifteen years ago and told me that yoga would profoundly alter my understanding of how my body, mind, and imagination cooperate with my writing process and style, I would have raised my eyebrow. So be ready to test things out. I had to.

As a writer, I've had a precarious relationship with my body. The summer after my freshman year in college, when I heaved stones under the hot Texas sun for my then brother-in-law's landscaping business, I wrote in a notebook one evening, my slight muscles throbbing, "I will be a writer." Anything to avoid that heat and that backbreaking labor. More than pain avoidance, of course, led me to make that peculiar and private declaration of independence, for a far more reasonable aspiration than to become a writer might've brought more reliable sources of pleasure. After two years spent under the tutelage of writing professors such as David Wevill and Thomas Whitbread, I also realized that I genuinely wanted to be an extraordinary writing teacher as much as a writer. Those two pursuits I followed with fervor during my twenties, a fervor that exacted a cost on my body.

During my twenties and early thirties, I had become wedded to my writing and to teaching writing. At different times, I taught creative writing courses and poetry seminars at three colleges and at three high schools, including one public high school ranked by *Newsweek* as among the nation's top twenty. As a consultant for the College Board and as part of a textbook company's mentor team, I often traveled throughout the Southwest to teach hundreds of writing teachers the art of teaching writing. I also cofounded and acted as first president on the board of Dallas's first literary nonprofit organization, WordSpace.

I was a working head. Smug with my vegetarianism and imbalanced asceticism, I had not made love in years, fell ill from stress at least three times a year, and by age twenty-eight had stress-induced bronchitis, chest pains, and a pinched nerve in my right trapezius muscle that often left me half-paralyzed flat on my back. With muscles aching chronically and a right arm shaking from too much writing and responding to students' writings, I'm surprised I didn't scribble in a notebook at the time, "I will become a stoneworker," which was starting to sound like more attractive work.

Not particularly athletic, I had intuited even at nineteen that I needed to be more aware of my body. As an undergraduate, I had sneaked off early one morning away from my roommates to take my first yoga class. That was in 1985 in Texas, where yoga among my friends was still relegated to one of the weird things people who wear funny beads and smoke funny weeds do. I knew it felt good. Unfortunately, for my body and my writing, for the next ten years I didn't stick with it consistently. No one in graduate school or in the writing workshops and conferences I attended suggested I tap into the body or breath to alter my writing or to help me understand why sometimes, when I wrote, images and ideas flowed effortlessly and yet other times I sat and doodle-wrote for hours, sure that I was a fraud and hack. Would that someone had.

By the time I returned to yoga regularly twelve or so years later, I was so wound up, balled up, and stressed that I had the tightest shoulders in my yoga class. I had leapt into a high-pressure job as English department chair of a high-profile school, where I developed a budding creative writing program and helped lead the nineteen eclectic English instructors—whom I also supervised, counseled, and evaluated—through the implementation of a new writing philosophy. Around the same time, I also had abandoned a stagnating relationship to leave myself alone again with writing and teaching. My consistent, dogged, maniacal writing had dwindled into an Anaïs Nin–style cataloging of all-night excursions, and even when I could write a publishable creative essay or poem beyond my own foggy perspective, something in my writing process and style felt untrue, labored, dried-up. And as much as I understood elements of writing craft and process and style, I had no clue how the physical vehicle and subtle faculties that allowed me to write—in short, my body, mind, and imagination—functioned. I wrote from chin up, my shoulders clinched around my ears as if to keep any awareness from seeping down to my torso.

Once I returned to a steady yoga practice, my imagination awakened to my body. In the middle of a yoga class, I'd see my body as an ancient home with vast corridors, as a cottage in the Austrian mountains; aqueducts and rivulets with paper cups floating in them pulsed somewhere in my legs; a stranger's face, an old woman with braids and a scratchy scarf, rummaged around in my chest. A yoga class felt like an LSD trip. It also felt like those few and increasingly rare moments I'd have at the desk that you might call "writer's flow" when your imagination cooperates with your intellect and lets words unfold with few sputters. Those visual experiences, the pleasurable pulsing in my brain, and the relief of the pinched nerve in my right shoulder were enough to keep me coming back to yoga three times a week.

But on my journey I would come to understand far more deeply what happens when I write and how to help other writers understand their process. When practicing the physical part of yoga, I intuited subtle shifts in my views of myself, my ability to harness my energy and faculties for my writing, and a gradual ability to let go of or to work with the major obstacles—interior and exterior—that obstructed me from writing the kind of prose and poetry I intuited I needed to write. Those experiences initiated a series of questions: How could the body be a limitless yet immediate muse for writing? How does the practice of yoga conduce to an authentic writing life? Those questions have led me through a deeper study of yoga philosophy, through two yoga teacher-training and certification programs, and to Greece and India to study with such generous, authentic yogis as Angela Farmer, Victor Van Kooten, and Sri T.K.V. Desikachar, whose father, T. S. Krishnamacharya, virtually birthed yoga in the West during the twentieth century. These studies and my own experience confirm that yoga is a philosophy and science for transformation. It's also a readily accessible practice that can address with openness our yearnings and needs as creative writers.

Now I teach yoga as much as I teach writing. I teach yoga classes in Woodstock, New York, and I also teach Yoga as Muse workshops to writers across the country in writing centers, universities, retreat centers, and yoga centers. In both venues—the yoga class and the Yoga as Muse workshop—I encourage students to be receptive to the subtle changes in perception, constitution, and energy that yoga most assuredly will promote. Each day yoga and writing wed with one another at my desk, on the mat, and on the street. My mat in fact resides beside my desk. This journey has led me back to my body and to the faculties I embody—intuition, the unconscious imagination, intellect, emotion—a descent that has altered

profoundly how I view, experience, and understand my writing practice and my writing life. This book shares with you my findings and
provides you the guidance, the yoga philosophies, and the yoga
practices to help you try things out for yourself.

Why yoga? Why not another form of meditation or some form
of physical exercise such as running, aerobics, or lifting weights?
Meditation alone certainly heightens concentration and relaxation,
but focusing directly on our thoughts drives some people crazy. Their
lower backs twitch, their noses itch, and their minds flutter. A writer
friend I know took a six-week meditation class to help him quiet
his jittery chatter. By the end of week one, he was ready to take literally the Zen saying, When you meet the Buddha, kill him. That's
one reason yogis developed the practices of physical poses (*āsana*)
and breath awareness (*prānāyāma*) over two thousand years ago and
why yogis later developed Hatha-Yoga, the science of breathing,
physical poses, and energy flow. The fifteenth-century text *The
Hatha-Yoga-Pradīpika* recommends that rather than tending directly
to thoughts we instead focus upon our breath's in-and-out flow and
on our body's careful movements; thoughts naturally will quiet down
as breath, body, mind, harmonize.

With consistent practice, yoga can alter how you breathe,
think, shift energy, and deal with emotions—all beneficial attributes, as this book will explain, to writers. And whereas physical
forms of exercise such as aerobics and running do benefit the brain
and body, yoga's principles and tools offer a practical philosophy
that does not exhaust the mind and body; instead, it efficiently en-
ergizes and centers the "body-mind-imagination" and deepens self-
understanding. Yoga is a philosophy and practice that emphasizes
less how you look on the mat and more how you live in the world.
To practice yoga as muse for authentic writing involves the physical postures (*āsanas*), breath awareness (*prānāyāma*), concentration
(*dharana*), meditation (*dhyana*), visualization (*bhavana*), and self-
study (*svādhyāya*). But yoga and authentic writing make use of
these tools not as an end in themselves but in the context of how
days take shape in our lives. Practicing yoga poses alone is no more
a full yoga practice than learning a few tricks about style is an authentic writing practice. I suggest you approach these philosophies

and practices not with rigidity but with a sense of play. Test things out. Read this book to trigger fresh ways of approaching your writing practice from a different space, a more abiding space, your center. The center.

The word *authentic* is an adjective that stems from the Greek *authentes*, "one who acts on his own authority." So, again, we circle around to Krishnamurti's wisdom: Use this book to test things out for yourself and write from that space of experimentation. I suggest you first read Chapter One because yoga can help you explore what truly matters to you as a writer and remember your authentic intention as you draft, revise, and publish. Then either jump to any chapter that seems to speak to your writing needs, or enjoy the book from beginning to end. Chapters Two through Four address some of the most common questions that writers ask me: "How do I find time to write?" and "How do I find the concentration and self-discipline to write consistently and effectively?" Yoga can strengthen your constitution and slow down your brain waves so you can endure intense writing projects with self-discipline, perseverance, and concentration.

Even your writing style can benefit from yoga, as Chapters Five through Thirteen explain. Most writers I know sense that words are harbored in their bodies and that something visceral among body, imagination, and language mixes in authentic writing. Through simple yoga tools you can access the layers of your *embodied* imagination to heighten your presence and to create what John Gardner called in *The Art of Fiction* the "fictional dream," the seamless web of redolent detail and sapid images a good writer often creates for readers. For many writers who begin practicing yoga, something rich happens, too, to the present moment of penning or typing word after word. With simple yoga practices, you can induce a creative frame of mind that can so open your imagination and body that the writing experience can become as satisfying as a day spent hiking through a newly discovered evergreen forest. And with yoga's tools for listening, you can regain your authentic voice, craft convincing dialogue, and write sentences whose music comes from the mix between brain and heart—literally.

Chapters Fourteen through Nineteen explain how yoga helps you as a writer face emotionally hazardous terrain. By deepening your emotional intelligence, yoga grants you resources to better handle that most primal emotion—fear—as well as its close cousin, anger. I'm not promising that yoga will make you a better person, but because yoga can help you practice compassion and truthfulness, you can learn to portray your subjects—yourself, other people, difficult fictional characters—with greater complexity and believability. And perhaps no part of the writing process so confounds writers as rewriting, but yoga can help here too. Chapters Twenty and Twenty-one offer you advice. If you already have a regular and advanced yoga practice, you might jump to and review Chapter Twenty-three. Its ideas and generalizations I offer there may inform your reading of the other chapters.

Each chapter shows you how either yoga principles or specific yoga tools can help you become a more versatile and authentic writer when addressing specific writing topics in your own practice. Most chapters include "TAKE A BREATH" exercises to guide you through *embodying* your writing practice. If an exercise requires a physical pose, you can use the appendix of photographs as a prompt. Several original Sanskrit terms—Sanskrit being yoga's language—may deepen your knowledge and understanding of this sacred tongue. To those ends, the book also offers a glossary of terms.

To write authentically is to write from a common source, a common center. Ancient Hatha-Yoga texts describe unique centers within certain parts of the body that guide facets of ourselves such as our emotions, physical energy, will, imagination, and vision. Some texts describe seven, some eight, some more. You'll learn in this book, though, how some of these centers help you write from one center.

When an anthropologist asked a yogi, "Where is the center of the universe?" the yogi looked across the plain where they stood, pointed at a mountain, and said, "There." Then he said, "If that's where you're standing." Then he pointed to his left at a tree and said, "There. If that's where you're standing." Then he pointed to the place beneath the anthropologist's feet and said, "There is the center of the universe for you at this moment." He paused again. "And there. It's always there," he said, pointing to the anthropologist's heart. He wasn't a relativist or a narcissist suggesting that the universe is simply a construct of a person's point of view, nor was he being clever or symbolic by pointing to the heart. The heart's location below our brain and in our torso can keep our awareness in our core, the Latin word for *heart*, from which we get *courage*. From that center, common to all of us, spirit and body and language align. When you write from the center, you write what your spirit, body, and language demand you write. It's a potentially hazardous and dangerous path because your protective ego may no longer be in as much control, and this writing can shake you out of your comfortable habits by forcing you to write the truth—regardless of genre. With persistence, though, you learn you can persevere, that you can write no other way.

Writing *is* a journey. When Margaret Atwood asked several novelists a few years ago what it felt like to write, they repeatedly used words evoking a journey through a dark place. Many of them felt almost blind along the way, yet they sensed that the movement forward would bring about vision. Atwood writes, "I was reminded of something a medical student said to me about the interior of the human body, forty years ago: 'It's dark in there.' "[1] And perhaps this is how I've remembered to live and to write authentically: to make love to the darkness instead of trying to kick it out of bed. To make love to the darkness a writer moves toward doubts and doesn't try to repress them or let them control her. Such a writer finds ways to spelunker into the body's and the imagination's subtle caverns and find hideous yet exquisite forms and names of oneself, of humanity, of God, and of whatever it is we call reality—the basic stuff of authentic writing and the basic stuff of yoga.

This book encourages you to enter that darkness. It does not pretend to be Virgil to all of the Dantes in the writing world. Writing is difficult. This book, however, does suggest new ways for you to use yoga's tools and live its philosophies, that you may find the courage, confidence, and skill to step into the darkness and so begin a journey to the center and then back to the page.

I.
MAKING A FEW
PREPARATIONS

CHAPTER ONE

Putting on the Robe: Exploring Your Intentions for Writing

An hour or so before dawn, the congress in my head that years ago would wake me by trumpeting the day's debates seems this morning cooperative and sedate. I creep from bed across the hall's squeaking hardwoods to my study. On one side of my study, the window above my desk looks like a blank blackboard that complements my computer screen's white sky. On the study's other side, my yoga mat waits for me to step on it like a diving board. If my mat be a diving board, then that white screen must be the sky into which I dive. (I'm not one of those gonzo writers who actually leaps from downed planes flying over, say, war-torn Liberia and live to write about it; metaphors placate my imagination just fine.) It's a precarious business, this writing life, one filled with little daily affirmation from other people that what you're spending your precious time and energy doing actually matters or is any good. No supervisor nods her head in approval. No customer survey rates your writing. No regular performance evaluation ranks you for writer of the month. Just the wide-open page and you, free-falling, twisting, teaching yourself how to shift your limbs to spin into airborne pirouettes, all with the faith that as you see some creative problem mount and the brown ground zooms toward your face, your parachute cord will work. More often than not when you write, although it feels at times as if you get caught in trees or hurt your knees, you land upright on your two feet, your soles refastened to earth. The next day you can't wait to begin again with a new page.

Why on earth, of all the ways to spend the morning, do I choose to write? While I was a temporary resident at the Zen Mountain Monastery, Vice-Abbess Bonnie Myotai Treace, Sensei, raised a question about practicing Zen that reminds me of an essential question for writers: "Why, given the endless possibilities of a morning, given dawn, put on a robe at the sound of a bell?"[1] Why put on your robe, indeed, and hobble to the desk? Why write? It seems like a good question for starters. Without a genuine motivation, we're possibly hobby writing, sky doodling. We got into this business of taking creative leaps for reasons other than an adrenaline rush.

Something I've learned from my yoga practice—to revisit a variation of the question "Why write?"—has changed the way I start things—my mornings, my classes and workshops, and my own writing sessions. Before practicing yoga, I set an intention. An intention is a conscious gesture to align your mind, heart, imagination, and body with whatever act you're about to begin—whether it's a series of physical poses, breathing awareness, a day of karma yoga and good acts, or a writing session. A yoga teacher and writer I know practices yoga to manifest her highest qualities. A friend of mine says he simply practices yoga to deepen his joy. Another friend practices yoga to perpetuate peace. Most of us take that first step onto the mat for personal reasons. An injury, the first signs of cellulite, loneliness, heartbreak, grief, addiction, or a gamut of physical and emotional ailments may propel us into downward dog pose and cobra pose. In her classic book *Awakening the Spine*, Vanda Scaravelli lays out her poetic reflections for a natural, egoless practice: "Yoga should not be a training for body control; on the contrary, it must bring freedom to the body, all the freedom it needs."[2] The highest motive to practice yoga may be liberation.

I don't know if writing will set us free, but I do know there's value in setting an intention as a writer. To begin each writing session and each workshop, I've rephrased the question "Why write?" to "What am I writing for?" A more private question than its more direct sibling, it's meant to be asked of and answered primarily to yourself and to whoever or whatever else can read your body, mind, and heart. No other yogi, writer, or professor will hear you. That fact alone may make all the difference in the answer that surfaces. You can respond with a justification, a defense, but you may be surprised by what happens. You'll feel more at ease about your writing as you start to connect your writing intention to your core identity as a writer. The phrasing "What am I writing for?" may even lead you to dedicate your writing practice to something or someone. In this way your writing may come from a source other than your ego. When successful, seasoned writers tell me "something is missing" from their writing practice, this simple gesture begins to satisfy some of their hunger.

No need to expect grand or immediate answers, though. Often only after years of writing do we have any perspective on why we've been spending the better part of our days following one word after another. This gesture of asking "What am I writing for?" to yourself, though, begins the process. Perhaps the answers that surface for you—today, tomorrow, next month—may reflect what other writers have said they write for. Jhumpa Lahiri, the youngest writer to receive the Pulitzer Prize, says she writes to confront and sort through the discrepancy between her Indian parents' worldview and her more American worldview with which she has grown up.[3] Sindiwe Magona, a novelist from South Africa and now working for the United Nations, says writing is therapeutic for her and for others.[4] Essayist Jean Bernstein says she must write because questions, voices, images, surface in her like "splinters," and writing essays is the best way she has found to pull out the really irritating ones.[5] These motives sustain writers and propel them to the desk each day.

What are you writing for? Perhaps, like many writers, you write to make sense of the world. If lucky, you can form some order out of chaotic human experience. For now, what you write for may be nothing more than the pleasure or wonder you've experienced when wielding words. Something related to a core principle also may stir you to write. If you hunger to make sense of how the taco-chain owner who migrated from Mexico twenty years ago is filthy rich and yet pays his illegal immigrant employees thirty-five dollars for fourteen-hour shifts, then exploring justice's complexities may be what you write for. Sometimes the reasons why we write seem as fleeting as the hidden blue jay cawing among the birches, but these more remote, at times ineffable, motives help us write from our center.

When checking in with this question, watch your ego. A thirty-

year-old writer, Elise, recently asked me to help her figure out a focus for her first novel. She had almost finished the first draft of the
story, which follows a young woman's emotional and political en-
tanglements as she avoids marriage to pursue her dreams of opening
an animal sanctuary, but Elise felt that the story, and she as a writer,
had started to lose direction. "What stirs you to write this book?" I
asked. She responded almost without hesitation: "To prove to my
mother I've accomplished something. I have three degrees in lan-
guages and have nothing to show for it." Oh, the mother motive.
I'd heard about it, although thankfully I've never had to wrestle
with this one myself. Elise's ego, I sensed, still clung too tightly to
her manuscript. She didn't trust her own authority. I suggested she
let the project rest for a while and instead explore a deeper motivation that leads her to write even when her mother's not approving
or disapproving; otherwise, she not only may censor herself when
drafting and rewriting, but she also may be sorely disappointed
when the book's completed, and her mother still doesn't nod her
head. Will the book, then, be a failure? Two months later she hadn't
taken my advice. Her mother's judgmental air still hovered over her
shoulder, and when she had worked on the book she still felt lost
and often uninspired. So, I took her through a fairly simple process
to slow down her thoughts, to ground her in her body, and to help
her locate an authentic drive that would both sustain her writing
and give it focus. Within a few minutes, she realized she was writing
her novel to satisfy an insatiable hunger to figure out some of her
own views on being a woman in this country, on living an ethical
livelihood, as well as on the conflicting loyalties between having
a family and following a personal dream. These issues mattered to
Elise, but she hadn't been able to acknowledge that her caring about
these puzzling topics was what had stirred her to write the novel.
The next day, Elise told me, she centered herself and kept in her
heart some of these intentions. The results? She finished a *second*
rewrite of the manuscript within six weeks and submitted it to her
agent.

Many writers appreciate admiration and approval, but that motivation can consume us. Nonfiction writer Michael Stephens has
admitted how, as a young writer trying to prove himself, spite and
competition in his writing group fueled his young blood at St. Marks

Poetry Project. Whether green or seasoned, we seek it. Nothing wrong with a little praise or ego drive, except that it can become an addiction that can steer us away from a more sustaining path. "Stop trying to get your audience to like you," writer Gerald Burns once told me and a group of other writers. Writing mainly to please someone—even an imagined audience—may sustain a writer for a while, but those exposed roots only extend so far.

When you privately ask "What am I writing for?" the ego can rest (and it's rare for our writers' egos to rest). You don't have to impress anyone. In this space, you can be more honest with yourself about what leads you to write. Recently, my father-in-law (a retired stockbroker), my wife, and I were talking about books and writers. My father-in-law said, "Well, you know, most writers publish books for one reason: to make money." My wife immediately disagreed. He looked at me and said, "Well, all right, Jeff, why do you write? When you're writing, aren't you thinking about making money?" I grinned and told him that I ask myself every morning why I write and never does "to make money" surface; otherwise, I would've stopped writing long ago. He smiled back and said, "You know, you'd make a lousy stockbroker." I didn't detail to him exactly what I write for, because sometimes the reasons are difficult to articulate, but I should have told him about my father's journal.

When I was five, my father gave me possibly the most important gift he's ever given me: one of my grandfather's datebooks that my father had used as his own daybook. It contains my father's scribbled boyhood descriptions of mowing the lawn and walking to the lake with his friends as well as such sketchy observations of my own as *I saw a hobo by the tracks today. I wonder where he goes. What he sees. I want to ride a train someday.* I've been riding the train of language and imagination ever since. With that journal, my father gave me the writing bug that never left my system. Fiction writer Ellen Gilchrist says there is next to "... nothing the outside world gives me in exchange for my writing that is of value to me. I do not take pleasure in other people's praise, and I don't believe their criticism."[6] Would that I could always be that clear. Gilchrist knows why she writes: She loves language. For some writers, it's as good a reason as any.

So, before I write, I stand before my desk, hold my hands at my heart, close my eyes, take at least two full breaths, and quietly ask, "What am I writing for?" This gesture prepares my body, mind, and imagination before I take a leap. The answer's content and nature often depend upon my writing project. Sometimes an answer wells up in fragments and phrases: "to help others," "to tell the truth," "to hold myself together," "to figure out what I think I think and what I think I know," or often even something as vague as "to follow language's currents." Sometimes, I have to wait for several minutes, and, granted, some mornings give me little more than faint images. Yet lately, voices more urgent have surfaced in the morning: "Fight the tide of complacency" and "Do something for peace." Words may not save us, but it's worth reminding ourselves of our words' intention. Doing so gives me hope.

I take students through two important parts to setting a writing intention. Once we've listened for a few breaths to whatever rises in response to our question about what we're writing for (the first part), we clarify the simple topic or specific focus for the day's writing session (the second part). Maybe it's something direct like "concentration to finish a book's chapter" or something juicier like "wild images for a new essay." This second part does not take away from writing's magic; it gives the magic direction. Sometimes, writers choose to keep this part general and say, "I'm open to the moment." Novelists such as Milan Kundera and Norman Rush often begin drafting a novel with little more than a faint voice, a shred of dialogue, or a character whose face won't leave the writer alone. In one of my workshops in New York City, a veteran short-story writer said she rarely writes with an intention, but doing so ironically prepares "her imagination's soil" so that she can be open to whatever happens in the moment of creating. Sometimes she starts with one intention and then follows another.

Other writers tell me that making a simple twofold intention grants them more ease while writing, and one writer in Portland, Oregon, says that setting this two-part intention lifts her out of what she calls her "morning neuroses" so she can promptly move on to "writing that matters." As a writer who can get lost in distractions and digressions, I enjoy the hazardous interplay between having an intention and not knowing where the train's taking me; the intention gives my wanderings some slight direction, like the pull of my mother's voice calling years ago whenever I had strayed miles away into the woods. Remembering both my larger intention of what I'm writing for, morning after morning, and the more specific intention of a single morning's session often brings me home.

Many of the exercises in the rest of this book will offer you possible specific intentions. Take them or leave them. They're there to help you focus your imagination and your mind.

Two last words about intentions, though: First, let go of the outcome. If, after one session, or if, after a week or a month, you still haven't written what you set out to write, don't fret. The writing likely took you somewhere you wouldn't have arrived had you avoided the desk altogether. On the other hand, if you do accomplish precisely what you had intended, relish it and move on. And this: Sometimes the answer about what you're writing for is right in front of you. One writer I met in a workshop in California last year said that one morning no answer was surfacing until she heard her four-year-old son's laughter in the next room. "To sustain that laughter," she said, "—that's what I'm writing my stories and essays for."

It's a little past dawn, the mountain mist rising with the sun. From the window above my desk I spot a wild turkey walking across my lawn, then two, three, soon eight baby turkeys with one adult leading and a second adult following. Like schoolchildren lined up on a field trip, the chicks are being led near the garden and beneath the oak to find their morning feed. This, I think, is as good a reason as any to rise early, put on my tattered robe, and sit at my desk: to watch hope manifested in ten awkward bodies hobbling across my lawn like words in a sentence in search of some small seeds of reassurance.

$\mathcal{T}$AKE A BREATH

It can be just this simple: Do what you need to do to settle some of your inner chatter. Sit comfortably in a chair, on the floor near your desk, or stand in front of your desk. See the Appendix for seating options. I usually prefer to stand in **MOUNTAIN POSE** *(tādāsana), my feet hip width apart, my spine long, my hands at my heart. Try it. As you*

breathe, focus on your lower body and feet to help ground yourself liter-
ally in your physical connection to the earth and to draw attention away
from your chatty head. Chuang Tzu noted, after all, that the venerable
teacher breathes with her heels.

Just breathe. Stand or sit for two minutes or so simply listening to
your breath. Take a deep inhalation from the base of your belly, and a
full exhalation. Do as a fiction writer in Connecticut told me she does:
Close your eyes and center on your heartbeat.

When your thoughts stop whirling long enough that you can follow
two full inhalations and exhalations, you're ready to set a twofold writing
intention. First, ask yourself with a quiet voice, "What am I writing
for?" You may remind yourself of something residing in your creative
wellspring that nourishes your writing. Listen. Don't force a response.
Let it bubble up.

Second, clarify a more immediate focus for your writing, a subject
(for example, my grandmother, the fourth scene of Chapter Eight in my
novel, fear) and/or an intention to receive insight (for example, to gain
insight into what motivated my grandmother in her later years, to get to
the heart of this scene's surprising conflict, to understand the complex
joys of fear). Then, while you're writing, you can return to those inten-
tions, to whatever invisible source rouses you to write.

An intention can be made in a simple or complex way. It's up to you.
Regardless of your intention's intricacy, practicing a gesture such as the
one described above can radically alter your writing process and connect
your source or your motivation for writing to something great and still
within.

CHAPTER TWO

Schedules and Rituals to Stretch Your Writing Time

An odyssey requires time. One way or another, as a writer, you have to make your peace with time, to stop fighting it, and to avoid bemoaning its apparent scarcity. There's plenty of time to be had, and if we can't change the way time works, then we can change the way we work with it.

To transform our conditioned habits of how we live in time, some of us need jolts to startle our whole being—mind, spirit, body. Yoga shook me up. Then Zen. During my residency at the Zen Mountain Monastery in the Catskills, the monks tossed me into the liturgy, the rituals, with little explanation. In the predawn haze, bells of different pitches rang on cue, a bass drum boomed on cue, and we bowed and prostrated on cue. As I fumbled and sweated in my new monastic robe, my skeptical mind's radar set off several red beeps: What are we bowing to? Why doesn't anyone explain the purpose of these movements and chants? Isn't all of this ritual meaningless routine? The monastery worked on me from the outside in. With no psychobabble or sweet talking, but instead with bells and sticks, with structures and strictures, the monastic experience helped me develop more of the discipline I needed at that time in my life. Although my life before then was fulfilling and spiritually grounded, many of my days had lacked authentic form; no genuine daily rituals anchored my awareness. Not so at the monastery. Every day had a distinct structure that varied occasionally: Awaken at 5:00 A.M. and walk in silence to the zendo, meditate, chant and bow at the dining hall, eat breakfast, chant in preparation for work, practice, work, chant and bow at the dining hall, eat lunch, rest, meditate, engage in art practice, study, rest, and so on until sleep. We slept for maybe six hours. The schedule exhausted me. Being aware is hard work.

The monastic experience hooked up well with my yoga practice to give me tools to hone my writing life: namely, structured days and rituals to mark transitions between activities. I have met too many writers to know that despite our well-defined resolutions to pursue projects, we often let other less inspiring projects assume priority and consume our time. Then we delay, we excuse, we neglect, and ultimately we forget the original idea. A writing practice, like any practice, requires self-discipline.

Discipline. There it is. Some of us lug baggage with that word stitched on it. A friend of mine in marketing recommended that I not mention or highlight the word *discipline* in my pieces about writing because this baggage would block the message. But discipline is the message. So, let's unload the baggage. The word *discipline*, like *disciple*, stems from the Latin *discere*, "to teach." When we cultivate self-discipline, we teach ourselves of our capabilities, of our body and imagination's inherent relationship, and of what external and internal tools work best to enact a personal and artistic alchemy. Without self-discipline, we'll only make half the journey, if that far.

To take a first step in cultivating self-discipline, consider your relationship to time. My writer friends and students usually fall into one of these two extremes: Either their days fill up quickly—with other work, errands, familial duties, social engagements—or their days have wide-open space bounded only by light and dark. Time Crunchers hunger for an hour or two every other day simply to sit with their thoughts and their laptop. They're busy and important people at their jobs who keep companies functioning; they're busy and important parents who keep their children fed and clothed and sheltered. They snarl and secretly envy my other friends whose lives fall into the latter category: the Time Stretchers. These few writers and aspiring writers, who either by wealth or by wit succeed in leading a simple life, are privileged to wake up when they wish, write when they wish, and sleep when they wish (with some regular exceptions, of course). On the other hand, these same writers, who avoid penciling in their activities like monks bowing on the hour to the bells on Wall Street, and have time to write, may be the more frustrated at deciding what to do with themselves and their days.

Such a writer recently asked me to help her. "I have all the time I need," she said, "but I won't write anything unless I have a deadline." As a masseuse with a few private clients, Brandice had hours each day to visit friends, read the mounds of books that lined her small apartment, and comb her imagination for her own book ideas. She had written for years for local and prominent national magazines, but she wanted to finish her first book proposal (something she had tried three times before). Every time she had started her book project in the past, something else headed the muse off at the pass. After I helped her sort through her manuscripts and determine her book's unique focus, I had her do two things: We cleared a space in her cluttered work area to "sanctify" her project, so to speak, and we pulled out her daybook. "Make an appointment with your writing," I suggested. In her near-blank daybook, she wrote in two-hour blocks for the Tuesday, Wednesday, and Friday of the following week. Six hours was a good start. "Keep these appointments," I suggested. "During these allotted times, refrain from checking e-mail. Don't go on a fall foliage tour. Don't even schedule a massage client. Don't write any articles. Write your book proposal." She did so—with some occasional "falls from the page," of course. But in a month she had shifted her habit of distraction into a habit of discipline.

Successful writers can be time crunchers or time stretchers, but both require some form of voluntary self-imposed external structure. One writer and well-known writing professor, Donald Murray, has composed most of his books ten or fifteen minutes at a time. Between classes and conferences, between errands and meetings, he writes in patches until gradually he has gathered enough material to stitch a book. He then makes more time to sit for longer stretches to weave the pieces together. How much less intimidating to pen a good paragraph for thirty minutes than to wrestle with twenty pages for eight hours.

Other writers, of course, have months each year to wrap themselves in words. Truman Capote wrote while lying down in bed or on a couch, always ready to assuage his appetite with cigarette and coffee (which, he claimed, turned later in the day to "mint tea to sherry to martinis"). He always wrote drafts longhand in pencil. Then he wrote another revision in pencil. And a third draft on a very special kind of yellow paper. Very disciplined. (But then, who knows? The lovely, froggy writer, who pioneered the popularity of "creative nonfiction," was known to fib and exaggerate.) Some writers float for days in that luscious write-space. While writing *Pilgrim at Tinker Creek*, Annie Dillard said she slept until noon, then would write at one sitting in the afternoon and then another sitting after dinner and a walk until midnight or later. Tales of such nights of the living imaginations sometimes feed our romantic notions of the writer's life. Living without regard for nutrition or respite or the rest of the whirling world sometimes is the writer's equivalent of living in a personal monastery or ashram—a *sat-sanga* of one.

SCHEDULES AND A REGULAR "PRACTICE"

To work on cue—whether we have a stint of fifteen minutes or a stretch of fifteen weeks to write—we need creative structure in our lives not unlike our body's creative structure. External structure, especially self-imposed structure, can liberate our muse.

"More than half of the practice is just showing up to the *zafu*," Abbot Daido Loori often said at the monastery. How many times had I heard that? Sri T.K.V. Desikachar talks about showing up at the yoga mat, and we writers must "show up" at the desk. To make time to show up, most writers will tell you the same thing: Sacrifice something. Not a virgin or a goat. Not your husband. Not your friendships. Forgo a movie here and there. A lunch here and there. Hide your television. How about starting with that voice that keeps telling you, "You can start on your own writing with more discipline as soon as . . ." As soon as what? As soon as you quit your job? As soon as you move to the Virgin Islands or whatever your idyll may be? As soon as your kids leave home? Put that voice on the altar today and relish slaying it.

To assist you with the sacrifice, make appointments with your writing. If long chunks of time intimidate you, think short and frequent. This suggestion may be this chapter's single most important one to heed. If you keep appointments with your hairstylist or with that friend who hounds you to have lunch each Wednesday, then why not keep regular weekly, if not daily, appointments with your muse? (She's probably more fun and less gossipy. Maybe.) I learned this simple fact from my yoga practice. It became a "practice" once I started practicing at home at least three afternoons a week. Soon, I was engaged in yoga on my own six or seven mornings a week and started tuning into what my body needed, how to use *āsanas* to relieve tension in my neck or to help me relax; the *āsanas* became assimilated into my own body and imagination instead of remaining forms that a teacher called out to me to execute. This regularity transferred to my writing habits.

Years ago, I would jot a page or two in the morning and sometimes write three pages madly into the night and every once in a while squeeze in twenty minutes in the afternoons. My writing practice suffered from the irregularity, and if a deadline wasn't pressing, weeks might pass without my writing at all. I changed my erratic ways. I started finding the joy and authenticity of meeting my muse at the same time of day at least four times a week—despite my then cluttered schedule. As a result, my body and mind calmed down on cue when I arrived at the desk each morning so my imagination could come out to play. Even when I didn't think I had anything to say or to write, I sat at the desk and wrote. My productivity has increased tenfold, and my muse appears far more regularly. My daily schedule includes setting an intention and practicing from thirty minutes to two hours of yoga and meditation, usually first thing in the morning (after, that is, I've fed my nineteen-year-old arthritic and demanding cat, Igrin). Typically, I pencil in chunks of four to eight hours for five days out of the week to write (sometimes with notes about which pieces I intend to work on) as well as times for my yoga classes, my writing classes, and miscellaneous business. I usually write for three hours in the early morning, break for breakfast, and write until noon. Then another two to three hours carries me into the afternoon. I don't always write with such time constraints, but for someone who has made his life deliberately unstructured from a conventional point of view, self-impositions help me work well.

Be flexible but regular. If developing a regular schedule is new to you, even if you've been writing for years, you might use this simple formula: 3-60-15. Write three times a week for sixty minutes each session for fifteen days (that is, three days a week for five weeks). Or this formula: 7-60-15. Seven days a week for sixty minutes for fifteen days. The fifteen days is a marker to see if this changed habit will stay; it provides a reachable end. If your schedule allows it, it's probably better to write for less time on several days each week (for example, one or two hours on three days a week) than to write for several hours only once a day each week. When you sit, just write. Recognize you have to wade through a lot of crap sometimes to get to the clear springs, but you'll benefit from scheduling appointments for the wading. When I suggested to one aspiring writer that she take only thirty minutes three times a week—that's all—to start her book and to do so diligently, she did. Thirty minutes became an hour. Then, she could not *not* write her book. Less than six months later she came to a workshop and told me, "That simple suggestion has changed my life. I'm almost through with the first draft of my book." She's not the only one.

And once you sit, stay put. If you've given yourself an hour to write, refrain from answering the phone, getting a snack, checking e-mails, or whatever other sneaky obstacles might try to keep you from your soul's work. If you have something on your desk to stabilize you—a stone works for some writers—gaze at it and remind yourself of your own ability to stay anchored in your seat and intention. A stick of incense helped one student I know. Three evenings a week when he came home from work, he'd turn on his computer and light a stick of incense on his desk. While the incense burned, he continued to write. When it extinguished, he could leave his desk (although he often stayed for more). Most incense sticks burn for an hour or ninety minutes, so try it.

Schedule breaks if you need to. During my breaks in the middle of long writing sessions, I regularly saunter along the nearby roads or through the woods, and without fail the walk produces something in my imagination that wouldn't have surfaced if I had stayed at my desk. Philosopher Immanuel Kant was renowned for walking the same route every day at precisely the same time in his small town. The locals allegedly could keep time according to when he strolled past their homes or shops. Poet and director of creative writing at Brandeis University Olga Broumas wrote three books while walking, she once told me in an interview. If not walking, then try running. Joyce Carol Oates runs for miles—has written and run since a pigtailed girl—to court her muse. Scheduling a break, as opposed to taking one at whim, often keeps my body and mind alert and my imagination fertile for another thirty, forty minutes until it's time to saunter.

SLOW *VINYASA* AND WRITERS' RITUALS

We could use a little slowing down. We speed-read, gobbling our words only to forget most of what we've consumed. As we read, so we live. The alarm clock rattles before dawn, and you're up and off to wake the kids, shower, shave, grab some toast, prod the kids to eat and dress, drop the kids off, dash to work, make your calls, grab a sandwich, glance at some headlines, do more work, pick up the dry cleaning and the kids, shuttle the kids to soccer practice, and you have forty-five minutes to yourself to eat or catch your breath before you pick them up again, bring them home, feed them, help them with their homework, and put them to bed. You didn't spend the day's allotted time; clearly, it spent you. And you and your days feel cheaper and cheaper by the week. With the world too much with you, you wonder how you ever thought you could manage the time to write.

My yoga practice of *vinyasa* has helped me not so much to manage time but to stretch it. Some people refer to *vinyasa* as a physical yoga system characterized by a quick yet artful sequence from one yoga pose to the next, as in Sri K. Pattabbi Jois's *Ashtanga Yoga* (headquartered in Mysore, India) and David Life and Sharon Gannon's *Jivamukti Yoga* (headquartered in New York City). Practicing *vinyasa* authentically, however, has less to do with speed and quantity of poses than with awareness and intention. *Vinyasa* is to flow with a body-mindful awareness from one situation (another translation of *āsanas*) or activity to the next.[1] I used to find myself shuttling from one thing to another, oblivious as to when lunch stopped

and work resumed. Now, I try to make more time to taste waking
up; to prepare breakfast and give thanks and to bow out when finished; to acknowledge the beginning, middle, and end of my writing time; to look someone in the eyes as I speak to her, notice her
breath, and say a genuine good-bye before we part. Yoga does indeed calm the mind's whirling fluctuations; it also, though, calms
our actions' whirls.

Practicing *vinyasa* by tending to the point when one activity,
like a poem's line, ends and the next one begins can help us stretch
time for our writing. We can frame our writing sessions with awareness from beginning to end. When we discipline ourselves to tend to
our days' and our writing sessions' transitions, then we move toward
living and writing from our center because our writing doesn't just
pass us by.

One way to tend to these transitions is to create very simple
rituals. Rituals, however small and personal, align our attention
with our body's action and open the barn door to our imagination.
It's no secret that writers are ritualistic creatures. Margaret Atwood
recently wrote of writing as a venture into utter darkness where a
writer ultimately encounters the dead. No surprise, then, that, as Atwood tells it, writers create their own rituals before making their dangerous descents where they'll meet darkness, the dead, their demons.
Isabel Allende, for instance, once lit a candle to honor her dead ancestors before each writing session.

In addition to setting a twofold writing intention, I also do a
couple of other things to open the gate. I pay homage to Ganesha,
the potbellied, elephant-headed god of writers and of auspicious beginnings. Ganesha embodies the wisdom of maneuvering success-
fully in this world with courage, grace, kindness, and resolve. I'm
not Hindu, but this big-eared, four-armed figure so enchants me
that I cannot help but have a simple place for him by my desk and
in my heart. Ganesha at once removes obstacles for me and places
them in my way; plus, he's the scribe of Yoga. No wonder writers
like him. Author Diane Johnson said when she was blocked while
writing her latest novel, *L'Affaire*, she sought out a guru who gave
her a mantra—a simple but charged chant—to help her. She still
uses it as a prewriting ritual. If you don't favor Ganesha or a chant,
you might do as several of my students have done and acknowledge

your own talisman, divinity, or good luck charm. Keep it simple but meaningful.

I also bow to my laptop. Well, not exactly. Ganesha sits next to my laptop, and before I write I bow to that quality to remove obstacles, so it looks as if I'm stooping to my laptop (an idea Michael Dell might like). I bow before I begin to write, invoke a brief chant that asks for the removal of obstacles, and bow as I end each session. You might do similarly. When you've finished your writing session, acknowledge the end. Let your computer or notebook hibernate while you incubate. Place a cover over your computer, or put your notebook away in a regular spot. Stack your papers. Put your books back. Polish your lucky stone. "To really complete work practice," abbot of Zen Mountain Monastery John Daido Loori writes, "requires cleaning up, putting the tools away, picking up the loose ends, 'leaving no trace.' "[2] Then, bow again, say something, or with your thoughts acknowledge whatever you invoked to begin your session. Blow out the candle. Once you've noticed at least two full breaths, then flow into your next activity.

Some of this talk of tending to the details may seem too precious for some of you, and (as I used to) you may feel at home not knowing when your writing stops and when checking e-mails begins, and you may think you work best by keeping manuscripts smeared with peanut butter stains from six months ago stacked or splayed out on your desk, but if you feel spent with your writing as if it's roamed the wild lands without direction for so long and hasn't gotten you anywhere lately and if you feel your writing is no longer coming from an authentic space, try something different. One man in Portland, Oregon, has been a writer for thirty years and yet had been recently discouraged. After trying some of these suggestions, he wrote me to say that the simple ritual of moving through some simple yoga poses before his writing session "helps me form a boundary of good energy around my writing time." We need creative boundaries.

Imagine two lambs. One lamb roams the wild for a few days before being devoured by a wolf. Another lamb roams a farm's four hundred acres among other lambs, knows when she'll be fed, her wool regularly groomed and transformed into heat-saving sweaters and socks. You can build handmade fences with beautiful gates around your thoughts. Feed them when they need it, and let your imagination roam free without being devoured by fear, doubt, anxiety, anger, ego obsessions, and self-criticism. Try a variation of *vinyasa* with a ritual.

Two friendly warnings, though: First, don't spend so much time constructing elaborate structures and rituals that you neglect the most important reason you may be reading this book: to write. Second, be flexible. I don't live a monk's life of absolute regularity. Surprises happen, and as with any enduring structure, I must be flexible. Once we set schedules and self-impose structures, we have to keep with them voluntarily and without feeling enslaved by or obsessed with them.

*T*AKE A BREATH

Keep your writing sessions simple but meaningful. Show up for your writing appointment at least three times a week. Align your mind and body with your imagination by setting a twofold intention. Once you've clarified your intention to check your ego, enact a simple ritual that will invite your muse to open a gate. Before the ritual, tend to your breath's rhythms and notice how you feel in your body. Aim to give each part of your body—from your crown to your soles (not just your thoughts)—to the ritual. A simple bow after two full breaths may suffice before you sit. Lighting a candle—with attention to the match and box, to the wick and flame—may help to frame your writing session. Stay with your appointment to write until the end. Then, with the same attention you gave your opening ritual, put away your things so you can begin the next session with openness and clarity. And bow out. Give thanks. Appreciate where you've been going during this session and where you're going next.

CHAPTER THREE

A Stoked Belly:
Mustering Perseverance
to Keep Writing

Once you make your sacrifices to create and stretch time for your writing, your body may not want to cooperate. When a writing problem persists, an image won't surface, or words scurry like mice away from your mind's light, your body may decide it's time to take a nap. Or maybe after you eat another row of Chips Ahoy!, your body reasons, you'll have more food for thought. This journey isn't easy, you realize. It requires work, if not a lot of knowledge about craft and skill. More to the point, writing requires persistence and perseverance.

I met perseverance while driving through East Texas. On one of my wayward excursions when I lived in the big state, I stopped to eat in a small town. The cook, a woman with rough and sweet eyes and big frosted hair tucked in a net, rustled for me a plate suitable for a Southern vegetarian—thick mashed potatoes swimming in butter, cornbread drenched in butter, green beans, cooked carrots, and squash all awash in butter. The man sitting on the diner barstool next to me introduced himself as Walter. A farmer. Now a widower, he was prompt to tell me.

"I'm sorry."

"No, don't be sorry. Etta was a great woman. One of a kind. Hard-working. And a pistol too. We had a good life," he said with the rhythm of hammering nails and with a slight smile and heavy eyes.

I asked him how he had kept going during the past year.

"Work. Work saves me." He had been building a fence around his entire farm from the best wood around. For the next fifteen minutes he detailed how he had chopped the wood, hauled the trees, shaved the posts, dug the holes, and wedged the limbs together. He still had miles to go, though, he said in so many words, and I was sensing he wanted me to help him build it if I had the time and inclination. "Wanna see it?"

I had nowhere in particular to go. Once I finished the last bite of melting mashed potatoes and tipped the big-haired waitress/cook, I followed Walter in his old Ford pickup for about five miles outside of town to his farm. Four hundred acres, and for four months he persistently had been replacing the collapsing wooden fence with a new oak one. Transformed from trees with ax and hand, sweat and grief, each log, wedged and secured like the cedar logs of a home-grown cabin, gave the landscape shape. Every morning, he told me, he awoke before dawn, gathered his materials and tools, and raised the fence one limb at a time. By noon, he'd have a significant line of fence in place; then he could spend the rest of the day tending to his farm. From his porch, I took in the vertical lines of pines, oaks, and elms that reached from earth to sky sliced and defined by Walter's oak fence. He could've rolled over and pulled the sheets over his head. He could've said, "To hell with it," dropped his tools, and walked away from what he'd started. But he didn't. What Walter had for fences and barns and porches, writers have for writing: namely fire.

Heat in Sanskrit is called *tapas*, possibly the singular most important quality for yoga (and authentic writing). *Tapas*, the earliest recorded yogic concept,[1] which translates also to "ardor" and "austerity," describes yogis' practices of burying their heads in the sand, or sitting nude in subzero weather to cultivate their "inner heat" that they may attain transformational powers. To each his own, but I'm not into this sort of thing. Luckily for us, Patanjali's *Yoga-Sutra* (c. 200 C.E.) and other yoga texts denounces these extreme measures as being ironically driven by pride and as destructive to the body—*not* yoga's aim. So as writers we take a more benign approach to *tapas* as perseverance.

Tapas describes that fire in the belly that propels us to work well and to persevere in the world. It is the burning enthusiasm that excites us when we discover a blue-sky idea, a delicious image, a tapestry woven plotline. We stay up an hour later concocting the story, or we may madly record in a notebook that vital detail, such as a dream we don't want to—nay, cannot—forget. The electric rush from our imagination gives our days an extra kick, and we may ramble like a daft man to strangers on the bus about our fantastic new idea. Some of us live and write for that rush. The problem is, the flame wanes. The novelty wears thin. Maybe what we thought was a startling, innovative story idea turns out to be a rehash of plotlines stretching from Dante to Dostoyevsky. The sustained fire that lets us write day after day even when our head hurts or even when we meet rejection upon rejection is also *tapas*. Once we've tapped into our *tapas*, how do we keep the heat burning? How do we avoid this intellectual, imaginative, spiritual burnout? Or if we're burnt already, how do we rise from the ashes?

We can begin practicing *tapas* by tending to how we talk about our writing. One student recently complained that she had been writing short stories for ten years but that recently every time she sat down to write she felt no spark. "I already know what's going to happen in my stories, so I'm not excited anymore to write," she said. I asked if she spent too much time thinking about how her stories would unfold before writing them—thus squelching the joy of being surprised as she wrote. "Maybe," she said, "but I think most about my stories as I talk them out with a friend of mine. We both share story ideas." There might be the problem, I suggested: Talking. The *Bhagavad Gita* (17.15) describes a type of *tapas* and control of speech called *van-maya-tapas*. The passage advises the yogi to speak the truth with kindness and with nonharmful honesty. I offered her a variation of how as a writer you can speak without harming your writing and to speak honestly about your writing: Speak about what you've written, not what you're going to write. A former acquaintance of mine used to spend each night at a coffee shop telling me and others about the fantastic novel he was going to write. For a few weeks, his eyes would open wide and his voice would grow animated as he described this marvelous plot about an escaped prisoner and an aide to the president of the United States. I loved to hear him talk about it. Yet, after a year, he hadn't budged beyond outlining some ideas. When I asked him when he was going to write the novel, he said, "Well, I think I've already written it by talking to everybody. It doesn't excite me so much anymore."

Let the surprise simmer and surface while you write, not while you talk.

I also suggest to students that three times a week, for at least a month, they try doing other things that they avoid besides writing. Call your mother. Try a handstand. Cook a meal (or ask your lover to cook a meal, depending on what you avoid). If you're a multitasker, what's difficult for you is simply to do nothing. So do nothing except gaze at a pond. We take a lifetime to learn how to do nothing, and to do it well. Sometimes, writers claim their writing practice must subtract from their living. I disagree. All things in balance. For once you meet your writing with vigor and persistence, then you may be even more willing and excited to dance until the early morning hours, to eat three-cheese lasagna for lunch, to climb a tree, to listen to Lou Reed play live, in short, to live with gusto and with the fullness of body and imagination that all of those activities merit. But doing a few things that you tend to avoid gradually can build stamina and help you persevere even when the writing gets tough.

Still, some of us must transform our constitution at a subtler level. We can change all of our external circumstances to help our writing: We can rearrange our schedules to write for an hour or more a day, we can change jobs, we can move to the Bahamas, we can build a studio in our backyard, but all of this changing and rearranging will come to nothing for most of us if we lack some inner heat. A student of mine several years ago said he used to flounder whenever he realized that a short story would require several more revisions to "get it right." After writing for seven years, he had expected it to get easier. When he still struggled, he often lacked the will to persist. Another student in the same class complained, "My last story has been rejected ten times." She lacked zeal as well. How do you keep writing? At the time, I could offer little other solace than to advise them to keep writing and to build resolve. I told the student frustrated with rejection to hold out for twenty rejections. When I had started sending off work to be published over sixteen years ago, the twentieth one was accepted. One in twenty is a fair ratio.

I realize now, though, that both of these students, both good writers, might have benefited not just from a reality check about the hardships of writing but also from some yogic *upaya* (tools) to alter their internal heat—tools that I now share with my students. Although lack of perseverance may be in part psychological, yoga also works on the psyche in part via the body—the physical body and the subtle body. These labels of "physical body" and "subtle body" come from how the ancient *Taittiraya-Upanishad* (Part II, 2.1–5.1), as well as some later yoga texts, describe our bodies as having three core layers: the physical (gross) body, the subtle body, and the causal body. For now, we'll consider only the first two. The most obvious body is the physical body of blood, bones, organs. Yoga poses most directly moderate the physical body's circulation, metabolism, cell production, organ function, and sensory stimulation. Beyond the physical body is the subtle body, the body of breath, emotion, intelligence, and knowledge. The subtle body, accessed by breath control and other yoga tools, helps yoga practitioners shift their energy—their physical, mental, and emotional energy. Several ancient yoga texts describe specific energy centers and energy channels in the physical body that can be manipulated and controlled. As "woo-woo" as it may sound to talk about energy outside the context of petrol, electricity, solar, or wind, biologists' and neurobiologists' recent research, as well as studies in acupuncture, are confirming the existence of some such energy conduits.[2]

Our inner fire simmers most pronouncedly in an energy center located approximately, but not literally, in our belly. Most of us have heard of the solar plexus, our inner sun, located near our navel, that can burn bright within throughout the day. To Hatha-Yogis and Tantra-Yogis, this region of the subtle body, called the *manipura cakra*, stores our ability to manifest will into action. Our English tongue's metaphors reinforce the idea: We must have "the guts" to walk across hot coals, or we must have a "strong stomach" to withstand hardship, or we might have "fire in the belly" that lets us act upon our deepest desires. Dead metaphors, like yogic symbols, suggest our ancestors had some intuition about how the body and psyche relate.

From just above your navel to your waist's left side, right next to the upper portion of your small intestine, resides your pancreas gland. Working in harmony with the pancreas and the liver, the pancreas's endocrine cells secrete the protein hormones insulin and glucagon, which together moderate blood sugar content. Healthy doses of insulin especially boost our energy by shuttling glucose across the livers' and muscles' cell membranes. To avoid energy stagnation, the pancreas's exocrine cells produce enzymes that aid the small intestine's digestion. One ancient cleansing process called **SHINING SKULL CLEANSING** (*kapāla-bhāti-kriya*) efficiently clears some of the body's passages to give you instant vigor and energy, like drinking a double espresso without the erratic brain activity or the caffeine letdown two hours later. Involving rapid, forceful exhalations and passive inhalations, this process also fires up the liver, spleen, and pancreas—all working for your digestion—so again the digestive tract can be restful to boost your stamina. Another practice that involves sucking in your abdominal walls is called **SOARING LOCK**, *uddīyāna bandha*—loosely translated as "a lock that lets energy fly up."[3] The subtle body contains over a hundred energy circuits called *nadis* that maintain the physical body. Since many of these energy circuits originate in or near the belly region, this practice can quickly rouse a dormant, sluggish body and a resistant psyche. In *uddīyāna bandha*, the energy flows from the lower abdomen up to the brain. When this region, then, is active and fluent, we have the stomach to confront what we avoid, to follow through on promises to ourselves and to our muse, and to transform wispy wishes and base dreams into elegant phrases, sentences, poems, stories, and books. We have heat to write what we need to write.

It was 4:30 the other morning, and I had been writing for three hours. When I can't sleep, I sense what my body and mind need to do. That morning, it was walking and writing, writing and walking. It's autumn, a season that often heightens my focus. The predawn autumn air's crispness collects the skin between my brows as it collects the energy in tree limbs. Chlorophyll-deprived, the birch and maple sleeves of our road have slowly grown golden and amber. In autumn my body feels as if its leaves change hue and gradually fall to a cold floor, forcing my mind and body to focus upon its remaining nutrients. Maybe the shortened daylight makes me fear, unconsciously, that time may be falling away and that I, thus, must work with more awareness and persistence. In this melancholy season, I welcome an internal heat. While walking toward town, I saw a glow from behind the local glassmaker's house, so I mothed my way toward it and found the young glassmaker in his shed blowing his torch. From the metal pipe, blue, orange, and yellow flames licked the liquid he kept in a vat. He looked up, nodded, and continued, concentrating on his work. I thought for a moment of Heraclitus, that pre-Socratic mountain dweller obsessed with flames, whose fragments on fire remain: "Lightning is the lord of everything" and "Everything becomes fire, and from fire everything is born." Within fifteen minutes, from his hands a vase with pecan-colored and goldenrod-tinted swirls was born.

So it is with writing. The *Shiva-Samhita* says that if you keep a sustained focus upon your *manipura-cakra*, you can make gold. The best writers I know are alchemists who make treasure from base words. What's alchemy's source? Heat.

$\mathcal{T}$AKE A BREATH #1: SHINE YOUR SKULL

A young man used to come to my house each week for writing lessons. A brilliant mind and a passionate musician, he also seemed rather lackluster. The weight of being young showed in his ponderous eyes and languid voice. When it came time for him to write during our sessions, either he'd ask 101 questions or sputter a word at a time. When he'd go home, sometimes his focus was even more scattered. So, I gave him the following suggestion to sharpen his mind and heat his belly. It worked. He would practice it to give himself a "charge," he said.

FRIENDLY WARNING:
Anyone with high blood pressure, poor lung capacity, ulcers, or eye or ear irritations should avoid this process. If pregnant, avoid these practices because of their pressure on the abdomen.

INTENTION:
Try this practice when you need to muster the resolve to write with vigor and perseverance.

SHINING SKULL CLEANSING BREATH (kapāla-bhāti-kriya) *gives you back your luster. Here's a way to practice: Before your writing* session, sit quietly for at least two full breaths, lengthening your spine in both directions. Set your twofold writing intention. Then, when ready, exhale vigorously through both nostrils, allowing the inhalation to take care of itself. Vigorous exhale, passive inhale, vigorous exhale, passive inhale. The exhalation should draw up your abdominal walls, which warms up the belly's sun and shoots rays of light, so to speak, to your skull. Then, relax your body and stomach as you begin your writing session. As you encounter challenging parts of your writing or as your energy wanes, redirect your focus to your inner sun. Try another round. After a week try three rounds of forty. Gradually build to three rounds of sixty and then one hundred and twenty.

$\mathcal{T}$AKE A BREATH #2: STOKE YOUR WRITER'S FIRE

Shandor Remete, a remarkable yogi and teacher from Australia, calls his yoga forms "Shadow of Yoga" (www.shadowyoga.com), a name he draws principally from the ancient text Shiva-Svarodaya. The following practice marks the very beginning of one of his forms he taught me in Boston. It's a variation of a traditional practice. You might review the illustrations for **SOARING LOCK** (uddīyāna bandha) in the Appendix.

Stand in **MOUNTAIN POSE** (tādāsana) next to your desk, feet a foot apart. Set your twofold writing intention. Then when ready, place your hands on your hips. Keep your soles and heels rooted. Take a full inhale. Then on the exhalation make the following simultaneous movements: As you bend your knees and slide your hands, arms straight, down your thighs with your fingers facing inward, exhale all of the air out of your lungs with your mouth open and your tongue stretched toward your chin as far as it will go. Drawing your tongue out naturally lifts the abdominal walls. Then, draw back your belly and lift it up or suck it in so your abdominal region will be slightly or significantly concave. Retain your breath for three seconds. Holding the abdominal lock and your breath, return slowly to **MOUNTAIN POSE**. Release the lock and inhale deeply and gracefully. Repeat at least three to five times. This process takes some getting used to. Be patient. Within a week or less, most writers adapt. While stimulating the abdominal walls as well as the internal organs of digestion, it also warms the belly's sun—the gastric glands.

Then, move from your mat to your desk to write what needs to be written from your belly. With each word unfolding on the screen or page, imagine the heat flowing from your belly through your limbs to keep you stoked even when the day and the practice get dark.

CHAPTER FOUR

Inspiration and Joyful Concentration: A Matter of Breath

Prolonged concentration seems a mystery to some writers. A writer I know can write for six hours straight on the same subject without budging from the screen. When I asked him how he does it, he said, "Oh, it's simple." Then he took a deep breath and held it. Is having concentration as easy as holding your breath? Not exactly. But consider the alternative perspective. Another writer recently told me she has Attention Deficit Disorder. We were discussing writing habits, and she—a writer and English professor for over twenty years—said she recently hasn't been able to sit still for over thirty minutes. Not that she doesn't *want* to: She has plenty of willpower. Not that her schedule won't allow it: She has lots of free time. Her mind, she said, won't allow it. When I asked her when she was diagnosed with ADD, she said she labeled herself. I've met other writers like her. Victims of their own minds and possibly of their own self-perception, some writers buy into the idea that we live in "the Age of Distraction." A book by that name came out a few years ago, a politician recently gave a speech called "Politics in the Age of Distraction," and another writer recently published a book titled *The Zen of Listening: Mindful Communication in the Age of Distraction*. When I tell other writers about this tag for our era, they nod their heads in recognition of lives cluttered with Palm Pilots, faxes, cell phones with a hundred programmed numbers, televisions with five hundred channels, and e-mail boxes with twenty Listserv messages coming every few hours. Who has time, a writer might wonder, to contemplate world peace, much less personal peace to write a novel?

We writers shouldn't feel, though, that we're special in our challenges to concentrate. The Age of Distraction has been going on since well before this era of gadgetry. The mind, a microcosm of the universe's perennial dance of change, naturally shifts and wanders as it reflects nature's inherent tendencies to be in flux. It's comforting for me to know so, since my mind still pings and pongs on some days from writing a paragraph to wanting to paint the barn to alphabetizing my novels by their first line. Still, to sustain this journey, we'd do well to find ways that keep our body-minds centered on the task at hand.

Yoga helps me to center my thoughts. I often return to a popular yoga text, the *Yoga-Sutra*, comprised of 195 aphorisms penned by yoga scholar Patanjali probably sometime around 200 c.e. Consider the second sutra, which reads *"Yogah-cittavrtti-nirodhah,"* "Yoga is the cessation of the mind's fluctuations." One of yoga's aims for over two thousand years has been to quiet and to harness our thoughts and inner chatter through *dharana*. *Dharana* describes a sophisticated form of concentration that advanced yogis achieve after several years of intricate practice.[1] I'm less interested in *dharana*'s esoteric dimensions, however, than I am in its practical application to help writers be at ease with a deliberate focus on word upon word. What I call joyful concentration is a way to be authentically centered upon our writing. As breath and body befriend a writer's mind, joyful concentration comes from openness and ease more than from force or will and is, dare I say it, inspiring.

Most experienced writers glare, if not sneer, when someone mentions inspiration. Faulkner said, "I don't know anything about inspiration, because I don't know what inspiration is—I've heard about it, but I never saw it." There's a certain truth to not being smug about the ease of one's writing, for often when I've thought my writing has gone swimmingly, I've in fact come close to drowning in delusion. We wizened scribes know that our work is toilsome, sweat wrenching, Sisyphean. Even when we have the flu or a migraine, we must push our monolithic manuscripts up the inclines of our personal underworlds. Only neophytes, we say, speak of and wait for chubby cherubs or dancing pixies or sword-wielding goddesses to visit before writing. But these inspiring visitations may not be sexy matters of magic; they may be simple matters of breath and body. In Anne Lamott's *Bird by Bird*, a delightful book on writing, the author mentions the importance of breathing to her writing practice: When she deliberately deepens and slows down her breathing, that incessant internal chatter that wants her to color-code her clothes or deep-clean the microwave dissipates, or at least quiets long enough for her to begin the necessary work of writing. In her simple breath work, the author has stumbled upon one of the most fundamental principles underlying the practice Hatha-Yoga and the attempt to gain some control over the mind's fluctuations. Yet she almost apologizes for even mentioning breathing in the context of writing for fear she might sound like her flighty New Age friends. To focus upon our breathing, however, need not lead to crystal healing and channeling Oscar Wilde; it can move us toward the center, concentration.

I have a basic theory about the bards who sang to the muses to inspire them. Homer asks the muse to "sing" to him of Odysseus, Ovid prays the gods "breathe" upon him the tales of the world's metamorphosis, and the Puritan poet Milton doesn't call upon God to sing of humanity's fall from Paradise but upon "Thou O Spirit." These bards—as they call for song, breath, spirit—may be praying to have what every writer deeply desires and needs to write well and long: the song of joyful concentration. Song is a wielding of words with heart-centered breath that praises and celebrates the human condition as well as informs our soul of reality's darker regions. These bards ask for this breath. When Milton called upon the Spirit instead of God, he must have sensed the root of *spirit*, the same as the root of *inspiration*: the Latin *spirare*, to breathe, and the Latin *spiritus*, the breath of life, soul.

When yogis speak of breath, they often speak of *prāna*. *Prāna* in Sanskrit is sort of the *chi* of yoga, the *spiritus*. What makes breath possible, *prāna* is that creative element that let Prometheus mix water and breath into clay and so create human beings, that births lotus flowers from muddy waters, that lets images and memories and words combust into epics or memoirs or novels. In short, *prāna* is creation, the in-breath of the gods and goddesses. To be inspired is to breathe in. *Prānāyāma* is the art of becoming aware of and harnessing breath to vitalize the body, to alter space within the body, and to increase concentration and awareness. To engage in *prāna* is to part the clouds—the clouds in your lungs and mind.

Breathing deeply, with our mind's attention on breath's fluent river, can tangibly alter our brain chemistry and shift the speed of our brain waves. Herbert Benson's research out of Harvard (*The Relaxation Response; The Breakout Principle*, Scribner, 2003) and several other neuroscientists' research is scientifically accounting for what yogis have known for millennia: working with the intricate layers of the body heightens human beings' creativity. *Nitric oxide* is a buzzword around science labs these days. It's a chemical that might account for much of what we call "mind." Some people call it the chemical of God. When released through meditation, controlled breathing, and physical exertion, it stimulates and releases endorphins and dopamines, the brain's neurotransmitters responsible for inducing pleasure, relieving pain, and arousing happiness to raise its sleepy head.[2] It also heightens creative thinking and imagining.

We can experience different states of awareness that correlate to the brain's wave patterns. Beta brain waves bounce and flip at about thirteen to thirty cycles per second. On an EEG (an electroencephalograph, or machine that maps the brain's electricity), beta waves look like jagged flames. When we're in "beta brain," we can multitask, chat to three people at once, or navigate busy sidewalks or streets to get to our next meeting. Beta brain is busy brain, and it's where many of us live most of the time. My friend Helen will begin a story about how her daughter landed a new job with a consulting firm, but before she can finish that story she's telling me another about the mouse she saw last night scurry across her kitchen floor and before she finishes telling me what her languid cat did in response she starts another story about the time her older sister tried to bury her in the backyard. I love trying to follow Helen's stories within stories, but she rarely gets to the punch line. Although she writes more coherent short stories, she often complains about how long they take her to write.

Alpha brain waves pulse at about eight to thirteen cycles per second, notably more slowly than their beta friends. In "alpha brain," we can concentrate on a single task, get "in the flow" that high achievers, runners, and writers describe. This state of awareness approaches what in yoga is called *ekagrata*—one-pointedness. Fewer of us reach this state regularly, but if you've ever been frustrated because you can't concentrate on a single page you're reading or center on what you're *writing* because your mind flutters like a moth from thought to thought, then you may have difficulty shifting from beta brain to alpha brain. Breathing from the diaphragm and abdomen particularly, versus breathing from the midback or thoracic level, is more likely to let brain patterns flow into alpha waves, those waves that induce more artistic surfing as stress floats out to tide.[3]

A couple of years ago a highly energetic person named Katie came to me with a book idea. Encumbered with bags of four-inch three-ring notebooks that tried to contain her mounds of notes and drafts and transcriptions, she sat down and for ninety minutes talked nonstop about her book idea, her work, her experiences leading up to the book, her marriage, her child, her sister-in-law, and so forth—all ostensibly related to her book idea and why she sought my guidance. When I read a draft of a story for Katie's book, the pace flustered me like her speech: The story was speaking *at* me, scenes were left incomplete, characters undeveloped, transitions almost invisible. "Any suggestions?" she asked. After I commended her on what was truly a compelling book topic, I said, "Let's practice breathing." She grinned and grimaced simultaneously ("grinnaced"?). I tactfully explained to Katie what I observed in her writing and recommended we focus upon her breathing patterns as a way to help her slow down her white-rapid thoughts. Luckily, she was open to the idea (or at least was open to humoring me). After introducing her to some breathing exercises, I suggested she practice them at home before and even as she wrote and revised her stories. For the next four weeks, at the beginning of our writing sessions we practiced breathing exercises for ten minutes.

The changes were subtle, yet significant. As she spoke, she caught and redirected her thoughts before they spiraled out of control. The pace of her writing allowed readers to dwell richly in key places. Images became fuller and more precise so the texture of her baby's moist hand versus her husband's coarse knuckles could enter her readers' imaginations. Katie told me, too, she felt more focused as she wrote and checked herself when she seemed to be speeding ahead to get finished. Heeding her breath, she said, helped her slow down and appreciate her writing as she wrote. She was, in essence, learning the tunes to her own song of concentration.

We can tap into this inner spring of joyful concentration by making slight readjustments not only in how we breathe but also in how we ground our thoughts in our lower bodies—instead of in our heads. Distraction may stem partially from blocked energy in our lower body. Near our sacrum and our tailbone is a plexus (system of nerves) that helps moderate our basic functions of urinating, defecating, and having sex. The perineum—our torso's base, located between our anus and genitals—along with this system of nerves comprises our root clearing or center, our *mūladhāra cakra.* *Mala* means "root" in Sanskrit as well as "firmly fixed, source or cause, basis, the foot, lowest part or bottom, foundation."[4] When we contract the perineum, we ground the lower body's energy in a lock called *mūla-bandha* (root lock). By engaging *mūla-bandha,* we also contract not only the pudendal nerves located near our genitals and the perineum but also a series of energy channels that in turn stimulate and moderate our liver, gall bladder, stomach, and spleen. When irritated or compressed, these passages affect how other parts of our body function. Consider the obvious: If food, that potential source of physical nourishment, does not run through us easily and does not provide our bodies with optimum energy, then our torso and brain's little helpers will scurry around, unable to focus clearly upon our writing afoot. Awakening this area can help us write from a steady place of sustenance instead of distraction.

So I suggest to my students some easy ways to awaken their lower bodies so their upper bodies—mostly their headful of thoughts—can rest a bit while they write with a far clearer stream of consciousness. With frequent practice, we can teach our mind to work for, not against, our writing. Recapturing our concentration need not be a struggle. Drawing our attention to our lower body quiets "writer's mind," and harnessing our breath can help us ride the alpha waves of joyful concentration.

*T*AKE A BREATH #1: RIDE THE ALPHA WAVES

This practice helps you use the ROOT LOCK *(mūla-bandha) and* EQUAL MOVEMENT BREATHING PRACTICE *(sama-vrtti prāṇā-yāma) to heighten concentration for your writing.*

INTENTION:
Engage this practice when you need extended concentration to write on a single subject for long periods of time.

Sit firm yet soft, grounded with the earth. Take one of four seated positions. If you can do so, sit comfortably in a kneeling position with your buttocks resting on your heels. You can place a pillow between your thighs and calves if you wish. This pose—called **ADAMANTINE POSE/ KNEELING POSE** *(vajrāsana)—opens the perineum and pelvic floor as well as piques the feet and legs. In this pose you may feel adamantine, glowing and stalwart. Or try to sit on a cushion with your knees out to the sides, your right heel tucked firmly beneath your perineum (the muscle at your torso's spine between your genitals), and your left heel resting in front of your right foot or ankle. This pose, a variation of* **ADEPT'S POSE** *(siddhāsana), also rouses the root area. Otherwise, sit either in an easy crossed-legged position (sukhāsana) or on the edge of a chair in* **WRITER'S FRIENDSHIP POSE** *(maitrīyāsana)—the latter being a perfect preparation for writing. Review the illustrations and captions for seated poses in the Appendix if you wish.*

Close your eyes and focus on your breath. If you're comfortable doing so, on each of the next five exhalations, direct the flow of your breath upward as you contract and draw up your perineum. You may have difficulty doing so without contracting your anus at first, which is a common way to start. This contraction is the root lock, mūla-bandha. Once you're comfortable with this lock, just focus again on your breath, and set your twofold intention. Once you remind yourself what you are writing for, you might set a specific intention such as "I need to recall and follow the sequential details of that horrific first date for my memoir" or "I need to give this central scene my best concentration for at least three hours." Let this intention matter to you. Feel its pleasurable weight in your body like a natural root extending from your torso's base that will keep you anchored so you can write what you need to write.

Doing nothing special with your breath, for a few minutes keep your eyes closed as you try to follow the stream of images—sights and sounds and associations and stories and voices—that float through your consciousness. Try not to impede the mighty stream's flow. Take a few minutes to observe their random movement. Don't edit. Now, let's try to shift the rhythm from beta brain to alpha brain waves. Keeping alert yet relaxed, breathe deeply. To a slow count of four, let your inhalation expand your diaphragm and belly like a balloon that floats up to your chest. Then, as you contract your perineum, to a count of four slowly let the breath's inner force float out your nose and down your torso as you imagine it massaging your organs. That inhalation and exhalation is one round. Keep this stream's motion between your root center and your chest moving steadily for ten full rounds. Anytime you sense the stream wishes to flow off course with a thought about your kids' supper or a deadline, return your attention to the breath. As you heed your breath, feel this stream deeply in your body.

When you open your eyes, keep your thoughts in that stream as you return to your writing intention. Begin then with that intention and write one breath at a time, steady from your body's base to your heart region, calmly, deliberately. When your thoughts flow off your pen's or word processor's course, focus on your breath and your root area, and guide your mind back to your page. Feel that your lower body befriends your mind to give your writing the concentration it deserves.

TAKE A BREATH #2:
HOLD YOUR BREATH TO MAKE SPACE

INTENTION:
For this practice, find a piece of your writing that needs expansion in a section. Maybe a dramatic scene between two lovers who are making love in an alley behind a grocery store needs a prolonged yet urgent pace. Possibly a section of an essay should describe the inside of a Russian kiosk but instead reads too rapidly and abstractly.

Settle in your seat, take two full breaths, and when ready set your twofold intention. Let your intention matter to your whole body as you breathe it in. Once you choose the piece you wish to rework, reread the section that needs expansion. As you read the section to yourself, pay attention to two key words or images. For instance, if you're writing a story about a boy who loves to rummage through an abandoned house down the road, a key word might be forage *and an image might be* "pearls" *(if that's what he finds). Just note them without "doing" anything* to them. Then, set aside your writing, recline on your back, knees bent or straight. Get comfortable, but stay alert and awake. This pose is called LYING RELEASE POSE/CORPSE POSE (savā-sana), and its supine position makes it a favorite among yogis and writers.

Rest and breathe normally and completely for a few breaths. With each slow exhalation imagine parts of your body sinking into earth. Feel the back of your neck melt. Your torso melds with the ground, as do your hips and heels. Now begin to see the two images from your chosen piece or hear the key words and phrases. Imagine them as the piece's bones. As you breathe fully, imagine the piece as a body in need of nutrients and a bit more "flesh" that your joyful concentration will provide.

> **FRIENDLY WARNING:**
> Breath retention is regarded in many ways to be the heart of ancient yoga practices. If you're a beginner to yoga, practice any kind of breath retention such as this one with caution. If you have untreated high or low blood pressure or a heart condition, avoid this breath retention unless under a holistic physician's supervision.

Then, after you let your breath fill your belly and lungs again, hold your breath. First for four seconds. Release slowly. Then, only if you feel comfortable doing so, try to hold again for six seconds. Then, only if you feel comfortable doing so, eight. Make the practice joyful even as you challenge yourself. As you make space in your lungs and rib cage by holding your breath, you also create space in constricted parts of your writing.

Breathing normally again, imagine the scene literally opening up as you see the key details and images that can grant your writing depth. Feel your whole body open up to give its resources to your piece of writing.

When ready, slowly open your eyes, keeping attention on your breath. Begin to rewrite the constricted piece of writing with the sensation that you're nourishing this writing and giving it the heartiness and full body it needs to be effective and authentic. When you notice your concentration waning, don't fight your mind. Instead, let simple breath expansion or retention move it toward single-pointedness—the single point being the moment of writing your scene.

II.
SETTING OUT

CHAPTER FIVE

Dummies and Self-Study: Creating an Authentic Voice

How did Billie Holiday cultivate a voice that conjures in one moment the image of an auto mechanic's oil mixed with whiskey and in the next the image of a sleek black panther that moves along a baobab branch invisible at night? As a young lady, did Bessie Smith notice the way her voice romped with the spirit of a robust bull gliding upon a river's lip? Did teachers tell little Janis Joplin that her voice vibrated people's sinews like a wild bird's caw? So I wondered one night as these vocalists' serenades haunted me. What distinguishes Smith, Holiday, and Joplin as vocalists, and not just singers, rests less with the songs they wrote or were given than with *how* their voices could mix the matter—words on sheet music. A vocalist's voice is will, spirit, and soul stirring breath's rhythms. So, too, in the lines of a fortunate writer who can mix the stuff that makes a writer's voice and gives it a timbre.

Perhaps no facet of writing seems as fleeting and strange to attain as that ephemeral quality we call "voice." Voice animates otherwise stagnant written words. It charges written words with personality and verve, or with reservation and gravitas. It is a writer's near-invisible signature on a page like a watermark. But if you hold a novel's page up to the light, you still won't find the secret traces of a writer's voice. So, how do writers, without the resources of vocalists, create distinct and authentic voices? Since writers can't whisper directly on the page like Marlene Dietrich or sneer like Ani di Franco, some rhetoricians suggest that we "write in the language of intelligent conversation" and that a writer's voice should sound "natural." But how do we sound "natural" with the written word? And who is to determine whether the speaking voice of William F.

Buckley, Jr., Howie Mandel, or Snoop Doggy Dogg is the better model for sounding "natural"?

Most writers I meet either have or hunger for a voice that they feel is real, authentic. We know that words on the page don't strike an audible chord; yet, when we read something written with an authentic voice, it often strikes an "unstruck sound," something deep within us. An unstruck sound, *anāhata* in Sanskrit, originates from the heart region, a region that yogis have realized for centuries is a source of authentic language. So to "write from the heart" can have a literal reality. Something in a careful ear that hears an "unstruck sound" can help us fashion a distinct, authentic voice on the page. Ultimately, with study and listening, we can write with confidence and courage as our work manifests our deepest intentions.

Students often ask how they can find their voice. Stop searching, I suggest. This idea of "finding" one true voice, as if it's hidden somewhere or as if we lost it as kids, frustrates writers, I think. Writers with an authentic voice have not so much "found" their *one* true voice as they have found their way with words, a combination of movements with favorite words and images, ways of thinking and structuring sentences and paragraphs (a Faulknerian sentence versus a Hemingwayesque one) that may in part distinguish their voice. They have grown intimate with their tongue long enough to help them move from word to word confidently and convincingly. They also have become intimate with that complex network of senses and thoughts and perceptions we call "self" that mixes up words for better or worse. There's nothing magic about this process. It just requires work and study.

The yoga practice of *svādhyāya* is "study," "self-study," and means more literally "moving into one's self." Identified in Patanjali's *Yoga-Sutra* (circa 200 c.e.) as an essential yoga practice, *svādhyāya* typically involves studying, memorizing, chanting, and reciting sacred texts to deepen our understanding of a higher self. Through this practice, we honor those teachers who have gone before us and have laid stepping-stones for us that we may eventually add our own stones. We also honor language's sacred capacity to inform our hearts. These modes of *svādhyāya* also work on the self the way being absorbed in literature does: We dissolve our ego needs into another text that something greater than the ego might be aroused to reflection and action. Some of us are drawn to read literature not only to study the self but also to allow the self's boundaries to expand, to be inclusive of far more than our ego may want. Similarly, some of us read ancient yoga texts to reflect upon what the "self" indeed is or is not. *Svādhyāya* for yogis has two turns: a turn toward texts and a turn toward one's own mind and heart, both to explore one's self. So, too, *svādhyāya* for writers, I suggest to students, has two turns: a turn toward texts and a turn toward the mind and heart.

Never stop reading and studying. Most writers who have mustered an authentic voice study or have studied certain texts that have preceded them—the sacred and the profane. On my bookshelves, the *Bhagavad-Gita* rests next to George Bernard Shaw's plays. The *Yoga-Sutra* informs my reading of *Crime and Punishment* and vice versa. Both texts can move you into uncomfortable parts of the self. Writers study writers whose voices they admire. When we read with the pace of a summer afternoon sentences deftly crafted, voices of the dead and of the present might mesh with what voice we deem our own. Such a process is more likely to lead a writer to developing a memorable writer's voice than listening solely to the way she speaks in intelligent conversation. I converse with the printed word. I converse with dead writers. And, I admit, they shape my voice.

Like trying on personas to see which one fits for an identity, we can try out other writers' voices to see which ones sound right. True, Emerson wrote that "imitation is suicide." Yet, the then-self-reliant zealot already had spent years imitating and emulating Carlyle and Lamb until the point that he at last developed a nearly inimitable voice as orator and essayist, a voice we now admiringly—or usually so—call "Emersonian." Eliot also wrote some of his best poems while immersed in reading the rhythms of Donne's poems, of Ovid's tales, of St. John's Gospel. Nobel Prize recipient Seamus Heaney has written about his "Hopkins ventriloquism," how Gerard Manley Hopkins's voice shaped young Heaney's ear.[1] Our identities are largely unique composites of other elements; so, too, most writers' writing voices. An authentic writer's voice, then, does not come ex nihilo from some ideal plane of pure originality; it is in part a voice we admit has been influenced by our teachers, our mentors.

Some writers are or become, as Emerson called essayists, "ventriloquists." So, for a while become a writer ventriloquist. It may seem counterintuitive to recommend that to develop an authentic voice you should study other voices, but that's precisely what I'm suggesting: "Throw your voice" to see what feels and sounds right in your heart.

I started to find my voice through ventriloquism. My grandfather had told me all about Edgar Bergen, the renowned ventriloquist who set one or both of his dummies, the gentlemanly and monocled Charlie McCarthy or the dimwitted and bucktoothed Mortimer Snerd, on his knees and breathed life into wood. After I saw television footage of Bergen doing his thing, I thought at age ten he could perform the most magical act: He could throw his voice. I imagined that if you were standing next to him and three other adults at a party engaged in intelligent conversation, he could utter something vulgar like "I've really got to fart" and make it sound as if it had come from the man standing across from you who sucks on his pipe and tries to look debonair. Bergen did all of this in the name of humor, but humor, I later would understand, in the best sense: His humor exposed the pretenses of civilized society and manners, and the foibles of our prejudices and ignorance.

The texts you study aren't dummies, but they can work like Charlie McCarthys. I've encouraged writers for years to seek out either a "remote" or a dead mentor. A remote mentor is a writer still living, yet who advises a writer solely via the mentor's texts. A dead mentor is the same, of course, just dead. So Scott Russell Sanders could be a remote mentor; Virginia Woolf, a dead one. Most of us *love* the writing of certain authors. You sense in that voice something kindred that kindles your heart, that may even register a visceral response. With this view of writers, you realize you exist in a huge *sat-sanga*, what in Sanskrit means a community of like-spirited individuals, with boundaries far superseding your home's space and your biographical age's time. Through such study, your writer's heart may never be alone.

When you've found such a mentor, find a passage—fifty words, a hundred words, may suffice. Then read and heed—slowly—the syllables, the twists in syntax, the edgy wit or bawdy humor, or the saturnine gravitas that drums through the paragraphs. Let the passage wash over and in you. Then begin to record, word by word, this passage. Notice how your body feels as you handwrite these sentences' rhythms. Your inner ear cannot help but tune in. Numerous writers keep notebooks full of such passages, not just for the passage's message but also for the qualities I've just noted: the cadences, the images, the twists, the tones.

Commit a few lines to memory. Choose something that you feel expands your sense of who you are as a writer, something that informs your own writer's voice. *Committed to Memory: 100 Best Poems to Memorize*, edited by John Hollander, is a good source. Although poetry with regular meter, sound, and form is easier for the brain to retain, some fiction and nonfiction merits memorization, if not recitation as well. You don't have to chant Molly Bloom's reveries or Raskolnikov's observations, as yogis do with sacred texts. Still, the process of memorization can bring a passage's essence into our hearts. You'll feel and hear those rhythms creeping into your writing. (So be careful what you choose to memorize.)

Begin an informal writers' study group. I know of a nonfiction writers' group formed from one of my workshops that gathered solely to read to one another not their own writings but the writings of authors from whom they had learned. Usually six to ten of them would alternate meeting at one another's homes and then each took turns to read a passage from E. B. White, Phillip Lopate, Jeanette Winterson, Terry Tempest Williams, Kenko—various nationalities and eras represented. When I cofounded the literary organization WordSpace in Dallas, one of my first projects was "PoetTalk." I invited a writer to prepare a talk and lead a discussion among other writers on the work of a certain poet. This practice is an enjoyable way both to deepen your knowledge of other writers' works and to honor these writers—contemporaries and predecessors alike—as teachers.

Study a few works by a mentor whose voice you want to imitate if not emulate. Michael Cunningham's novel *The Hours* is an extended study of emulation and an homage to one of his dead mentors, Virginia Woolf. In your study, be receptive to the writer's sensibilities to language, to experience, to humanity. Consider some of these questions: What about the writer's work reveals truths about our complex emotions? How does this writing allow you to descend

into the questions that keep you awake at night? Why, with this author's book in your hands, do you tremble with self-recognition and
self-realization? How is your sense of self altered or challenged? Consider some fundamental questions of style too: On what subjects
does the writer often focus? What types of characters? Themes? Are
the writer's sentences typically long or short? How are they varied for
effect? Is the writer's vocabulary typically lifted from the streets or bor-
rowed from literary dens? Do images and metaphors pepper the writing,
or is it seemingly plain spoken? You're not demystifying the magic of
that mentor's voice. You're discovering some tangible ways to honor
that voice via imitation and emulation—the highest compliment.

Then, choose a subject—maybe a twist on what this writer
might choose—and write the passage as if you wrote with the other
writer's voice. That is, throw your voice, and write whatever you
want to. The other writer's voice becomes an intelligent dummy, so
to speak, for your self to fill out, for your voice to breathe into without fear of too much self-disclosure. You can hide behind your mentor's voice like a ventriliquist. And such hiding is fine, as long as
you know you're doing so. Have fun saying what you want about
whatever you want in this other voice. One student chose Annie
Proulx as a mentor, and then wrote a fictional piece about sex—its
mishaps and disappointments, some exquisite fantasies—as if Proulx
had written it. If you've feared exploring some dreadful feelings
about your existence or your work's illusory nature, and if your
mentor is Barbara Kingsolver, then write a piece from a desperate
character's point of view as if it were in a Kingsolver novel. You'll
know you're finished when you reread the piece and can't believe
you wrote it. And when you read it to your writers' group, your
friends won't believe you wrote it either. *You* didn't write it, you'll
claim. Proulx or Kingsolver did. Yeah, *she* wrote it. Not me. And
yet, you did write it. And you expanded "you."

At some point, though, we make the second turn of *svādhyāya*
as we learn to listen to that still, small voice in our heart, that
source of our own authenticity unmediated by mentors.

I first heard that voice when I was eight and taught my cousin
Donna how to pray. I attended church; she never had. "How do you
pray?" she asked. We got on our knees beside her bed, bowed our
heads, cupped our hands. "Don't speak out loud," I said. "Just talk

in your head without speaking and say whatever you want to say to God." I concentrated and waited. I don't recall what I tried to discuss with the Almighty, but I did hear a voice, confident and kind, knowledgeable and unassuming. "Yep," I said to Donna, "I can hear God speak." She didn't believe me. "Listen, just keep your eyes shut, and listen," I said. Smirking, she tried it. Perhaps not to be one-upped, or possibly blessed with a window opening within, she said, "Yeah! I hear Him." For the first time I had become aware of a steady, guiding voice that later became part of my writing voice.

Pat Conroy said he first heard his voice when eighteen years old. Conroy's father ruled his house with a domineering, abusive voice, and then his high school basketball coach's similar voice tore talented young men's confidence into pulp. While the coach was blowing out one of his tirades, Conroy recalls hearing a strong voice within him say, in essence, "Don't listen to that voice. You have your own voice that will guide you." Listening to that voice, Conroy said, would later serve him well as a writer. I suspect it helped him later listen to what his heart needed to say, not to what his ego wanted and not, when he wrote the novel *The Great Santini*, largely based on his father, what his father's ego would've wanted. To hear and to distinguish one authentic voice among the chorus that fills most of our thoughts is not schizophrenic; it is an essential part of unfolding your writer's voice.

We must speak to ourselves, for writing is largely a solitary art. We must release our mind's exhaust upon occasion that we can hear not just *what* our inner voice says but also *how* it rumbles, flows, stutters. Only if I can hear myself think can I muster the courage and clarity to write one decent sentence after another. The rhythm and pace, the hesitation and repetition, of how an inner voice stitches phrases and clauses is, I suspect, different from those qualities of an outer voice.

Many of us may be terrified to sit with ourselves for too long. It's noisy in there. Yet it's a habit that can allow our minds to discern when we're writing from our ego or when we're writing from the heart. Writing habitually from the heart allows our body's natural rhythms to guide our subjects, word choices, metaphors, sounds, and sentences. Gradually a style ensues that we feel pumps from our cells and fits our skin; gradually an authentic voice emerges.

I know there's a voice that visits me when my awareness seems to hover between consciousness and unconsciousness, a twilight voice so lucid and direct, yet so compact—as if it were lecturing in haikus—that I rarely can translate its message word for word. Instead, I just listen and trust that when I need its words or images at the desk, they'll come to me. I trust, too, that had I not just sat and listened and watched within, then the conditions might not have been set for these words later to surface.

As our voices change and assume so many textures over the years, we may wonder if any of us writes with what we call our own voice. But don't fret. We can find pleasure and authenticity not so much in refining some fixed singular voice but in plunging into our own dark ponds' bottoms where thoughts and images mix in the silt with voices of the dead, spawn words, and surface as a voice. Just try not to hang on to any one voice for too long or even to call it your "own." Listen. Respond. Hook it and reel it in, playing it for all it has to give. Then let it go.

$\mathcal{T}$AKE A BREATH: STRIKE YOUR UNSTRUCK AUTHENTIC VOICE

INTENTION:
This practice can help you hear and feel your authentic writer's voice coming from your heart.

Come into a comfortable seated position. Any seated pose or even sitting in a chair is fine. Lengthen your spine in both directions as your body becomes alert, yet at ease. Draw your inhalation to your heart region as your chest expands. After at least two full breaths, ask yourself, "What am I writing for?" Tune your ear to your heart to hear whatever inner voice or image bubbles up, but don't try to force anything into shape. Just listen and watch. When you feel the response sufficiently sink into your heart, clarify your specific writing intention for this session. You might acknowledge that you wish to write with your authentic voice for a specific subject or scene—either one you've been writing about or a new one.

Bring your palms together, slightly cupped, at your heart. This mudrā, *or hand gesture, is called* anjali-mudrā, *a common gesture of respect*

(See Appendix). Close your eyes, and again let your in-breath fill your heart space. On the exhalation, imagine your breath pushing your palms apart as you open your forearms, elbows still bent, to each side so that your palms face forward on either side of your shoulders (see **SEATED EVEN-HEARTED POSE** *in the Appendix). Let the next inhalation naturally draw your palms back together at your heart. Continue this movement between your palms and your breath until you're comfortable with the rhythm.*

Then, imagine in your heart you have a second mouth, ear, and eye that inform the primary sense organs in your skull. Your heart's mouth, with your hands' and inner ears' aid, breathes in and out the rhythms of your authentic writer's voice. Imagine that with each inhalation your hands are drawing into your inner ear and heart whatever you deeply need to say—images, sounds, stories, words. With each exhalation, imagine your heart is guiding that expression, that movement outward. Repeat this rhythm until you feel you've brought sufficient energy into your heart space before writing. Then, just sit for a few minutes and listen to what your heart says for you to write. What does it need you to write? Notice how the voice sounds. Its tenor and tone may even register a visual image. Maybe she speaks like Billie Holiday. Just honor what you hear or see.

If nothing surfaces, relax.

Then begin to write. As you write, imagine a line of communication extending between your heart and your hands. Continue with each breath to write with the interplay between taking something in and giving something out. Ease into the words and sentences, the images and metaphors, that naturally unfold.

When you've finished drafting, you might revise anything that seems forced or not quite the language of your heart. Then read it aloud. Notice if it registers the same texture that you felt, heard, or saw when you listened to your heart while sitting still. Try this practice for at least fifteen consecutive sessions. You will find within a few weeks or months that how you write stems from another, richer source than before, a source that may be best described as your heart center. Anāhata.

CHAPTER SIX

Practicing Presence:
Ways to Heed and Harness
Your Senses

Perched in a tree, I'm trying to expand the present moment by holding my breath through a bloody nose. It's my ninth summer. Small boned, soft faced, blond, and the only boy in my neighborhood with long hair, I had been in a fistfight earlier in the day with a kid a couple of years older. He had called me "girl" or "hippie," I don't remember which, but with a quiet confidence, I released my unexplained rage through my fists. This kid outsized me, though, and a man from down the road had to pull him off of my sprawling body.

I sucked up my pride and the blood from my nose and retreated to the wooded lot down the street. The wooded lot where we kids built tree houses made of slabs the nearby developers left out at night, where we buried *Playboys* for secret viewings, and where we rode our Schwinn and Huffy "motorcycles" to help us flee police. My haven. I found my tree—a fortress unto itself, a huge tree with a gray ash trunk that not even three of me could circle with clasped hands if we tried. With simple wood blocks, I had nailed steps up its trunk until I could reach its strong limbs. This afternoon, here, I have crawled to almost the highest bough until I can see above most of the other trees. The light seems lighter, as does the air. A blackbird swoops by and caws, and suddenly twenty or more blackbirds lift from the limbs of a nearby tree, and another twenty and another twenty until my patch of sky looks black with blue dots speckled across it, black mixed with blue, birds mixed with sky.

Without warning, my body slips, my chin hits a branch, and my little hand, still caked in blood, looses its grip as I tumble to the ground. I had tried to hold the moment. This featherweight moment, suspended on a limb with me above my friends and family and strangers, floating somewhere between the ground where older boys could catch me and the sky where birds could catch me, gave me my first premonition of what it's like to be in the present. I had guessed that if I held my breath I could hold this moment. So while the day's memories floated past with the clouds, I must have stopped my breath until I lost awareness and my grip. A scraped forehead added to my bloody nose.

Being present in this world doesn't have to wound us. Thoreau, that perpetual present-moment monger and chanticleer to the blind and busy, wrote perhaps the most beautiful and influential ode to the life-altering benefits of heeding the present. In the chapter "Where I Lived and What I Lived For" of *Walden*, after taking note of the woods' vital sounds and sights about him, he writes that in comparison with sculpting clay or carving statues "it is far more glorious to carve and paint the very atmosphere and medium through which we look, which morally we can do. To affect the quality of the day, that is the highest of the arts." Granted, we don't have to assume, as did Thoreau, that practicing presence is a moral enterprise.

Still, I think every writer would be wise to try it. Why? Existentially, so you can live in such a way that no day slips past your imagination. Pragmatically, so you can write in a way that your readers' imaginations can enter. To be able to write about the cracks in a basketball player's knuckles or the patches of dirt beneath a gardener's fingernails might require having a useful imagination and memory that can store and then recall images in the moment of writing. But how do we develop a useful imagination and memory? How do we begin? Why not begin with reassessing how you spend each day, or, rather, how each day spends you? How much of the bird talk or office chatter do you hear? How much of the asparagus tips do you taste? Perhaps, we need to pay more attention to the phenomenological world of hiccups and paper cups and paper cuts. We don't have to sweat the small stuff. We just need to heed it. Breathe it. If I wish to muster in my imagination the marmalade pace of my mother's voice (which pronounces *ham* with three syllables), then I must listen. If I wish to muster from memory the velvet feel of my great-grandfather's left hand, I need to touch and remember how to touch.

In both writing and yoga, we move toward the center by grounding ourselves where we are: here in our bodies, in our minds, in this world. Heeding this world's physical currency can help you not only to reembrace and explore your intricately physical existence; it may give you the sensibilities to craft original writing from an authentic source.

Writers of all genres know or intuit two key traits of authentic writing that come from practicing presence: particularity and sensuousness. Your life's details—your mother's goofy patchwork dress that she wore to your elementary school's open house, your dog's distinct chlorine-cedar odor—matter in embodied writing. Ezra Pound implored a young writer in essence, Don't write "red." Write "rose" or "rust" or "ruddy." Toni Morrison's character Milkman in *Song of Solomon* remains with me in part because of how he earned his nickname (a man saw him being nursed by his mother—when the boy was ten years old). Barbara Kingsolver's fictional Africa in *The Poisonwood Bible* remains in my memory for the unique, subjective way she transformed it through five distinct female perspectives. The novel revolves around a missionary family from Georgia that travels to the Congo. That the first daughter to narrate the story says in her first sentence, "We came from Bethlehem, Georgia, bearing Betty Crocker cake mixes into the jungle," says a mouthful about the family and especially the mother. We learn that the mother also packs "a dozen cans of Underwood deviled ham; Rachel's ivory plastic hand mirror with powdered-wig ladies on the back; a stainless-steel thimble; a good pair of scissors; a dozen number-2 pencils; a world of Band-Aids, Anacin, Absorbine Jr.; and a fever thermometer."[1] What we carry with us betrays parts of our identity. These intimate details are what I call "particularities"—they are the details of your or of your characters' unique experience and identity. They won't readily be duplicated by your readers' experience, but they will invite your readers into the rich textures of the singular world you're creating for them.

Authentic writing also is grounded in sensuousness and sensuality. Verbs lick us. Images ignite our imaginations. Suggestive and connotative diction caresses us. An image in writing is often defined as a word or words that appeal to one or more of our senses; but an image does not merely appeal to our senses. An image triggers our inner senses and can make a deep impression (*samskāra* in Sanskrit) upon our own and our audience's imagination. By inviting themselves into our imagination's inner sanctum, images dissolve some of the distance between writer, reader, and language. William Carlos Williams said decades ago, "No ideas but in things." Although the quotation has been misappropriated frequently from this author of poems about red wheelbarrows and broken glass to mean that one should simply describe things and not think about ideas, he was onto something that cognitive scientists now are onto: Ideas, like language, stem from our physical reality.[2] I'm curious, then, to explore this intricately wired vehicle that shapes so much of my experience, for our bodies are hard-wired to proffer us the particular details and images that form the foundation of an authentic style. We might rewrite Williams's quotation as "No ideas but in the body."

Senses—all five or six or one hundred of them—are your body's tentacles to the physical world of lightbulbs and sunlight. Your sense receptors connect parts of your body with your brain and, like breath, to nature. Senses are the most influential factors on a person's perception of reality; thus, yogis often consider it an essential first step in their practice to experience fully and then to control the core five sense organs (in Sanskrit, *jnāna-indriya* or the cognitive senses). Since yogis have realized for centuries that the world can oversense us near numb, blind, and deaf, it's no wonder that one ancient yoga text says simply that the senses lead a person to heaven or hell: heaven if a person can harness them, hell if not.[3]

We don't have to deny ourselves of this world by retreating to caves and living on thistleweed tea to write authentically and to practice presence (or to practice yoga). After the Buddhist monk Saraha of Bengali (circa tenth century) left the monastery, he allegedly met a spiritual companion, a Tantric yogini who taught him the wisdom of this world's pleasures. His new discoveries spawned this verse: "Without meditation, without renouncing the world,/ Stay at home in the company of your mate./Perfect knowledge can only be attained/While one is enjoying the pleasures of the senses."[4] Rather racy wisdom for a tenth-century Buddhist monk. Similarly, the *Kalcakra-Tantra* recounts how King Sucandra asked Buddha for a Yoga that would help people in his troubled time. The Buddha's response was simple: Appreciate our bodies as temples and delight in this world as a manifestation of and extension of our nature.[5] This wisdom sums up much of Hatha-Yoga's philosophy for us as writers in the twenty-first century. We find practical ways to heighten and to harness the senses without being driven by them and without being driven away from the world.

Your senses impress themselves upon your imagination. And your imagination has layers, I think, that correlate to what ancient yoga texts describe as the body's three main layers or sheaths (*koshas*): physical, subtle, and causal. Being present as writers and learning to engage the outer and inner senses involve especially the first two layers. The physical body is the gross body of organs, muscles, and bones, and what I call a writer's **physical imagination** accounts for our external senses' ability to register and to shelve images in our memory's storehouse. Look at something in the room where you're presently reading this book: a picture frame, a lamp base. Gaze at it, taking in a few details. Close your eyes, and see the object with your "inner eye." This ability to recast an image with our inner senses comes from our physical imagination, the gross level of the imagination that allows us to receive information from the physical world.

Other visual images, as well as inner sounds and smells, can surface without clear reference to a memory. These images well up from the spring of our **subtle imagination**. Whereas an image from the physical imagination stems almost solely from impressions made by outer senses, an image from the subtle imagination can be influenced more directly by the mixing of a writer's breath, intellect, emotions, and unconscious. These images manifest themselves in dreams and often appear like ghosts on our consciousness's periphery. You've had the experience before. You're talking to the woman who sells you flowers and herbs down the road. Without your knowing why, the sound of a baby crying to the tune of a bullfrog or an image of a man sprouting from a water lily surfaces in your subtle imagination. You continue talking to the woman about azaleas and marigolds, but as soon as you get in your car, you might pen a note to yourself on your receipt: "baby bullfrog" or "water lily man." Maybe the image won't amount to anything worth writing about, but you know the habit of heeding these peripheral images keeps you in frequent contact with your unconscious. Writers—as do most creative people in their fields—pay more attention than other people to the images on the margins of awareness.

Yoga allows writers to do the same thing with a more systematic intensity. By exploring the subtle body—a subtle layer of emotion, intellect, breath, and energy enveloping and pervading the physical body—we can delve into layers of the imagination and unconscious that remain dormant in most people. We begin this journey by paying attention to and using sensations and tensions within the physical and subtle bodies.[6] You can imagine an ache or sensation richly. Maybe you're weary of feeling tired and achy, broken and bruised. But rather than reach for the aspirin, try to ignore it, or complain to your partner, try a fourth option: become increasingly aware of the ache and sensation. When you increase awareness of your body's subtle aches and sensations, you can not only improve your yoga practice; you also can tap into a whole new source of writing. **Proprioception** is awareness of one's proprioceptors—specialized receptors that note what's happening with tendons, muscles, and joints. Thanks to these receptors we have that touchy sense. Heeding their subtle signals activates our brain's cerebrum in conjunction with the imagination, which lets us see in our mind's eye what might be happening and where within and on our body. So, let your imagination get on your nerves. This subtle work trains the inner senses as well. The mix between the physical and subtle imaginations may be the basis for enduring fiction writing, as well as for the memorable imagery rife in so much creative nonfiction and poetry.

I offer my students several suggestions for awakening to this world that work and busyness has dulled them to. Recapture your childhood imagination, for starters. During the next week, allow the world's minutiae—the hues of the sun as it bleeds behind clouds, the melody of a child's whine—to ignite your imagination. Let the world of physical stuff hold your imagination captive till you heed whatever is calling you. Forget whoever might be watching you. In a journal or notebook, record your initial observations in detail. With a relaxed body, render subtle textures and tints with vivid verbs and images. Or follow your nose. In a notebook, track what you smell from the moment you awaken to the moment you drift to sleep. From your lover's hair to the cilantro in your omelet to your wet cedar deck, sniff out those hidden smells and similes, and record the images. Some writers also log what they detest and delight in. That is, take note of what sounds, what ditty bells, you enjoy versus what sounds, what clamorous bells, you despise. Of course, you'll log those tintinnabular combinations of notes and syllables that delight and disgust simply because of the sounds themselves, but you also may note those sounds that, because of their messenger, their context, their personal resonance, make you crinkle your nose or cringe. Be particular, personal, quirky. Celebrate and censor. If logging sounds sounds dull, try tastes, touches, sights, or smells.

Or experience a day like a Picasso model. Picasso's Cubist and post-Cubist portraits placed ears where we'd expect a nose and mouths where we'd expect an eye. I imagine if such models literally existed as Picasso portrayed them, they would know firsthand "synesthesia," that heightened capacity to experience senses simultaneously and in overlapping categories. We smell sounds. We taste color. We feel a smell's texture. So try to see the colors and shapes of cardinal clicks. Listen to the pitch and tone of morning light upon tree leaves. Stroke the skin of midnight air. Most of us must force our brains to reexperience the world in this way. So, if it helps you, first note a sense in its typical category (sight, sound, et cetera), then try to shift categories. How would this taste sound? How would this sound look? Write at least ten a day for the next fifteen days.

All of these practices are just that: practice. They're ways to retrain your senses to be alert and to fill your physical and subtle imaginations' storehouses with material, so when you're writing you can retrieve readily the appropriate image or detail. Your words and phrases may have a texture more akin to a homemade cup of Chinese hyssop than of Lipton. Practicing presence can help you remember the splendor of your outer senses and rediscover the mystery of your inner ones, for words can work magic upon our intellects, imaginations, and emotions in ways that enlarge our inner senses and our sense of an embodied self.

$\mathcal{T}$AKE A BREATH:
LET YOUR IMAGINATION GET ON YOUR NERVES

If you're not familiar with the following four simple yoga poses— MOUNTAIN POSE, STANDING FORWARD BEND, KNEELING POSE, *and* LYING RELEASE POSE—*I suggest you review them in the Appendix so you're not caught up in getting poses "right." You might try the poses twice without regard to the prompts, and on the third time try the sequence with your eyes closed. Treat the poses as catalysts to awaken your physical and subtle imaginations.*

INTENTION:
Generate fresh ideas and enrich your writing's particularity and sensuousness by heightening your outer and inner senses.

Come into a comfortable MOUNTAIN/STANDING POSE (tādāsana). *Anchor your body in both feet, close your eyes, and focus on your breath for at least two full inhalations and exhalations. When ready, set your twofold intention first by asking yourself, "What am I writing for?" Let words or images, of whatever kind, surface naturally and honor them. Then, be specific with this session's writing intention. Perhaps you want to be open to the present and see what happens with your embodied physical and subtle imaginations. Perhaps you want to project and transfer what you experience into the body of one of your fictional characters. Or if you write personal essays, this practice can offer surprises about the stories latent in your body's pages.*

Once comfortable with your intention, tend to each sense organ. Look around your room and notice what's happening with your sight at this very moment. With eyes fixed on something, notice how your body feels as you appreciate how light transfers data through your eyes and registers signals in your brain, which in turn sends signals scurrying throughout your body's cells and nerves. Then, close your eyes and notice how you can, if you wish, recall images of the room's objects. With eyes still shut, open your ears and hear what's rustling outside of you. Then, try to hear what's stirring inside your body: breath, heartbeat, something subtler. As you breathe, take in scents, however distinct or faint, and appreciate how smells and breath constantly energize your body down to your soles. Notice your tongue and how the residue of taste lingers in the back of your throat or, like lost words, on the tip of your tongue. And heed some of the millions of touch receptors from your head to your toes, your body an electric vibration of constant sensory information. Stand and embrace that fact for a few breaths.

Then, when ready, begin to notice any slight sensations at the muscular level or at the nerve level, and let one sensation direct your imagination's focus. Perhaps there's a sensation in the back of your neck or something on your left foot. Or in your right hip. Let your imagination go there. How would you describe this sensation? Be with it for a few breaths. Then, with part of your imagination still on that sensation, inhale, and exhale as you bend from your waist down into **STANDING FORWARD BEND POSE** (uttanāsana). Bend your knees, if needed, to avoid strain. Stay here for a few breaths, and notice if the sensation changes, moves, transforms. Breathe with it. As you're in this pose, notice what image might surface. Avoid forcing anything. It might come from your physical imagination of memory or from a subtler and as yet inexplicable source. A person's face or body. A scene. A building. Something moving. Absorb its particular textures and shapes.

When ready, take a full exhalation, bend your knees, and come onto your shins, tops of feet on the mat, into **ADAMANTINE POSE/ KNEELING POSE** (vajrāsana). Then, bring your heels together and rest your hips on your heels, your hands resting on your thighs. For more comfort, place a blanket between your thighs and calves. Keep your eyes closed. Is the sensation the same? Has the image developed, moved, or become something else? Can you stay with the image and let it unfold, move, shift shapes if need be? Try to stay with it for several breaths and let it soak your body.

When ready, rest on your back in **LYING RELEASE POSE/ CORPSE POSE** (savāsana). As you release your back body into the ground, try to feel the images residing in the physical space of your sensation. How do these images feel? Stay with these new sensations for several breaths. Then, be open to how your original physical sensation and these images might relate in some intuitive way. These connections between your physical sensations and the imagery may be part of your story, your character, your self. There may be a cause-and-effect relationship, a symbolic relationship, or something as of yet undisclosed that only writing may reveal.

When ready, open your eyes, and write a piece of fiction, nonfiction, or poetry that explores the feelings and significance of a physical sensation. Based upon your intention, assume either your own point of view or another person's or a character's point of view. You might begin by describing a character—or yourself—in an imagined or actual situation or by describing the physical sensation. What particular details and words could render the character, the sensation, the situation, unique? What core images could impress your readers' imaginations? Gradually and subtly honor and explore the bridges, the connections, between the physical sensation and the imagery. The connections need not be overt and obvious. It might be best to keep them on the subtle level.

CHAPTER SEVEN

Writing with Wonder and an Awakened Imagination

Thoreau allegedly took children huckleberry hunting through Walden Woods. Imagining woolly Thoreau traipsing through the trees with a gaggle of little ones tagging along inspired me several years ago to take my then six-year-old niece in search of these special berries. In the fields of North Texas, you won't find many actual huckleberries, but I didn't let on to Megan. After we arrived at the field, we walked along the cracked-earth paths lined by brush. "They could be anywhere," I said, and raised my eyebrows and widened my eyes as if I might spy a berry any moment. Megan followed suit, her blue eyes alert for a huckleberry head to peep out from behind the wildflowers. "There!" I yelled. "Where?" "Right there! Do you see it?" "No!"

I dashed off the path and across the weeds, and squatted by some stones. "Here's a bushel!" My fingers reached down just above the stones and moved as if picking off berries. After I reached into the air and picked more of the invisible fruit, Megan leapt to my side and gazed as I unfolded my right fingers and with my left fingers picked an invisible berry, lifted it to my lips, and savored it bit by bit. "Cherry," I said, "a cherry huckleberry." She relished one by one the treasure I proffered and then, with a big grin, dashed to the foot of a sycamore. "I found some too," she said. "Tastes like bubblegum!" For over an hour, we hunted and shared huckleberries of all flavors.

In almost every writing class and workshop I teach, at least a handful of writers say they hunger to reclaim some part of their childhood imagination and write with wonder. Having a sense of wonder opens us up to a day's quirks, which in turn can give us unique writing topics as well as uncommon angles and untrodden insights on familiar subjects. To be seized by wonder is to experience our worlds—the outer one and the inner one—anew through a child's mind, imagination, and body. Poet Charles Baudelaire once wrote that "genius is the capacity to recapture childhood at will." Replace "genius" with "to write with wonder." It is to understand as writers that our imaginations, our physical existence, and our most mundane moments give us infinite possibilities to create for our readers fresh worlds made of words. For such is the stuff linguistic dreams are made of.

What we want from our writing—just as from our reading—is authentic novelty. This newness not only keeps us, as writers, held in writing's grip as we wonder where the words will take us around the next page's bend; it also holds our readers' imagination, word by captivating word. Authentic freshness lacks gimmicks or cheap trick endings or gratuitous experimentation, showing its cleverness for cleverness's sake. Its novelty instead might provoke readers to view their own world and reality anew, to consider being human in a new light, or to open their hearts and imaginations to someone else's perspective. With regular practice, your imagination may find new stepping-stones for your characters to hop across. Your fictional plots, your nonfiction narratives, and your poetic situations may stay alive because you let your imagination romp and wander into the land of "What if?" and, to borrow Borges's title, into the garden of forking paths of possibilities.

When we talk about wonder, I tell my students, in no mystical terms, about a text called the *Shiva-Sutra*. Written in the ninth century, the *Shiva-Sutra*[1] offers some fundamental suggestions that can help us cultivate and write with authentic wonder. The text discusses "joy-filled amazement," the state of being "wonderstruck" with life, awareness, and reality; called *vismaya* in Sanskrit, it's an essential though rarely discussed quality for yogis and writers. To experience this wonder, it helps to understand what this text describes as four levels of awareness: waking reality (*jāgrat*), dreaming reality (*svapna*), deep sleep (*nidra*), and the fourth ultimate reality (*turiya*). As writers, we'll explore primarily the relationship between the first two levels—waking and dreaming realities—and the third level to a lesser extent. The fourth level we'll save for another chapter. In the first level of waking reality, *jagrat*, we're aware especially of the outside world of things—apple trees, construction cranes, and traffic jams—when awake. Awareness of this world helps us later reconstruct settings and situations for our writing. Being alert to the details of *jāgrat* helps us cultivate presence but also lets us retrieve details from memory to create the basis of, say, Yoknapatawpha County. But the details that—whether in fiction, nonfiction, or poetry—help writers create compelling "alternative realities" for our imagination don't come solely from memories of the waking world. For instance, in dream reality, *svapna*, we connect with that world of imagery that inhabits our unconscious—a veritable treasure trove for enriching our writing.

Writing with wonder, though, comes from being open to how these two realities, waking and dreaming, overlap. When we experience and *enjoy* simultaneously the waking world and the dream world, according to *Shiva-Sutra* I.11, in essence we can harness if not control our intellect, imagination, and emotions. To do so is to be conscious while dreaming and to be dreaming while awake. For instance, when you dream, you can become aware that you're dreaming, as in lucid dreaming ("awake" while in the dream state), and thus have the ability to influence what actually happens in your dreams.[2] Conversely, while working during the day, fully awake, you can be aware of the random imagery bubbling up from your subtle imagination. For instance, your eyes might be centered upon the oak chair before you as your imagination concocts images of termites burrowing holes and corridors inside it, and while you stare at an ivy plant, your dreamlike imagination might imagine the vines reaching out like arms as you invent a gothic story of a "still life" living room grown wild. When you're consciously entertaining random imagery while awake, you're not daydreaming (or hallucinating, you hope) as much as you're living in the reverie of being a writer. Your imagination animates this physical world. Not only are possessing joy-filled amazement (*vismaya*) and being given to play (*kaimura*) precisely tell-tale traits of the yogi who experiences these simultaneous and overlapping realities; they also may characterize the writer given to wondering about and questioning reality.

Whether you subscribe to the *Shiva-Sutra*'s descriptions of reality or not, these teachings are potent ways of engaging what is real, what is imagined, and what is created in an authentic way so that our writing in turn piques in us and our readers that delightful wonder of being human and alive.

To awaken wonder in our writing, we can find the uncanny in familiar places and ordinary situations. In yogic terms, we can see a dreamlike and playful nature in what we perceive while awake. Essayists such as G. K. Chesterton (1874–1936) have a ready wonder with the real. In the essay "A Piece of Chalk," the British writer describes himself in despair because he came to a hill to draw with his colored chalk onto brown paper only to realize that he's forgotten "the most exquisite and essential chalk": the white piece. This leads him to argue—nay, to wonder in such a way that we almost cannot help but agree—that drawing with white chalk on brown paper illustrates that white *is* a color, a *positive presence* of color, not an absence of color. This assertion then sends his mind inventing a moral analogy that a virtue is not an *absence of vice* but a positive action: "Chastity does not mean abstention from sexual wrong; it means something flaming, like Joan of Arc." From personal fact to inventive assertion to risky analogy, this writer kept his boyish imagination alive throughout his writing life. So, too, can we.

Fiction writers also love surprises. Emmett, the forty-five-year-old narrator and protagonist of Nicholson Baker's novel *The Box of Matches*, works as a medical textbook editor at his Maine home, where he lives with his wife, two children, cat, and newly acquired duck, Greta. Life couldn't be more ordinary and uneventful. Each chapter follows Emmett's morning ritual: He wakes up before dawn, slips out of bed, keeps the lights out to maintain that delicious twilight state of awareness, makes coffee, lights a match to start a fire, and then begins his morning rhapsodies. The pleasure of how a dishwasher's top rack rolls out, the strategies of being a male and trying to pee in a toilet with the lights out, or the exhilaration of scrubbing first thing in the morning a dish left out overnight ("smiling with the clenched-teeth smile of the joyful scrubber")— these uneventful moments provide Emmett and his readers with fodder for daily astonishment. I imagine Baker not completely unlike Emmett as he tends to his own kitchen's secret treasures and his own fireplace's mysteries. The character sprang, I suspect, from some part of Baker's lifelong childlike imagination that relishes upon occasion crazy yet revealing observations of ordinary waking reality.[3]

We can keep our writing fresh, too, by questioning our own constructs of reality. How we view time and space, our notions of "inner" and "outer," the material and immaterial, may be turned inside out and upside down. Jorge Luis Borges, like a curious boy, poses "What if?" questions and then lets his stories work them out to their logical or absurd conclusion. In "The Circular Ruins" the trickster author explores not only "What if a magician could imagine a boy into being?" but also "What if the magician were dreamed into being?" Which leads us to wonder, "What if we each are someone else's image?" All characters do, and in some sense each of us does, indeed exist in someone else's imagination. Gabriel García Márquez also blends the fantastic with the ordinary in the oft-anthologized short story "The Very Old Man with Enormous Wings." Set in an impoverished South American village, the story is fueled by the question "What if an angel appeared in our own village?" Most readers may experience complex feelings, including disgust, when a poor couple cages the creature and sells tickets to view him, but we also likely feel strange wonder when the very old man, perhaps content that the couple with a new baby has made a stash of cash, rises from the sand and soars off.

To practice as a writer openness to surprise and wonder can be simple. Play with your waking awareness (*jāgrat*), and allow the ordinary waking world to seize you. Drop this book. Look around you right now. Let something—a candle's hue, a watch's shape—take your imagination hostage for a few minutes. Begin describing the object. Follow your memory in relation to the object of your gaze. Imagine it speaking. What does it tell you about itself and who inhabits this space? What does it perceive each day? Don't be embarrassed. You have nothing to lose and only your imagination and your *vismaya* to recapture. Or see a familiar place anew. Walk through your house and see it as if you had never seen it before, as if you didn't live there. Put a stranger, someone from another country or another time, here. Let a character from someone else's novel—Madame Bovary, Raskolnikov, Gatsby—drop in. What would beguile them? Fascinate them? Which objects get regular attention? Which seem neglected? If you go to a place for work each day, see it afresh. Ferns in the hallways, prints on the walls, memos on a bulletin board, all can become "signs" of meaning. How did these things get here? How long will they be here? How did *you* get here? Wonder. These exercises might give you novel plot premises and twists, richer observations in fiction and nonfiction, and characters with fuller interior lives.

Any place, any moment, can suspend us in surprise. I was once standing naked—except for my robe—in the middle of our road and staring at the glowing moon and blowing mist. I hadn't planned to stop there. I had intended to find the owners of a manic barking dog that kept interrupting my dreams, but once I stepped into the road, unable to follow the rude mongrel's path, I looked up and was struck by the hazy moonlight and translucent sheets of mist, by the buzzing power lines and power box in front of our neighbor's house, and by the street's stillness. For a moment everything floated as if the street had become an ocean floor, and I wondered if I were back in bed asleep and finally dreaming. But I was not. I don't think. Maybe the delirium of dreams and dogs' voices filtered my perception, but I savor such small surprises that inform much of how I write. Try it: Get up in the middle of the night. Walk through your house in the dark. Walk down your street at 3:00 A.M. You might feel as if you're walking through someone else's dream. Write about your house or street's night side.

Or log a day and night. Keep a list of observations from the moment you arise, recalling brief dream images from the night before, then incidents of your morning routine, and then work, and then to dinner, and finally dreams, again. Wonder in your writing like Nicholson Baker's Emmett about the miracle of such small stuff. If at day's end you have fewer than twelve entries, don't flagellate yourself for not heeding everything; congratulate yourself for altering your awareness even slightly. Be persistent. Try more the next day. In Gladys Cardiff's poem "Combing," her contemplation upon the simple ritual of caring for her daughter's hair reminds her of her mother and of her grandmother. This ritual, she concludes, is what women do for one another, "plaiting the generations."[4] Tend to the moment's depth. As you write about such a moment in whatever genre you choose, refrain from overanalyzing and straining for an epiphany (unless such tendencies suit your fictional narrator's proclivity). Keep it simple like the act itself you're performing.

Or try this: Watch a stranger. This suggestion is one of my students' favorites because most of us enjoy observing other people. One December day, Eudora Welty, while sitting in a town square, watched her neighbors scurry to buy Christmas gifts. In the distance, an elderly African-American woman, wearing disheveled clothes and remaining removed from the hubbub, sauntered and whistled on her merry way. That observation mixed with Welty's wondering, "Who is she?" and "Where is she going?" became the genesis of possibly Welty's most famous character, Phoenix Jackson, in the short story "A Worn Path." So, at the grocery store or yoga class or deli, notice somebody you don't know. Note the worn spot on her brown jacket's elbow. Note his chafed loafers. Note how she slices her tomatoes. Then, imagine. What's her name? What does he do for a living? What's her favorite memory? His worst? Where has she traveled? What does he dream? You have the beginnings of a character study and a possible story. You can begin a story by dropping this person in action and seeing where the new character will take you.

When engaged with this waking world, regularly ask yourself, "What is real?" and "What if?" I suggest to my fiction and nonfiction students they get in the habit of listing a series of playful questions about reality. What if deer attacked people? (Horror story.) What if the older woman down the street fell in love with your husband? (Fiction, you hope.) What if we ate with our ears? What if mud made us cleaner than water? How do rose petals swim? (Lyrical poetry.) Pablo Neruda filled a volume with such thought problems, titled *The Book of Questions*. Alan Lightman's novella *Einstein's Dreams* is structured as if each chapter were one of the physicist's dreams about time. Each chapter then plays out the dream, fueled by one of Lightman's time questions: "What if time were at the center of town?" "What if in a village time ran backward?" Writers never stop asking questions (which is one reason we're so dangerous to people with unchecked power and so annoying to our friends).

Dreams also can be an immediate resource for questioning what is real and possible. I'm not into mind trips, but dreams still fascinate me, as they do other writers, because they stir up unconscious stuff that writing can play out sometimes without our readers ever knowing we're drawing from our dreams. Twilight time—that state we usually experience either just as we're falling asleep or as we're waking up—is a rich time for me to try to draw dream images for my writing. Where the waking state (*jāgrat*) and dreaming state (*svapna*) overlap, this twilight time also can be induced through meditative yoga movements and breathwork.

Dream state is mostly theta brain-wave state. Slower than the beta brain waves and the alpha brain waves discussed earlier in this book in the context of concentration, theta waves glide to a rhythm of four to eight cycles per second. When in "theta brain" we can have "waking dreams," so to speak. Usually, we can be in a waking state with both alpha and theta waves when our consciousness shifts back and forth between a dream state and a waking state as if we were having a lucid dream while awake. In fact, for us to recall unconscious imagery or memories, our brains must contain some alpha brain waves mixed with the theta. When advanced yogis, inventors, writers, artists, scientists, and others report thinking lucidly in images, their brains likely shift between low alpha waves and high theta waves.[5] Neuropsychologist Erik Hoffman, who led a study on eleven experienced yoga teachers in Scandinavia, used an EEG and follow-up psychological measurements to measure the yogis' brain-wave activity after two hours of a form of yoga called Kriya Yoga. The study revealed significant theta-wave activity in both hemispheres, especially in the less dominant right hemisphere, often, but not always, associated with more intuitive functions. Some neuroscientists claim that practices that induce an alert theta-wave state help people access their unconscious feelings, images, and memories. Neuroscientists call this experience a hypnagogic state. Yogis might call it approaching the fourth state, *turiya*, *samādhi*, bliss. Some writers might call it "writer's flow."

In a state of "writer's flow," writers experience easier access to thinking in images—the heart of creative language. Writers access a "storehouse of images," said poet William Butler Yeats. Any writer can access this storehouse. One study suggested that 70–77 percent of people experience this hypnagogic state but aren't aware of it, yet through some simple yoga tools writers can become aware of their interior storehouse to enrich their writing style and engage their readers' imaginations.

A few months ago while practicing breath work, I saw this image that lasted all of twenty seconds: A round-faced man sits among Zen monks and says, "So, you're not really rich, are you? You're not corrupt? I thought you guys all pretended to be simple and austere but actually had a harem with big-screen TVs in the back of your meditation hall. But you're just like me. I see, I see. I had it all wrong." The monks sit still in silent disbelief. So began a short story about Marvin, a charming but self-deluded "spiritual seeker" who, while halfheartedly trying out the monk life at a Zen monastery, creates all kinds of creative turmoil with his naïve perspective and unbridled questioning. He eventually is asked to leave because he can't practice silence.

But beware when drawing from random images and dreams: Weirdness alone won't sustain a piece's quality or an audience's motivation to keep reading. "So what?" most readers will ask. And the answer usually must be more than simply revealing something quirky about the writer's imagination, personality, or "id." Most of us don't read to psychoanalyze writers, and writers usually don't write as dream therapy. When we ask, "So what?" we're wanting some glimmer, even if it's ambiguous, about being human and what we think is real.

To sleep, perchance to dream; to dream perchance to see what is real, that's what your writing does for your readers. The imagination offers us an entryway into, not an escape hatch from, reality's marvelous corridors. And the imagination's creative work, your writing, lets your readers find huckleberries growing in sidewalk cracks and beneath their own back porch.

$\mathcal{T}$AKE A BREATH: DREAM A ROUTINE

INTENTION:
With the following practice, explore different states of reality to charge your imagination and wonder. It's most effective when you're just waking up, approaching going to sleep, or starting to engage in regular routines.

List some daily routines you do around the house that would take no more than ten minutes to complete. *Brushing your teeth, checking your e-mail, washing dishes, making oatmeal, hugging someone.* Preferably, perform the following practice right before you engage in one of these routines.

Begin in a comfortable **LYING RELEASE/CORPSE POSE** (savāsana) by resting on your back, knees bent or straight. As your back body melds with the earth, breathe two full inhalations and exhalations. Let this breath clear space for your intention. When ready, ask yourself, "What am I writing for?" After you've let a response bubble up, clarify your specific writing intention. You may want to keep wholly open to the experience as it grants you brand new ideas for new material. You may want to resuscitate a near-dead story, essay, or poem that lacks fresh insight or imagination. You may wish to embody a character's point of view. Let that intention emanate throughout your body, not just in your head.

Once you've set your twofold intention, become aware of how your breath travels through your body. Imagine its path like a colored subway coursing through your nostrils, down your throat, and into your lungs. Imagine you breathe in through your body's left side and nostril and breathe out through the right, creating a circle of breath that for a moment dissipates tension and worry. Feel your breath glide in this circle along your body's inner and outer surfaces—around your organs as well as on your skin.

As you focus on your breath, imagine yourself dreaming at this moment. You're dreaming of yourself resting on your back here in this room. Don't rush this part. Try to slow down your breath and let it be easy and smooth. When ready, actually open your eyes, yet continue to imagine you're dreaming. With slow, easy breathing, stand up, notebook in hand, and walk around your house to begin your routine. You may feel slightly light-headed, but notice how your surroundings look, and notice how parts of your body feel as you walk. As you turn the bathroom doorknob, for instance, notice how loose the knob is and how its metallic coolness almost stings your fingers. Perhaps the room you've entered sounds notably louder or quieter than usual. Engage in the routine with as much awareness as possible but with a child's delight, as if you're hunting for huckleberries in your own bathroom or kitchen.

While in the routine, pose a playful question to yourself that might bring delight: "What if hair grew teeth?" "Who is dreaming me here?" "What if I were an eleven-year-old girl? How would I experience this act? What if I were an eighty-year-old man?" Embody that question in *this dreamlike routine. If peripheral images or voices surface, you might note them and carry on (you may be getting signals from your subtle imagination).*

Once you've finished—the exercise should last no more than ten minutes—begin writing by writing yourself or a fictional character, gifted with this wondrous awareness, into the routine. Don't be shy. Let your readers know rather quickly what you or the character is doing—that is, refrain from making the piece sound like a mysterious dream or riddle. It's your piquant description mixed with authentic playful wonder (vismaya)—not trying to be "weird"—that will tantalize your readers. Enjoy the description, the playful speculation, the voice of pensive whimsy.

CHAPTER EIGHT

Embodied Metaphors and Symbols: The Brain's Yearning for Unity

Rain, Hurricane Isabel's gift blown in from the Eastern coast, pours on a pond's skin, each drop rippling shivers through the pond's body. *More, more,* the pond utters as it drifts between waking and sleep, lulled by the rain's caress. With each absorbed drop, the pond expands itself to test just how much rain it can contain. Slowly, its surface swells over its edges as its water bleeds into the soil and grass, the roots of goldenrod and cattails, and, as if relinquishing a part of itself in near sleep, releases water to the nearby brook. As rain subsides after several hours, the body rests again, content to house the three box turtles that bark at passersby, the carp that feed off its weeds, and the few frogs whose bellow brings on dusk. It's a good life this pond has.

I swim in this pond each week, but the above description didn't come directly from a swim. It came from this morning's yoga session. While rain relentlessly fell on the roof and meadows, I set my twofold intention to focus upon letting my body grant me some new metaphorical understanding. I flowed through a series of poses, focused on my breath, and then after an hour rested in LYING RELEASE POSE (*savāsana*). My body relinquished the morning's tension as my thoughts centered at once on the sound of my breath and that of rain. For a fleeting moment an image of the pond in my torso surfaced, the rain popping on my chest and arms, my back melting into muddy waters. Just for a moment. I didn't force images, and I didn't fight occasional self-conscious intrusions that analyzed them; instead, I just absorbed what I could. After sitting in meditation for only twenty minutes or so, I went to the desk, turned on the computer, and tried out a few sentences. The experience, primed by my yoga practice, gave me a new view of this pond I hold so dear.

Metaphors, most writers learn, are implied comparisons between two unlike things, as in "The *long-necked* ballerina *glided* across the stage" (ballerina to a swan). Similes, another kind of metaphor, make more direct comparisons by using *like* or *as*, such as "The *unbridled* child *loped* across the room like a wild horse." Symbols, simply put, are tangible things—objects, people, places, animals, events—invested with a meaning larger than what they literally are. Simple words or images or moments become signs to read. An antique writing desk owned by your grandfather means something more to you than treated pieces of wood fashioned into furniture. A friend of mine once said he distrusted poetry with metaphors and symbols. Direct and plain language he equates with honesty; metaphors, with showiness. When not harnessed, metaphors indeed might distort a piece of writing and hide rather than express a writer's authentic voice.

Authentic metaphors and symbols, however, are far more than ornaments to decorate an otherwise dully clothed page. They may be an expression of the body and the brain's innate yearning for meaning as well as for connectedness and interrelatedness among the universe's disparate things. Understood this way, authentic metaphors and symbols may reflect our embodied reality and can give us a powerful way to deepen and to alter our readers' understanding of our subject.

Consider that each of us may be wired for metaphor making. Our brains' synapses seem to delight in making new connections, in having new thoughts, as some neurological research has shown that a brain's plasticity increases when a person forms new ideas and concepts. The process of making a metaphor stimulates significant regions of both the left and right hemispheres—regions that far surpass the Broca's brain region responsible for the simple utterance of literal words. In turn, when both hemispheres are stimulated, our brains can become primed for such linguistic novelty. In *The Midnight Disease*, neurologist Alice W. Flaherty suggests that metaphors' potency stems in part from the fact that producing and reading metaphors stimulate the brain's more rational cerebral cortex as well as the more affective limbic system. Thought and feeling entwine. Metaphors then can alter not just our minds and physical imaginations; they can alter our brain's shape as they play with our neuronal paths and our cellular dance. As they do for us, so they can do for our readers.

Our bodies shape our perceptions. Exploring the nature of our embodied perception can help us understand why and how we naturally create authentic metaphors. Metaphors are a form of novel categorization and recategorization, and the way our brains operate makes us "categorizing" beings. As George Lakoff and Mark Johnson contend in their book *Philosophy in the Flesh: The Embodied Mind and Its Challenge to Western Thought*, the human eye, for instance, contains a hundred million light-sensing cells but only one million fibers to connect sensations to the brain.[1] Just as a crowd of a thousand people wanting to buy plane tickets may stand efficiently in ten lines according to their last names, so the brain naturally categorizes sensory impulses via certain "fiber lines." The very nature of our bodies, Lakoff and Johnson suggest, make us categorize; it's what we're wired to do. Even how we formulate complex metaphors, they argue, stems from our physical experience. For instance, "Love is a journey" depends largely upon our direct encounters in taking trips, having mishaps, discovering joyful surprises, and questioning whether or not a trip's hardships were worth the trouble. That physical experience gives us the basis for understanding something as abstract as love, also rife with mishaps, surprises, and questions.[2]

Our minds constantly shift from receiving sensory input from the exterior world (what was introduced as *jāgrat*, the waking state, in the previous chapter) to entertaining thoughts and feelings and images in the interior world (*svapna*, the dreaming state). Our imaginations often link an impression from the exterior world to a feeling or thought. A writer's imagination may latch on to the uprooted birch behind his cottage because he's moved recently from his home state of California to Vermont. Much Zen poetry, including haikus, blur these distinctions between inner and outer worlds through subtle metaphor. Ezra Pound's haikulike Imagist poem "In a Station at the Metro" concisely captures this aesthetic: "The apparition of these faces in a crowd;/petals on a wet, black bough." The speaker ostensibly glimpses a faint mass of anonymous faces in Paris's subway station (clue from the title), and imagination's memory and metaphor-making ability links the mass of faces to a branch's petals. Crowd and bough, their sound and concept, bind the two lines and images. Metaphors connect realms of interior and exterior, subjective and objective.

One day within the next week, notice how you're feeling or what you're thinking or what you're imagining. Then, while feeling inward, get in the habit of looking outward. One student, for instance, was writing a story about a male character, sixty years old, who was unsure about getting married a second time. As she took a lunch break in Union Square, she noticed she was feeling queasy herself about starting a new job. Then, she looked around her and just noted what she saw: among other things, a man eating a hot dog, a dachshund licking its owner's fingers, and an old oak about to keel over. She penned in her notebook, "Ralph stood in the park, wondering how he could begin this next phase of his life—to remarry. A young man with shaved head sat on the bench next to him. He chuckled as he fed a dachshund bits of a hot dog. Suddenly Ralph felt his limbs about to fall off, his torso hollow and dried out, his whole body leaning, as if about to keel over, uprooted, unable to stand straight and steady. The young guy continued to laugh as the little dog gobbled shreds of processed cow parts." She projected her own queasiness about starting a new job onto her character and used the image of the dachshund munching on a wiener to suggest, comically, that feeling.

I encourage students to explore their constructs of reality in relation to metaphor- and symbol-making. Some principles from yoga philosophy, from Vedanta to Shaivism, can help us understand how metaphors can express the nature of reality (although I know few writers who are unified about what is the nature of reality). "Yoga," notes the Yoga-Bija, "is said to be the unification of the web of dualities." Most of us begin yoga by working with body and breath. We can become increasingly sensitive to the ways the outside world affects and reflects the inside one and vice versa. We can become attuned to how our mind's habitual thoughts and images shape how we act and what we do in the world, and likewise we might note how the changes in our physical body begin to change the habitual patterns of our emotions, our thoughts, our images—in short, our subtle body. If our bodies influence our perceptions, then when we change our physiology and the ways our brains function, our whole worldview can follow suit.[3] Although our bodies seem bilateral—a left side and a right side—our physiological functions illustrate how these divisions overlap and complement one another. For instance, breathing through the left nostril has been shown to stimulate the brain's right hemisphere and vice versa. The left nostril, often associated with the cool moon, also stimulates a channel of energy called the "comfort channel" (*ida-nāḍī*) that correlates to the para-sympathetic nervous system, which in turn "cools down" a person's energy. The right nostril, which stimulates the brain's left hemisphere, connects to a path of energy associated with the hot sun called the "tawdry channel" (*piṅgalā-nāḍi*). Breathing solely through the right nostril has been shown to quicken the sympathetic nervous system and thus heat up the body.[4] These two lines of energy, according to texts such as the *Hatha-Yoga-Pradipika*, spiral up and down on either side of the spine (not unlike, incidentally, a DNA double helix or like the two winding serpents in Hippocrates' caduceus—the ancient emblem of healing and now the symbol for Western medicine). The practice of yoga harmonizes these seeming dualities of body and energy. In fact, one esoteric translation of *Hatha*, as in "Hatha-Yoga," is "sun-moon" (*ha*=sun; *tha*=moon). Through yoga, we gradually may be able to experience how what we perceive as light is dark, how we find ourselves in getting lost, for we, too, embody metaphor and paradox.

This complex nondualistic thinking and imagining has been verified not only by yogis' experiences for millennia but also by some quantum physicists' recent descriptions of the universe. The more intricately physicists delve into the universe's laws, the more paradoxical it becomes. Chaos brings order and life, and time may be timeless, as Nobel Prize–winner Ilya Prigogine's research indicates. Nature replicates its patterns, a fact that suggests to several scientists the inherent interrelatedness of all things. A leaf's veins branch out like a tree's limbs. A tree's limbs feather out like a bird's wings or like a brain's neuronal folds. The patterns we find in some snowflakes reflect the patterns that sound vibrations can create in sand. No wonder, then, physicists and science writers recognize that metaphors are not simply flourishes, extraneous to the language of logic, but are expressions of our embodied perception and, perhaps, of nature's nature.

As writers we express parts of this reality through paradox— another kind of metaphor that weds seeming opposites into a poetic truth. William Blake explored a similar reality in his poetic essay "The Marriage of Heaven and Hell," and Nathaniel Hawthorne's metaphorical imagination created a tapestry of paradoxical metaphors and symbols in his canonized novel *The Scarlet Letter* as, for instance, a symbol of Puritan punishment becomes an artistic emblem of personal pride. Hawthorne, as do other writers, sought to create a text that would not lead to simplistic, dualistic thinking of "good" and "evil," "love" and "hate." Authentic metaphors and symbols, like yoga, can break down conceptual boundaries and bridge conceptual worlds in our minds—the tangible and the intangible, the interior and the exterior, the familiar and the unfamiliar. Most of us taste such nonduality only in passing moments, if at all, but in the act of expressing and creating authentic metaphors and symbols, we can give ourselves and our readers a hint at such connectivity without our writing sounding forced into mysticism.

Authentic metaphors bring us delight, then, perhaps because they can alter the ways we and our readers view concepts and constructs of reality. In the essay "Transfiguration," from Annie Dillard's book *Holy the Firm*, the author recounts how she, seeking solitude and rejuvenation as a writer, camped alone for a few days and took with her to reread *The Day on Fire*, a novel about the meteoric poet Arthur Rimbaud, who nearly burned out his creative light by age nineteen. While Dillard read by candlelight, a moth kept flying closer and closer to the flame until, at last, it found the light literally, its body aflame:

> The wax rose in the moth's body from her soaking abdomen to her thorax to the jagged hole where her head should be, and widened into flame, a **saffron-yellow** flame that **robed** her to the ground like any **immolating monk**. . . . She burned for two

hours . . . glowing within, like a building fire glimpsed through silhouetted walls, like a **hollow saint**, like a **flame-faced virgin gone to God**, while I read by her light, kindled, while Rimbaud in Paris burnt out his brains in a thousand poems, while night pooled wetly at my feet.[5]

The religious metaphors (emphasis mine) compare the moth to a saint sacrificing herself to God's light, and—by extension of the author's desire for rejuvenation and her reading of the Rimbaud book—the moth symbolizes the sacrifice sometimes necessary to be a writer, to be transfigured. In the essay's next section, Dillard asks her writing students which of them will sacrifice their lives to become writers. Her metaphors create a bridge within us between our vaporous ideas of "religious sacrifice" and tangible things like a moth flying into a candle. With these metaphors, familiar distinctions break down.

I imagine Dillard opening up a window to see which metaphors fly and feel right on the page's white sky. I suggest to students that if, *while drafting*, they sense that something beckons for a fresh fashioning, they keep open to that subject's myriad metaphorical possibilities. One day I brought in a thin branch to a writing class and asked students to brainstorm as many possible visual metaphors as they could: *a hand, telephone power line, half a spider, duck toes without the webbing*. Then, together we created a piece of writing that incorporated several of the metaphors. The exercise reminded them not only how pleasurable creating metaphors can be; it also showed them how natural doing so felt. Then, I shared with them a passage from *Walden* to illustrate how some prose writers stay perennially open to the world as metaphor. When the spring air thaws Walden Pond's ice, Thoreau gazes at the sand that flows down to the pond. At first he compares the shapes the sand makes to lava, lichen, coral, leopards' paws, "brains or lungs or bowels." As he watches sand shoot from earth and form leaflike shapes, his imagination leads him to an observation that a quantum physicist or yogi would appreciate: "No wonder that the earth expresses itself outwardly in leaves, it so labors with the idea inwardly." He continues in the next passage to perceive numerous interconnections that suggest the inherent relationship among earth, the body, and language:

Internally, whether in the globe or animal body, [the leaf] is a moist thick *lobe*, a word especially applicable to the liver and lungs and the *leaves* of fat . . . *externally* a dry thick *leaf*, even as the *f* and *v* are a pressed and dried *b*. The radicals of lobe are *lb*, the soft mass of the *b* (single lobed, or B, double lobed,). . . .[6]

Writing itself heightens Thoreau's ability to perceive the metaphorical reality as he sees and hears the lobes of letters. He intuits both much of yoga's wisdom exploring the intricate interrelationships among language, sound, nature, and consciousness—which preceded Thoreau by nearly two thousand years—and the insight of quantum physicists who follow Thoreau by nearly 150 years. After reading this passage, most students are eager at once to get outdoors and then to get into their writing's indoors.

So take a walk and try to find at least ten leaves not on or from trees. That is, try to find ten things whose shape and/or function resembles trees' leaves. Or seek out ten things whose shape resembles a hand or a face. Look up, down, upside down. Doing so will remind you of nature's and our bodies' self-replicating patterns. Then, write a prose description of the items, in which you seek to explore their metaphorical reality. As you write, start heeding the words you employ to refer to the things in the world. How does the word *tree* relate to the wooden form with leaves we call tree? How does the word *sidewalk* relate to the squares of cement we call, without thinking, sidewalks? What other concepts nest inside *tree* or *trunk*? What's the root of *tree*? Play with the words to see what surprising revelations and connections surface.

Thoreau practiced something else essential that I encourage students to do: Dig around in words' roots. My students often unearth words' metaphorical origins and discover language's metaphorical nature, a realization that readies them to derive the most charge from their words. Rummage through a source such as Eric Partridge's *Origins: A Short Etymological Dictionary of Modern English*, and you'll discover that many words, born from our physical and sensory experiences, reveal a metaphorical base. The root of *courage*, for instance, is the Latin *cor*, meaning "heart." I imagine some twelve hundred years after the Romans named the physical organ, the Medieval French—based upon their immediate wartime experience of blood rushing through them, chests swelling, and brains reeling—formed a word that may translate to "full of heart": *curage*, which gave the English not only *courage* but the siblings *encourage* and *discourage*. Similarly, after the Romans named the mouth's slippery but tangible organ *lingua*, the French named the abstract phenomenon of words uttered from the mouth and tongue *langue*, which gave us the English "language." The tongue gives us language. *Capital* as in "first" or "primary" stems from the Latin *cap*, meaning "head." Hence, we may ask a houseguest to remove his *cap* before coming into our home (although we likely wouldn't *decapitate* him even if he wore out his stay). Many of us may know our words' roots. My point is, though, that we form words that express abstract concepts quite often from immediate, concrete experience. Our body's myriad nerve endings and our brain's sensory receptors, imagination, and intellect compel us to generate, utter, sputter, and write metaphors.

Language is metaphorical. A story among some Northeastern American Indian tribes tells of a young man asking a wisewoman, "What does the earth rest on?" "A turtle's shell," she said. "And what does that turtle stand on?" "Another turtle," she said. "It's turtles all the way down." A friend of mine once said the same thing about language and its reflection of reality: "It's metaphors all the way down." All words are symbolic representations of ideas or things or feelings; all words, when spoken or written, manifest something otherwise invisible. The authentic metaphors we discover in fiction, nonfiction, and poetry express language's nature in an artful and pleasurable way that can change how our readers feel and think, how their bodies and brains respond to the words our bodies write.

A final observation about metaphors and symbols: Just as personal symbols emerge naturally from our own experience and environment, so, too, do some authentic metaphors and symbols in writing emerge from the body of work itself, from the act of writing itself, and from a story's context and language. In Flannery O'Connor's short story "Good Country People," for instance, a girl has a wooden leg. O'Connor said that while writing the story, she didn't know the leg would become symbolic of the girl's vulnerability and limitations. But by the time O'Connor was writing the climactic scene, in which a con man dupes her by posing as a Bible salesman, has sex with her, and then takes her leg and leaves her, O'Connor knew the leg had become symbolic. Similarly, many of the moth metaphors and symbols from Dillard's experience came only years later when Dillard felt compelled to revisit her journal's notes and begin weaving her memory's images into the essay. Each of those religious metaphors contributes to the others' meaning, and they wouldn't have the same resonance without Dillard's situation of seeking some insight to rekindle her spark to write. An authentic metaphor derives its charged meaning from its relationship to other words within the same piece, just as part of a body functions in accord with the other parts. Otherwise, lavish metaphors and symbols seem forced and disembodied, or removed from the text's body.

We inhabit one complex, shape-shifting metaphor: the body. Recognize it for the metaphor reservoir that it is.

$\mathcal{T}$AKE A BREATH #1:
MINE THE MOMENT FOR A METAPHOR

INTENTION:
Engage this practice when you need for a writing subject an original metaphor that comes directly from your environment. You may simply wish to heighten your innate ability to create metaphors. This practice asks you to try ALTERNATE NOSTRIL BREATHING (*nādī-shodhana prānāyāma*), which can harmonize the brain's hemispheres and, thus, prime your brain and body for metaphor making.

Sit comfortably. EASY CROSS-LEGGED POSE (sukhāsana) *or* ADAMANTINE POSE/KNEELING POSE (vajrāsana) *or even sitting in a chair (see Appendix) will work. Take in at least two full breaths. Then, ask yourself why you write. Once you feel you've sufficiently absorbed a response, clarify to yourself your specific writing subject. Try to simplify the subject into a core noun, abstract or concrete, such as* Mother, Gerald, basketball, heavy metal music, grief. *Clarify, too, that you seek metaphorical insight into this subject.*

Now, with eyes still closed, hear with your inner ear the noun for your subject, and notice how it feels as the word courses through your body with your breath. Notice if it sticks anywhere in your body. Let it settle there.

With your subject sufficiently embodied, lengthen your spine, and rest your left hand on your thigh and lift your right hand. Fold the index and middle finger in toward the thumb base, and bring your right hand to your nose. (See Appendix.) Set your thumb tip on the outside of the right nostril; your ring and little finger along the left. Close your eyes. Close the left nostril, and slowly exhale through the right. Fill your lungs with an inhalation through the right nostril. Close the right nostril, open the left, and exhale all of the way through the left nostril. Inhale fully through the left nostril. Repeat continuously three to five times.

Sit for a few more breaths, and fine-tune your outer senses. Begin to hear what's going on outside of you. Take in the aroma of the air with your next inhalation. Coat your tongue with saliva. Feel your skin. Then focus on the backs of your eyelids.

When you open your eyes' windows, notice what object, sound, smell, taste, or sensation seizes your imagination. A cardinal's chirp near dusk. The slant of smoggy light sneaking through the window slats. Whatever the sensation, absorb it for a few breaths.

When ready, begin writing a piece of prose or poetry that metaphorically links your subject to whatever seizes you. Refrain from forcing obvious connections. You can begin by describing the subject and trusting that a link to the external sensation will surface. You can begin by describing the sensation and find your way to your subject. Or you can begin with a direct sentence such as "My mother stretches and looms like the hickory in our front yard" or "Grief spreads out and dampens the ground, the aftermath of a good rain that has cooled you down, brought you down to the soil." Then proceed to allow connections to surface from your imagination, body, and the language itself. Be receptive to the piece of writing's context so that the metaphors spring naturally both from your body and from the body of words.

When you feel comfortable with the piece, let someone read it and ask him or her how it feels to read the piece. Ask him or her what slightly new understanding of the subject the writing brings.

TAKE A BREATH #2: REIMAGINE A BODY

INTENTION:
Try the following pose to reimagine metaphorically the nature of
your body or the nature of a character's body for your writing.

Come onto your hands and knees, aligned beneath your shoulders and
hips respectively. Let the tops of your feet rest on your mat or blanket.
(See Appendix for marjarāsana.) Eyes closed, take at least two full
breaths. Set your intention by asking yourself what you are writing for.
Once you feel the answer sufficiently in your body, clarify your more
specific writing intention. If you're writing personally, set out to imagine
your body metaphorically, or, if you're writing about someone else or a
fictional character, ready yourself to project your experiences into his or
her perspective. Take another three full breaths as you feel the connection
between earth and your hands.

While you center on your breath's movements, sense what it feels like
to inhabit this body. Does it move with grace and ease like a river or a
greased machine? If it had its choice, what would be its preferred mode of
travel? Flying? Crawling? Swimming? Hang gliding?

Keeping firm in your hands' mounds and base knuckles, experiment
with moving in this pose: Inhale to let your back curve as your heart sinks
toward the mat and as your tailbone arches upward; exhale to arch your
upper back toward the ceiling and drop your tailbone. Then, look over
your left shoulder while you curve the side of your torso to the right and
repeat on the other side. You can drop your hips toward the floor on each
side to stretch your torso and the hips' external muscles, and you can
bring your hips toward your heels to stretch your shoulder girdles. Intuit
how this body wants to move the self that inhabits it. If the body wishes to
shift the pose in some way, follow it.

As you glide in each position and from one to the next, appreciate the
sensations in your body and any images from your physical or subtle
imagination that may surface. What is this body? What is this body like
that resonates with your authentic self or with the authentic self of your
subject? Does an animal inhabit this body? Is it something from the natural world? Could something from the city express its core? For several

breaths, just move with this pose, your body, imagination, and the language that surfaces.

The pose you've been playing with is called **CAT POSE** (marjarāsana). So you might explore whether or not this body metaphorically could curl up on branches or tops of doors and whether or not it could chase after birds and mice. This body may creak a bit like my nineteen-year-old black cat's arthritic body that still musters enough courage, enough heart, to fend off dogs and deer. If so, acknowledge it.

When you've had enough fun, begin writing a piece that explores one of the metaphorical connections that seemed most authentic. I suggest you place your narrator or character in a situation or place to give the writing context. Describe the subject's body in action and let the metaphorical connections unfold naturally. As you write a piece of prose, fiction, or poetry, be open to how each word's nuance may proffer new insight. Assume whatever tone—serious, humorous, a favorite cat's point of view—that suits your experience and your intention.

CHAPTER NINE

Bliss in a Toothbrush

You can become, if only for a fleeting moment, a birch tree, standing stalwart on a hill, whose limbs the animate air invigorates, a beet in a lover's salad that drips with passion, a humble stone rubbed against another that sparks messages from its inner walls. You can be in bliss. To be in bliss, to be bliss, has been one of yoga's ancient ends, possibly *the* end. To be in bliss is not simply to be giddy with delight, nor is it something that needs to be mystified. Bliss, *samādhi*, is a state of being wholly content while connected with, not transcendent of, this material world of toothbrushes and turnips.[1] We enter bliss when, even if only for a breath or two, the ego self releases its conventional view of reality, we glimpse the essential nature of some object, and our thoughts merge with the thing and its referent. Borders between subject and object dissolve. Thus, one of the oldest and most effective ways for being in bliss is to concentrate on an object.

To be in bliss as a writer you need not go into trances or have visions of deities. And let me say up front that I would never promise that you will or even *should* be in bliss. I'll just posit that it's possible and desirable as a writer. To write in bliss is a natural way to extend what we've considered in earlier chapters: concentration, presence, wonder, metaphor.

Reality—a word whose root is *res*, Latin for "thing"—involves our awareness of thoughts and of the material world. This interplay between thought and thing prompts many of us to write, for writing is an open inquiry into the nature of reality, however seriously or comically we wish to approach that inquiry. Our writing, in turn, can become a vehicle that prompts our readers to reflect upon their own reality, the way in which their own thoughts weave through this world of things.

Around a hundred years ago, poet Rainer Maria Rilke, in his early thirties, received some advice from the sculptor Auguste Rodin that changed Rilke's view of reality and writing. He told Rilke to stop thinking in the abstract and to work with his eyes, to learn from his eyes. He took the advice to heart and wrote to a lover-friend, "Somehow I, too, must come to make things; not plastic, but written things—*realities* that emerge from handwork." And so Rilke did. In the next six years he would write about two hundred such poems, whose subjects range from a panther in a zoo, to a candle, a bed, and a statue of Adonis. The writer's task, Rilke writes in his *Duino Elegies*, is to imagine and to say this world's objects in ways that not even the objects themselves could imagine being. Bridge. Tree. Jug. These become the poet's subjects.

During the twentieth century, a century of mass production, numerous writers heard Rilke's cry to tend to these things. Francis Ponge. Zbigniew Herbert. Wysalla Zymborska. Jane Hirschfield. These poets also let a world of objects float in their hearts. Fiction writers such as Nabokov, Tom Robbins, Nicholson Baker, and nonfiction writers such as Annie Dillard and Nancy Mairs so illuminate this world of small things that as the writer's eye and tongue and imagination play with and identify with the object, your sense of self, if only for a moment, can shift, heighten, even dissolve.

Your discovery of bliss in being a writer won't happen necessarily in a meditation hall or even in a yoga class. A meditation cushion and a mat can prime your body, imagination, and spirit for the real deal, which often visits writers in the living room, on a street or basketball court, and at the desk. In Lucille Clifton's poem "Cutting Greens," the speaker, preparing a meal, loses herself for a moment, in love with the blackness of everything around her and on her, including her skin, feeling "the bond of live things everywhere." The speaker experiences a flash of bliss in the flesh. Maxine Kumin feels the bond while raking horse dung in "The Excrement Poem." Infinity is in the ordinary—a flower bed, a bowl of oatmeal, your blouse, a letter. Although we don't have to spend six months meditating in a cave, we do spend years priming our imagination with ordinary things. So goggle and gaze, squint and blink, think with your eyes. Lose yourself in reverie, in the textures of cherry bark or of a fresh croissant. Allowing your gaze to render with a painter's precision the rich surfaces of the plastic toothbrush you've used to scrub the tub for five years can prime you. If you want to "find" bliss, I suggest you not spend too much time seeking it. Instead, learn to look and to inquire into the nature of things.

Your description of toilet paper or crepe myrtle anchors your readers in a bathroom or the South. They get their bearings. But an extended description of a thing also can become a form of aesthetic concentration and meditation in which the writer artfully follows the ways thing and thought relate. Take the protagonist in Nicholson Baker's *The Mezzanine*. The entire action of the novella takes place during a young businessman's escalator ride as he returns from his lunch hour. One escalator ride, 130 pages. The first eight pages detail why he asked a clerk for a plastic bag. Another eight pages follow his thoughts on broken shoelaces. Near the novel's middle, he observes his own crisp dry-cleaned shirt, which prompts him to describe for eight pages a memory of putting on one of the five shirts, newly dry cleaned, that he owned when he first got his job. The memory of opening the package leads him to observe, among many other facets of dry-cleaned shirts, that they were "wrinkled with positive kinds of semiintentional knife-edge creases and perpendicular fold-lines that only heightened the impression of ironedness, having come about either as a result of the occasionally indiscriminate force of the pressing and starching machines (such as the crow's-feet on the sleeve near the cuffs) or as a result of the final careful foldup."[2] This guy loves the textures of things.

In this same memory, he recalls how on the subway to work he had had a startling self-realization: He's the sort of person who doesn't think about, say, economics or politics or even his own personal demons, but about buttering raisin toast. As Baker's characters think thoroughly about superficial surfaces—a contemporary Proust with a busier life and less predictable wit—his descriptions and trains of thought keep us suspended in pregnant present moments whose edges round out like bowls around the past and future. As delightfully self-conscious and hyperobservant as Baker's protagonists may seem, they're also quite content, if not blissful. No pages here of psychoanalysis, of anxious fretting about the world's or a marriage's end, of guilt-laden confessions. They—and by extension, we the readers—find bliss in this world of things. We could do worse as writers whose grandest epiphanies have to do with, say, dog smells instead of God's scent. It's easy to bemoan this world of things; more challenging to praise it.

Although gazing on and receiving objects actually is an ancient yoga practice, if practiced well, it can constitute a new encounter each time. Think about what can happen when you direct your thoughts toward an object. Mind and object engage in a reciprocal communication. We practice one-pointed concentration (*ekagrata*). If you concentrate on the lampshade on your desk, your eyes, fingers, and your brain's nerve receptors take in the thin, smooth, barklike lines of the cloth stretched from end to end. You consider the word *lamp*, and subtle thoughts and images may surface as you explore its relationship to the desk, the electric current buzzing through its body, its willing gift of light. Memory may intervene as you recall your poor grandmother's house full of shadeless lamps, this being one of them, the naked bulbs exposed and proud. Awareness of the future illuminates that in a hundred years this lamp may be disposed of and disassembled into so many glass shards, screws, and wires. Your mind and imagination reveal the thing's nature, and it in turn reveals your nature—ephemeral yet part of the same basic atomic stuff.

This contemplation is the first step of what Patanjali calls in the *Yoga-Sutra* "bliss with support" (*samprajnāta samādhi*). Possibly, for a moment, these associations, analogies, temporal references, and thoughts such as "I am observing a lamp" vanish while thoughts merge with the thing, and the thing's essential meaning reveals itself. When you approach an object anew, when you forget your preconceptions of a thing—its typical function, its socially constructed significance—you also can awaken a dormant part of your consciousness that offers you insight, however poignant or banal, into the nature of a thing and into material reality. Blake sensed it in a grain of sand, Whitman in a blade of grass, Ginsberg in a building's bricks. Now, what that revelation is—or "epiphany," to evoke Joyce's similar process based on St. Thomas Aquinas's ideas—will be, should be, unique for each of us in each new encounter.

Our brains must love such fresh insight. As mentioned before, several studies performed on advanced meditators indicate that their brain waves slowed down to the alpha state with some traces of theta brain waves (four to eight cycles per second). In this state, a sort of drowsy yet alert state, the embodied unconscious raises random images and impressions to awareness. Such suggestions may be the stuff of what in yoga we call *dhiti* or revelation. Some recent studies show how, when highly creative people are engaged in creative work, cerebral blood flow increases significantly, the activity stimulates considerably more parts of the brain to cooperate, and nitric oxide releases neurotransmitters that release endorphins, the brain chemicals that induce deep pleasure and contentment. Similar physiological responses have been measured in people in deep relaxation.[3] Another study in Holland illustrates that nitric oxide, abundant in the sinuses, can be stimulated through conscious nasal breathing and humming on the exhalation. No wonder being creative and breathing deeply can be blissful. Bliss has some biological basis. Certain yoga practices that increase cerebral blood flow, stimulate nitric oxide, and slow down our brain's waves can be ideal ways to prime our bodies and imagination for bliss.

Your writing itself can be blissful. Of course, it can be excruciating as well and involves a heck of a lot of clipping, cutting, grimacing, complaining, and tossing. But if we're open to the possibility and prepare our bodies, we also can have at least a few moments of unmediated bliss. Sustained observation causes images to be stored in the physical imagination. In the writing process, as the brain and the body's cells and nerve receptors orchestrate a concert for a piece of writing, these stored images can mix your immediate experience with words on the page, as well as with your subtle imagination's seemingly random associations and imagery. The self gets out of the way, and language and imagination take over. Fresh images, metaphors, and music arise to bring things together, to unify, to make bliss. It's usually in writing anyway that I discover, by chance or revelation, whatever fresh insight I may proffer. We don't need to mystify these "experiences," for they're rare for me and other writers I know, mixed between a lot of patient pushing and waiting, of tinkering with and trashing drafts. Yet, something significant occasionally does stir me in the moment of writing as thought merges with words—the sense, the sounds, the innuendos—and rather than pushing words up a hill like a chugging locomotive, the train of thought and the words and images and their referents themselves carry my self to forgotten villages. And then it's back to the joys of clipping, cutting, pasting, deleting.

We can avoid mystifying writing while at the same time celebrating ordinary life's mysteries. That's my main caveat here and elsewhere in this book. To chase after bliss or mystical moments at the expense of this life, this world, this sentence, both misses the point and sets you up for disappointment and frustration. I think of Edward in Eugene O'Neill's *Long Day's Journey Into Night*, who pines to his father about how all he wants is to experience again what he experienced on a boat years before: with the wind howling like a hungry dog, mist flying from the waves that rocked the boat, the sky dark and vast above him, his body meshed with everything. He was everything. He was bliss. As his father sneers that Edward's idealism will doom him, Edward recites Baudelaire's poem "Be Intoxicated." Sure, you can take Baudelaire's advice and get drunk with wine, with poetry, with virtue, or with altered states of consciousness, but a startling sobriety that awakens you to this world of things isn't such a bad path either.

It's a humbling act. Giving your attention for several minutes, hours even, to coffee grains or worn-out socks rather than to "big" ideas like global warming or economics sends your ego and mind a message: "Be small." The ego can quiet down as it stops trying to figure out things and instead appreciates and receives *a* thing; our sense of separation from the world's things changes and potentially widens our heart's field. So, the frequent turn of the gaze toward the hammer or keyboard, the partition wall or bulletin board, potentially can alter how you relate to the multiple things that occupy your world. In a sense, you become them; they, you. You may slow down that fretful ego's to-do-list mentality long enough to create a more richly textured world of words for you and your reader. By asking us to humble ourselves to live among, and as, this world of small objects and small words—suitcase, apricot, bread—our writing itself asks us to stop trying to control nature, language, one another. Self and thing and word, in their nature, identify with one another. Maybe the habit at least will lead us to treat the things around us with a bit more reverence.

$\mathcal{T}$AKE A BREATH: GAZE

INTENTION:
This practice can increase your cerebral blood flow, slow down your brain waves, and prepare your embodied imagination for a fresh perspective into the nature of an object, the nature of thinking and of consciousness—the nature of reality.

Choose an object, or, better, let one choose you. A kitchen utensil, a tool, a pair of socks, something without preconceived sentimental value, works best. Or step into some woods or on a street. Walk with your breath until you happen upon a simple totem—a river stone stranded beneath some leaves, a turtle shell becoming dust, a tossed mailbox half-buried in the soil, a piece of bark shaped like your home state. Sit before it. **ADAMANTINE POSE** *(vajrāsana) or* **ADEPT'S POSE** *(siddhāsana) works best for this practice, but please choose a pose in which you can feel at ease but alert for several minutes. (See the Appendix for more options.) Close your eyes. Grow firm but soft in your seat. After taking at least two full breaths, ask yourself quietly, "What am I writing for?" Be patient with the response. Then, clarify that you intend to see some thing anew.*

Open your eyes and practice nonattached looking. For two breaths, move your eyes up between your eyebrows without looking. Then for two breaths, shift your eyes as far to the right as they will go without looking or fixing eyes and thoughts on anything. Then do the same by moving your eyes down, then to the left.

When ready, close your eyes and perform the same rotation measured by two breaths each. You're cleansing your eyeballs of preconceptions' dust and lint.

After five breaths, open your eyes normally, and as you let your thoughts hover upon the object's general outline, acknowledge the common word used to refer to it. Take in its shell in form and name. Close your eyes, and let the image's imprint rest on the insides of your eyelids.

From physical imagination's memory, fill out its edges and colors, its textures and surfaces. Imagine its form expanding and contracting with your breath. Then, open your eyes halfway and scan the object from left to right, up and down, noting each nook, crevice, scratch, shift in shade. While you hold your gaze like a rock in a stream, let your thoughts float by like sticks in a stream. Begin imagining its history. Its origins. Its multiple functions and roles in the world and its future.

Close your eyes again, and imagine its interior life. Breathe deeply and let roll from your subtle imagination a stream of visual and other metaphors that illuminate the thing's thingness, its rasa, or essence. Then, follow your breath from your belly's base to your third eye as you envision the object as yourself. You may see the object overlapped upon your body's form or vice versa. You may imagine yourself as having no form, only some essence that enters the object's form. Stay with this image for several breaths and observe what it feels like to be this thing without forcing its qualities into the human realm, without projecting your personality into it. Instead, let it enter you.

Whenever you're ready, open your eyes and write a prose piece or poem in which you try to capture in imagery and rhythm this thing's nature in relation to "I." Yet, do so with a natural voice, without seeming cryptic or obtuse. I offer you numerous options. A **NARRATIVE PIECE** may recount parts of what your narrator just experienced or may follow the thing's history. A **LYRICAL PIECE** may begin praising the thing's qualities. An **EXPLORATORY PIECE** may move back and forth in perspective between your narrator's "self" and the thing. Perhaps there are moments of mergence and of separation. Maybe metaphor links the two. Of course, you can experiment with point of view as well, particularly if you're writing fiction. You might aim to describe the object's essence. Select concrete, sensuous words, and honor the object's uniqueness by finding the particular details that distinguish it. Try not to follow personal streams of association or sentiment. Instead, try to honor the object on its own terms.

Or have a dialogue of sorts. You can begin by describing the object on its own terms. Then, introduce your "I" and how it relates—and attempts to relate—to this object. Where and how do the two meet? Where and how do the two divide? Metaphors build conceptual bridges between those two realms we call "inner" and "outer." The word house in a poem might signify the oak structure with a gabled roof in which a person *lives, but, depending on the context, it also might signify some invisible space in which ideas, images, dreams, voices, and memories live and daily cross thresholds. Metaphorical language lets our perception move outward and inward simultaneously. Thus, metaphors can rearrange the walls of our self-awareness and our self-identity.*

Be open to the bliss of writing itself. Let one word, one image, one sound, lead you to the next, not knowing exactly which cobblestone streets or cedar-chipped flower beds words will take you to.

CHAPTER TEN

Tuning In to Your Prose's Embodied Sounds

I'm a fool for sweet sounds. Rain "thwapping" between evergreens and service berries dots the early autumn forest floor of fallen leaves. Its sound beats irregularly against the steady stream that falls over the small dammed wall a few yards away. My car's transmission could drop to the street, a tree could fall on my roof, but if I can walk into the woods to listen to nature sweet-talk me, then all is right, and I'm in love with the world again.

Most of us, I suspect, are suckers for such sounds because they vibrate us on a core level we usually don't feel in our workaday world. A million people a year visit Niagara Falls, not only because of the spectacle but also, I surmise, because of the audible. Its water drum hypnotizes us, and because we're physically composed of dancing atoms, it makes us quiver on some subtle level beyond bringing pleasure. Some combinations of sounds remind us of the universe's creation. The Judeo-Christian Yahweh uttered speech to create the world in six days, St. John's famous book suggests "the Word" (the Greek *logos*) started spinning things into shape, and the Hindu Shiva's rattling drum beat into being the patterned matter of creation (imagine how we'd dance together in the streets if Yahweh could sing to Shiva's drum). Some scientists contend it all started with a loud sound, a bang. Pythagoras, that figure who haunted our geometry classes, intuited this music of the spheres, as did the scientist Johannes Kepler. Whether that sound was God's voice, Shiva's drum, or exploding atoms, this planet we inhabit nonetheless circles to a series of musical rhythms latent within its rivers and stones, even within its roads and streets, possibly the same sonic stuff of which we are made—our veins and bones, our cells and biofeedback loops. Our bone marrow may contain the melody of a stream, the cacophony of a street, or the symphony of a star.

No wonder certain words, combined in a sentence or series of sentences, ring true and bring joy. The first sentence of Joyce's *Portrait of the Artist as a Young Man* suggests a primordial relationship between narrative's music and the birth of consciousness: "Once upon a time and a very good time it was there was a moocow coming down along the road and this moocow that was down along the road met a nicens little body name baby tuckoo. . . ."[1] Such was Stephen Daedalus's earliest memory, we can surmise—a story his father invented and near-sang. Several writers sense that combinations and repetitions of sounds in prose or poetry, repeated with the right regularity, bring us delight or delirium.

You may think you have a tin ear. "I just don't hear the music," a student once bemoaned. "I guess my ears don't work that way." Actually, each of us has an inner ear that lets us hear how words work on the inner vestibule. When we tune in to prose's music, we can create rich texts in which sense and sound play off of one another. We can learn the ways words work in our inner ears and how repetition of sounds in our writing strums the strings of our spines. In an immediate encounter among words, music, matter, and body, we can write with authentic musicality. Really, the process of hearing prose's music is more mechanical than mystical.

To attune our ears to language's music, we must acknowledge that this sound stuff isn't just a poet's province; the best prose writers sense it too. True, poets who work in set forms, of course, have the advantage of setting off important words at the beginning or ending of lines, but some novelists also follow words' undulations and not just their definitions, as Faulkner so often did. In the following passage from his short story "The Bear," the boy protagonist stands next to his mentor, Sam Fathers, who has taught him for years how to navigate the woods among men so he might spy the mighty bear that his father and his father's father have hunted for generations. The boy suddenly feels in his body the looming meaning of hunting the bear. It's a terrifyingly exhilarating feeling of primal wilderness itself, that part of ourselves connected to the natural world that is raw strength and courage and instinct:

Then, standing beside Sam in the thick **great gloo**m of ancient **woo**ds and the winter's dying after**noo**n, he **loo**ked quietly down at the rotted **log** scored and gutted with claw-marks and, in the wet earth beside it, the print of the enormous warped two-toed **foot**. Now **he** knew what **he had heard** in the **hounds'** voices in the **woo**ds that morning and what he had smelled when he peered under the kitchen where they hud**d**led. It was in him, too, a little different because they were brute beasts and he was not, but only a little different. . . .[2]

The woods' atmosphere, combined with the sight of the bear's spoors—the gutted log and the footprint—trigger in the boy a visceral sensation that connects him to what the hunting dogs feel and know. In the first sentence, the hard "oo" of *gloom* and *afternoon* plus the soft "oo" of *woods, looked,* and *foot* hold these words together in their mutual combined effect on the boy. His connection with the hounds' instinct is reinforced subtly in the second sentence through the repeated whispering *h*'s and the thudding *d*'s. Words' sounds as much as sense hold together this passage's effect.

Some sounds, though, can just crack us up. The following not-so-subtle excerpt comes from the closing of humorist Suzanne Britt's essay "That Lean and Hungry Look," in which she reverses stereotypes about fat people versus skinny people:

Fat people will **g**rab, **g**iggle, **g**uffaw, **g**allumph, **g**yrate, and **g**ossip. They are **g**enerous, **g**iving, and **g**allant. They are **g**luttonous and **g**oodly and **g**reat. What you want when you're down is soft and jiggly, not muscled and stable. Fat people know this. Fat people have plenty of room. Fat people will take you in.[3]

The last paragraph's repetition of sounds builds upon the essay's rhythm to a comical climax. The repeated hard *g* sound almost imitates the gurgling chortle and jiggling gut of the essay's heroic Everyfatperson. Too, we can't help but notice how she reverses the stereotypical virtues of our Protestant work ethic and Catholic cardinal sins when she conjoins "gluttonous and goodly and great," the added *and*s echoing the King James Bible's incantatory cadences. Repeat this sentence with your inner ear. Imagine its vibrations on your vestibule. You may chuckle as these sentences plant a series of an aunt's sloppy kisses on your pudgy cheeks.

Your writing can generate an audible experience for readers. When immersed in reading a creative text, we suspend our normal daily awareness and enter a virtual world of words or a richly textured linguistic universe that engrosses our embodied imaginations and minds. We may feel wholly absorbed in the present of reading. When we process written words whose sounds reverberate off of one another, our mind makes meaning of a passage not just horizontally (that is, in the left-to-right direction our eyes trace when reading a text); our mind also processes the words vertically and diagonally. In the chapter "The Present" from Annie Dillard's Pulitzer Prize–winning nonfiction *Pilgrim at Tinker Creek*, Dillard stops at a gas station for some coffee after hours of driving along a mind-numbing freeway. There, she steps behind the station, pets someone's puppy, and watches the sun set. Suddenly, the present strikes and absorbs her consciousness. Whereas describing a sunset could be material for clichéd reverie, in Dillard's hands and imagination the description becomes a way to give readers a dazzling experience of being—and reading—in "the present":

> Shadows lope along the mountain's rumpled flanks; they elongate like root tips, like lobes of spilling water, faster and faster. A warm purple pigment pools in each ruck and tuck of the rock. . . . As the purple vaults and slides, it tricks out the unleafed forest and rumpled rock in gilt, in shape-shifting patches of glow. . . . The air cools; the puppy's skin is hot. I am more alive than all the world.[4]

Your mind unconsciously may draw virtual lines among *shadows*, *lope*, *lobes*, and *glow* because of the *l*'s and the long *o*'s. The first sentence actually contains six more *l* sounds. This moment of shifting light at once envelopes the landscape and Dillard's perception, and strings together the landscape's disparate parts—the rock and water and mountain and light. So the *puhs* and the *ucks* and the *ruhs* and *shs* also string together the various words in the reader's inner ear.

But what intrigues me about *how* Dillard writes is that I suspect she hears words' internal sounds *as* she writes. So as she writes or types *shadows*, she hears the long *o* which suggests to her imagination the metaphorical *lope*, which then triggers *lobes*. The same thing happens in the next sentence with the alliteration of *p*'s and the consonance of *k*. The sound of *ruck*—which means an indistinguishable jumble and thus makes a perfect word for how, at dusk, forms begin to meld into one another—leads her to *tuck*—which at once suggests a rock's pocket in which light could be tucked, as well as the definition of a drumbeat. "Ruck and tuck of a rock" reverberates with meaning and reflects a focus on the feast of writing itself: Sometimes we worry less about translating an experience into denotative words and center more intuitively upon letting one word's sounds unfold another word.

These sound combinations, then, can be more than simple "devices" that amateur poets employ for flourish. For starters, our musical prose and poetry stimulate more parts of the brain than plain, literal language. Writer and former *Kenyon Review* editor Frederick Turner is cofounder of the international poetry movement Natural Classicism, based in part on his extensive research with neurologist Eric Poppol on poetic meter and the brain. Their research suggests the human brain is genetically coded to need measured narrative, for his research reveals that narrative meter with regularly paced lines especially stimulates the forebrain—the brain's bridge between left and right hemispheric functions.

Yogis have experienced for over two thousand years how the consistent repetition of some sound combinations can so resonate and vibrate within the physical and subtle-emotional body that they can influence our state of mind. Similar to Pythagoras's view of the music of the spheres, the ancient Indian text *The Upanishads* claims that patterns of sound lie latent in the universe's rhythms (I hear the first *über*-note of Strauss's tone-poem *Also Sprach Zarathustra*). The Vedic bards, called rishis, tuned their ears to hear these pulses that they, then, translated into mantras. *Mantra* is an instrumental sound wedded to thought and intention (*man* meaning "to think"); it is a charged combination of sacred sounds and syllables that shape energy. Although Mantra Yoga can entail an elaborate system of necessary steps to take—sixteen according to one yoga text—for mantras to manifest their sacred power, I'm more interested in mantra as a way to help us hear how words, even seemingly ordinary words, emanate from our authentic embodied self and so can carry charged sound when bounced with other words' sounds. The practice of mantra can help us cultivate a writer's inner ear for words' authentic music *as we write*.

I've had writers play with four of Sanskrit's mantra seed (*bija*) syllables to help them embody sounds and to feel how words originate from and vibrate parts of their bodies other than their mouths. Seed (*bija*) syllables rouse specific energy centers in our subtle body. Most of us are familiar with the seed syllable with which we begin, *om*. After my students get in a comfortable seat and follow their breath for a few minutes, we focus on the third eye region between our eyebrows and utter *om*. The *m* sound vibrates from our mouth's roof to the pineal gland located near the third eye. Then we drop our focus to the throat and try *ham*—pronounced "haum." The *h* sound, originating from the throat, shivers our sound tunnel. The next floor down in our body's building is the heart space where we can feel the seed syllable *yam*—pronounced "yaum"—vibrate. And, finally, we experience how the seed syllable *ram* ("raum") gently draws our abdomen back and so stimulates our belly region or solar plexus. Then, we try to vibrate these places by repeating each syllable to ourselves. In *mantra* practice, we learn to speak a mantra out loud (*ucca*), whisper it (*upamshu*), and then speak it within (*manasa*). Repeating it and keeping its sounds vibrating within your inner vestibule at once heightens the word's energy and helps you adjust your inner ear.

After I led a group through this practice, the same writer who had told me she couldn't hear the music said that despite the fact that she had been writing nonfiction for eleven years, she'd never noticed how physical language can be. She later wrote me to say that not only does she take more pleasure, if not measure, in speaking, but her writing experience, now, seems more visceral as she can hear how words hum from her body to the page.

Start with something simple. Take at least two full breaths just to quiet your inner noise and to make space for music. Aim quietly to voice a word's wondrous sounds, to let them vibrate in ways you've never felt before. Take the word *reuniting*. Forget for now its meaning and just enjoy its sound as if you spoke it for the first time. Speak it out loud five times. Let your mouth, your word-organ, play the invisible word's notes one rebounding syllable at a time as your tongue and breath, your throat and lungs and heart and belly, all work together. Now, without moving your mouth or making an audible sound, hear the word being uttered within over and over. If doing so triggers an image or another word, heed it. You might write a brief sketch, a vignette, devoted to exploring this word's unique power or that of any word you choose. You can begin such a sketch by describing its sounds and then proceeding to what significant associations the word—its sound or sense—trigger within your imagination. It may lead you to memory or metaphor.

Read a passage by a prose writer who listens to words' music. Something by William Gass, Constance Hale (editor of *Wired* magazine), G. K. Chesterton, Arundhati Roy, Rick Moody, or Toni Morrison should suffice. First, put the passage's sense in the background, and its sound in the foreground. Read it aloud with the same savor you did with the word *reuniting* and notice what parts of your body seem especially tweaked. Then reread it to yourself to hear and feel how sense and sound in the passage may work together. Notice if one word's sound plays off of another and how your brain and imagination both walk along horizontal planks and climb ladders to connect one word to another.

Listen to and utter words whose meanings you don't know. At the Zen Mountain Monastery, we chanted *dhvanis* ("sound" in Sanskrit), chants whose words mean nothing other than their sounds. I relished just letting my tongue roll with my eased mind and breath. A friend of mine who taught English in Japan for a few years experienced firsthand how we delight in seemingly senseless sound. A friend invited her to sing at a Japanese wedding any song she knew in English. She was invited solely because she was American and could speak English, and she obliged even though she only knew the words to one song. Most of the people at the wedding spoke little or no English, but her presence, mixed with what they heard as the beauty of English, must have seemed a blessing to this union. It's probably just as well they didn't understand the song's lyrics. She sang "All of Me," the classic lounge song of romantic breakup. So, read a story or poem in a tongue you don't know. Read some of it out loud. Then let its sounds sink into your skin.

There's something to be said, too, for stepping outdoors to listen. Sometimes, numbed by the computer buzzing and my head humming, I have to walk out to the mountain stream near our farmhouse and sit. And listen. If I wish to recall the baseball bat's sonic *pock* that smacked the ball the one time I got a triple as a Little Leaguer, then I must listen. Likewise, if I wish to hear the symphonic cadence or the traffic-jam halt of my sentences, then I must listen. So, practice listening outdoors. A street may suffice as much as a stream. Then, move inward.

TAKE A BREATH: SOUND OUT YOUR EMBODIED WRITING

INTENTION:
Find a piece of your writing whose thudding sounds you'd like to tune up. Maybe the piece needs fine tuning for tone or mood, and changing its sound quality may just do the trick. Or you might simply want to sound out a new piece.

For this practice, you may either sit in a comfortable position and let your spine lengthen up and down, or you may recline in **LYING RELEASE POSE** *(savāsana). Feel your breath draw in and out as your belly expands and contracts. After at least two full breaths, ask yourself, "What am I writing for?" Tune your ear to whatever inner sounds or sights emerge, but don't try to force anything into shape. Listen and watch. When you feel the response sufficiently, clarify your specific writing intention for this session. You might acknowledge that you wish to hear the innate sounds of words for a specific subject or scene—either one you've been writing about or a new one.*

When ready, take a deep inhalation, and as you exhale hum with lips and eyes closed for as long as you can. As you do so four more times, play with the pitches and tones your throat, mouth, and breath can create. Focus on the third eye region between your eyebrows, and voice om ("aum"). Notice where in your skull the vowels and humming consonant vibrate. Then focus on the throat and hum ham, "haum." Notice how the h sound tweaks your throat. Then in your heart you can feel the shake of the syllable yam, pronounced "yaum." And, finally, the fiery seed syllable ram ("raum") pulls your abdomen back and so arouses your solar plexus, your inner sun. After you've played with and felt the sounds for a few minutes, breathe and quietly try to re-create some of the sounds internally.

Then, with your inner vestibule tuned up, heed and hear a core word or two that pertain to your writing subject or scene. What core words and syllables seem to be essential to your writing piece? Maybe mother and cutlery or angel and desperate suddenly surface. Sound out each one in your mouth. For the sake of experimentation, notice how their different sounds might vibrate different parts of your body. Then, as you breathe fully, hear a new line or a sentence for your subject or scene that surfaces naturally. For now heed sound more than sense.

With eyes open, slowly write down that line or sentence. As you do so, do as Dillard and hear each word's sounds that may trigger another word whose sounds may rebound off of yet another. The sound of mother may trigger mutter, and angel may lead you to bagel. Continue to write this way, following each syllable like a foot's beat, tending to sound more than sense, for several minutes or longer. When you've finished, read the piece aloud and hear how parts of it sing and vibrate. Double-check your words' meanings to see if their sense and sound wed. If some parts seem too forced, a tank of tintinnabulation roaring through your ear like lines from a Poe poem, rewrite it for subtlety.

CHAPTER ELEVEN

The Pulse of a Sentence
and the Yoga of Syntax

Syntactical patterns haunt and shape our thinking. Sentence rhythms that we hear and read can recall, in our brain's neuronal wiring, the ebb and flow in which predecessors uttered first syllables and words. Over years of thinking, of breathing, of listening and of reading, in certain patterns, we're drawn back along ancestral waves to interior caves where we write in patterns that we've unconsciously inherited.

Irish writer Seamus Heaney knows it's so. The Nobel Prize–winner says that as he struggled with the translation of *Beowulf*, he intuited a deep need to sustain the project as he realized that the project involved his "own linguistic and literary origins": "I had noticed, for example, that without any conscious intent on my part certain lines in the first poem in my first book conformed to the requirements of Anglo-Saxon metrics."[1] In other words, decades before Heaney started the translation project of the classic Anglo-Saxon poem, the Anglo-Saxon syntax—rooted as much in the Irish soil, in the Ulster taverns and farms, as in any book's pages—had shaped how Heaney heard words and rhythm bead together in his earliest poems. We inherit syntax.

Syntax, simply defined, is the patterned structure of words in a sentence. Over centuries, each language's speakers develop, consciously or not, what they consider predictable patterns and unpredictable patterns, what they regard as regular and irregular, pleasurable and annoying. Syntax is not an arbitrary term devised by rhetoricians; it is a natural expression and translation of our body's (especially our central nervous system's) rhythms. Our body's natural rhythms suggest that we're formed as much for sentence shaping as for lovemaking.

Although thinking about sentence structures while enjoying writing might seem like being on vacation with an uptight lover obsessed with rigid rules, tending to the syntax of things actually may liberate us from unconscious patterns of thinking and writing. Words and sentences are writers' raw material, and if a writer has no love of them, then her writing likely may never move beyond the transliteral or the purplish. Our sentences may pucker up and peck or be way too much tongue and saliva, but a writer tuned into syntax's rhythms may be able to wield sentences that will kiss a reader from cell to sole.

Each of us likely begins to write a sentence, any sentence, somewhere safe, a sort of toe-dipping by word and then phrase. Until we can glide across the page in a breast stroke and dolphin kick, we may be unwittingly content to dog-paddle in the shallow end of simplistic sentence patterns. Tending to and shifting undesired unconscious patterns is the heart of my yoga practice. Ninety-five percent of our thoughts are unconscious.[2] What's more, these unconscious thoughts shape the sentences that our conscious thoughts, imaginings, and feelings assume when they dive on the page. These unconscious impressions that shape our actions—"subliminal impressions," as B.K.S. Iyengar describes them—are called *samskāra*. Part of my yoga practice aims to do three basic things with *samskāra*: help detect these impressions' patterns, learn how to use them, and learn how to alter them. Learning the ins and outs of syntax can follow a similar process.

First, we recognize an obvious grammatical pattern engrained, consciously or unconsciously, in our minds if not in our brains. The English language's most fundamental sentence pattern is the S-V-O, or Subject-Verb-Object. Here are some simple examples:

The singer (subject) belts (verb) her tune (object).
Jonathan (subject) broke (verb) his leg (object).

This dog-paddle pattern locks in many writers' thinking. Their thinking plods in the same rhythms. Their sentences follow the same beat. Fine, if you intend to do so to make a point or to arouse monotony in your reader. But once aware of this basic pattern, you can create limitless variations of it to bring forth not just *what* your authentic voice needs to say but also *how* it needs to say it.

If we can hear syntax's rhythms, we can learn how to use or vary them according to our intent. A sentence often spirals or shrivels depending upon its rhythm—a sentence's basic unit that gives it musicality. Rhythm is patterned repetition. A sentence can repeat words, phrases, or clauses for a consistent musical rhythm and for emphasis of ideas or feelings; a sentence can repeat grammatical structures and parts of speech, too, to play upon readers' conscious or unconscious expectations of what idea or impression will come next.

So, there's merit in some repetition. Sometimes our writer's body and authentic voice need us to repeat this subject-verb grammatical structure to emphasize an idea or to evoke a feeling. The opening of Don DeLillo's *The Body Artist* describes the morning routine of a couple who has been married only for a few years: "**She poured** milk into the bowl. **He sat** down and got up. **He went** to the fridge and got the orange juice and stood in the middle of the room shaking the carton to float the pulp and make the juice thicker. **He** never **remembered** the juice until the toast was done."[3] These sentences' repeated subject-verb structure hammers the drudgery of the husband and wife's physically monotonous and parallel lives that only occasionally, if not accidentally, collide. She pours. He moves. She shakes. He pours. She nor he pays much attention to the syntax (or *samskāra*) of things, and neither (we can infer) has wholly kissed the other in quite some time.

But some writers' sentences do kiss. In *A Natural History of the Senses*, Dianne Ackerman recounts how in the early sixties many girls made kissing an art form:

> [W]e **kissed inventively,** clutching our boyfriends from behind as we straddled motorcycles, whose vibrations turned our hips to jelly; **we kissed extravagantly** beside a turtlearium in the park, or at the local rose garden or zoo; **we kissed delicately,** in waves of sipping and puckering; **we kissed torridly,** with tongues like hot pokers. . . .[4]

Ackerman knows how to kiss with her lips and with her tongue (her language, that is). The repeated subject-verb-adverb pattern torques her idea and reinforces how inventive the teenagers were with their kisses just as the writer is with her sentences. The opening of Rick Moody's *Purple America* uses a similar pattern for a different effect: The repetition of the arcane "whosoever" elevates the protagonist's personal sacrifice to something religious and reinforces the overwhelming nature of being a middle-aged son who must care for, in every way, his debilitated mother:

> **Whosoever knows** the folds and complexities of his own mother's body, *he shall never die*. **Whosoever knows** the latitudes of his mother's body, **whosoever has taken** her into his arms and immersed her baptismally in the first-floor tub, lifting one of her alabaster legs and then the other over its lip, **whosoever** bathes her with Woolworth's soaps in sample sizes . . . *he shall never die.*[5]

That last sentence runs for four pages, its momentum overwhelming the reader. Nonetheless, this sentence's kiss is so tender, so complex, so angry and confused and loving.

How I get writers and writing students to explore the syntax that rings right with their bodies and voice is not unlike what Bhakti yogis do. Bhakti is an ancient form of yoga devoted to praising the self's qualities by chanting. Quite often, Bhakti yogis chant in what is called a *kirtan* style—one person (often a teacher) calls out a chant to a certain rhythm and pitch, and the group (usually the students) responds by repeating the chant in the same rhythm and pitch. The predictable patterns give each voice a form in which to soar, and you learn that a chant's basic structure can have limitless variations.

So, too, with how I encourage my writing students. I "call out" a syntactical pattern, and they repeat it in their writing. I ask them to become aware again of the basic subject-verb pattern and then to feel in their writing how repetition with this structure gives our writing bodies some new strokes. Then, once your body and brain assimilate the patterns, you can learn to vary according to *how* your voice most needs to express an idea or feeling.

We start with parallelism. Possibly the foundational riff for writing musical prose, **parallelism** is the similarity of structure in a pair or series of related words, phrases, or clauses. In parallelism, we usually express a balance of ideas and images. In both of the following examples, notice the similar length of each unit, a quality that adds to each sentence's harmony. This simple student example repeats verbs to emphasize the bird's grace as it hunts: "The <u>eagle</u> <u>glides</u>, <u>swoops</u>, and <u>grabs</u> its meal." I encourage students to take their own subject ("my husband," "the waitress," "my body") and write a similar sentence: <u>X</u> <u>verb 1</u>, <u>verb 2</u>, and <u>verb 3</u>. An object can follow or not depending upon the verbs. We then take the pattern a step further and construct parallel phrases that begin with verbs (verb phrases). Read the following example and let your own subject soar:

The <u>sparrow</u>   <u>sings</u> <u>its song</u>,   <u>flings</u> <u>its feed</u>, and   <u>flicks</u> <u>its wings</u>.
<u>X</u>   <u>verb</u> <u>phrase 1</u>, <u>verb</u> <u>phrase 2</u>, and <u>verb</u> <u>phrase 3</u>.

For a dissonant effect or for surprise, make the third one stand out in length, meaning, or sound, such as this student sample: "The chef sliced the rutabagas, stirred the broth, and concocted new recipes to leave her lover." These rhythms can lull our readers asleep or rock them awake depending upon our intention. They surface naturally in our writing when our whole body seems to beat to the suite of our sentences in a desire for balance.

We can find balance, though, not just in harmony but also in contrast. Thus, writers also find **antithesis** useful. A type of parallel sentence in which two parallel elements contrast one another, antithesis can register in us a subtle pleasure when we define something by what it's not: "My mother taught me that my color was <u>not</u> <u>a mask</u> *but* <u>a shield</u>," writes Alice Walker, and in Clinton's early days of optimism he said, "We must be <u>the architects of our children's future</u>, *not* <u>the demolitionists of their dreams</u>." More than one scholar recently has pointed out that in Lincoln's Second Inaugural Speech, his voice latched on to antithesis as an artful rhetorical tool to try to bridge divisive factions during the Civil War. To try out antithesis, write your subject in the first blank of the following line. Think of two contrasting metaphors or images to describe your subject:

_____ is _____, not _____.
   [subject]   [metaphor 1]   [contrasting
                                         metaphor]

It's as if the subject's pull and push, in and out, work together.

Sometimes, we write with such fury or reverie, disgust or jubilation, that our voice beckons us to repeat phrases and clauses. In such writing, our writing bodies and voice may need the shapes of **anaphora** or **epistrophe**. Ackerman's kissing sentences and Moody's caretaking sentences excerpted earlier in this chapter employed **anaphora**, the repetition of the same word or group of words at the beginnings of successive clauses or sentences. One student wrote the following sentence, not to evoke emotion but to describe a character's obsession: "She writes at dawn; she writes at noon; she writes at dusk." **Epistrophe** is the repetition of the same word or group of words at the *ends* of successive clauses or sentences, as in Franklin D. Roosevelt's example that aroused Americans' feelings of unfairness: "In 1931, ten years ago, Japan invaded Manchukuo— without warning. In 1935, Italy invaded Ethiopia—without warning. In 1938, Hitler occupied Austria—without warning. In 1939, Hitler invaded Czechoslovakia—without warning. Later in 1939, Hitler invaded Poland—without warning. And now Japan has attacked Malaya and Thailand—and the United States—without warning." A student wrote the following sentence in a creative essay about the virtues of living in uncertainty and dealing with ambiguity: "Gravediggers work in the dark; politicians speak in the dark; poets live in the dark." Learning this structure is easy. Take your subject, feel a phrase that will resonate each time it's repeated like a song's refrain, and follow a form similar to this one: X verb 1 phrase 1; subject 2 verb 2 phrase 1; subject 3 verb 3 phrase 1.

But to write from our syntactical core, so to speak, requires more than learning twisty, tricky patterns just as practicing yoga requires more than learning twisty, tricky poses or chants. To start exploring how our bodies' authentic rhythms may influence our writing's rhythms, we work with breath because breath is easier to notice and manipulate than, say, thought patterns or biofeedback loops. We breathe about 23,040 times a day. The palpable fact of breath's rhythms reminds us of our body's rhythms. An inhalation brings oxygen to our cells; our cells release carbon dioxide to our blood capillaries; our blood capillaries send carbon dioxide to our heart; our filtering heart, drumming our destiny's beat, gives oxygen back to the blood; our veins channel oxygen throughout our bodies' cellular makeup. Our whole body breathes; our whole body beats. Its tempo, subtle and individual. My mother's body steps to the beat of a different drummer than mine, than yours, than your daughter's, than Thoreau's.

You played with your breath when a boy or girl. You'd hold your breath underwater or challenge your friends to breath-holding contests. You'd hold your breath so long you made yourself dizzy, and the world's form for a moment jiggled like Jell-O—your first taste of altering your own state of body-mind-imagination. *Prānāyāma* is the yogic art of becoming aware of, using, and altering breath to vitalize the body, to alter space within the body, and to extend the life force. Once we learn our breath's basic structure, then we can begin to work and play with it, not so much for child's play but for writer's playful work.

Just as a sentence has a structure, so, too, does our breathing have a basic three-unit structure: inhalation, exhalation, retention. Simple, it would seem. But as you read this paragraph, notice from where your inhalation begins. Are you still breathing primarily in your chest? Can you drop your breath's point of origin below your rib cage? Three fingertips below your navel? Place one or both hands below your navel, and on the inhalation let your belly expand and blossom. As you exhale, keep your fingers on your belly and lightly draw in your navel toward your spine. Keep your awareness on this movement for five breaths. Appreciate any differences you feel when breathing from this place versus from your throat or chest.

Retaining your breath on the exhalation (*bahya kumbhaka*) is the next step in harnessing breath. We taste stillness for a moment as our lungs rest and as our inner ears grow quiet. When we suspend our breath for a few seconds, we train our minds to heed our thoughts as well. By suspending our breath, we can almost suspend our thoughts like a diver caught in midair. An advanced yoga practice is to catch a thought in midair and reverse it like a film image of a diver who almost reaches the pool lip before the film projector halts the image and then lifts the diver right back up to the diving board. For those of us whose thoughts constantly plunge into the deep end and who find ourselves almost drowning from exhaustion, this practice can help us harness thoughts into the shaped sentences our authentic body and voice need.

Be cautious, though: It's best to practice *prānāyāma* on an empty stomach so the body and mind's focus is not divided. Begin *prānāyāma* cautiously, noting your limits as you proceed. Refrain from retaining your breath until you've worked for a few weeks with elongating your inhalation and exhalation. Also, refrain from re-taining your breath after the inhalation (*antarā kumbhaka*) until you're comfortable with doing so after the inhalation; otherwise, you may disrupt your nervous system. If you have high blood pres-sure or heart ailments, forgo retaining your breath at all. You can *re-train* your breath without retaining it.

Now, let's have some fun with breath and writing. As you read the following lines from Maxine Kumin's "Morning Swim," try to read as you heed the rhythms of your breath. That is, inhale as you read the first line, exhale as you read the second, and so forth:

> *and in the rhythm of the swim*
> *I hummed a two-four-time slow hymn.*

> *I hummed "Abide with Me." The beat*
> *rose in the fine thrash of my feet.*

> *rose in the bubbles I put out*
> *slantwise, trailing through my mouth.*[6]

The line's steady length and rhythm reinforce the speaker's bodily rhythms and the song's rhythms. Notice how each line's pace fol-lows your breath's pace and that each inhalation and exhalation's length is approximately a four-count. Most of this poem is written in what is called iambic tetrameter. An iamb is a measured unit of language made up of two syllables—an unstressed syllable followed by a stressed syllable. A line of poetry composed of four iambs is tagged iambic tetrameter. *Tetra* is Latin for "four," and *meter* simply means "measure," so *iambic tetrameter* translates to "A line of poetry measured with four iambs." Before you break out into a cold fever as you fret over marking a poem's rhythms, simply notice and hear the iambs in the poem's first line (with the stressed syllables italicized): and *in*/the *rhy-*/thm *of*/the *swim*. That English-writing poets for cen-turies have written verse so often in these four-beat and five-beat (*penta*meter) lines should be no surprise: They wrote with what came natural to their breath and with what brought the most em-bodied pleasure to their audiences.

Most prose writers also know the value of writing with measured rhythm. "The mass of men lead lives of quiet desperation," Thoreau wrote, wittingly or not, in a mostly iambic beat. And whereas the following sentence from Annie Dillard's *Pilgrim at Tinker Creek* follows a more complex measure (mostly iambs and what are called anapests), it does have a steady beat: "The sign on my body could have been an emblem or a stain, the keys to the kingdom or the mark of Cain."[7] The prose sentence's rhyme of *stain* and *Cain* is a bonus for the inner ear, the rhyme words' meanings reinforcing one another as much as their sounds.

Once we sense how a basic sentence's fundamental rhythms work, we can play with our sentences' breath (so to speak) by repetition and length. When we deliberately alter such patterns, we move to the third step of working with *samskāra*, those subtle impressions. This step involves consciously *altering* thought patterns. As with our breath, so, too, our syntax. It can expand or contract depending upon how we work and play with its rhythms. Each sentence breathes. Some stutter. Raspy heaves. Hacks. Other sentences blow on, their momentum carried by a phrase's or a clause's wind, sometimes their subject, hidden behind a flock of geese or an amateur glider, separated from its action.

Once writers set up patterns—as we've explored—they break them. Vary them. Twist them. Writers do riffs on the basic Subject-Verb-Object structure like a guitarist who can play variations of C for five minutes or longer. Sometimes the order of the subject, verb, and object writers invert—as in this sentence (O-S-V). Sometimes a subject, modified by a flighty image or breezy phrase, gets separated from the verb—as in this one. A writer or narrator's worldview, aesthetic tastes, and philosophical disposition can each influence sentence lengths and structures. The first paragraph of Hemingway's short story "In Another Country," for instance, contains all compound sentences. The narrator is wounded, physically and emotionally. He makes observations that are equally conjoined, and no thought ventures a complex cause-effect relationship. The past was then, and now is the present. Things just seem to happen, and the narrator just seems to blow in the wind. Faulkner, on the other hand, with the weight of the past and the weight of place always bearing on his protagonists' shoulders, exhales sentences that go on for two pages or more. In some writing, shorter sentences constrict. We feel tense. Or we feel relief. A character's fragmented thoughts might follow short patterns, whereas the thoughts of an effusive narrator, excited or outraged and openly expressive like a wild mare loping across a page's prairie, can only be reflected accurately in longer, rambling sentences.

With practice, we get the hang of some basic patterns, and then we alter them. As we learn to respond to how our body, breath, and imagination need a thought and image to unfold, writing memorable sentences that swim into our reader's unconscious, while still a miracle, may no longer be such a mystery.

$\mathcal{T}$AKE A BREATH 1: FINDING A STEADY RHYTHM

INTENTION:
Try this practice if you have difficulty hearing your prose's pace and your sentences' cadences. Try it also when you're writing about something whose steady rhythm you wish to capture in steady syntax. A character walking to the store, a conversation, a sunrise, people in a subway station, a character's morning routine.

This practice, which asks you to practice EQUAL MOVEMENT BREATHING PRACTICE *(sama vrtti prāṇāyāma), helps you harmonize your inhalation and exhalation. Using this practice to start tuning into the length of your sentences' units—the phrases and clauses—can create a steady rhythm. Once you can hear the steadiness, you can artfully vary and break up the patterns.*

Come into a comfortable seated position, spine extended. (See Appendix for options.) Breathe completely at least twice, noting where in your body your inhalation originates. When you feel your thoughts quiet down, ask yourself, "What am I writing for?" Let your whole body take in that question and the ensuing reply, whether in image or word(s). Then clarify that you intend to write intuitively according to the rhythms of your specific subject and your sentences as they flow with your breath's rhythms.

Once your intentions seem suitably embodied, balance the lengths of your inhalations and exhalations. Beginning the inhalation from your diaphragm, breathe in to a count of four. Then, drawing in the navel, breathe out to a count of four. In four counts, out four counts. Try this practice for five cycles, then seven, then ten. You're beginning to control your breath's basic dual structure, the in and the out.

With your writing subject surfing your breath's wave, take in another full inhalation, and hear a short sentence related to your subject that you can complete within an inhalation, followed by a sentence you can complete within an exhalation. You might begin with the basic Subject-Verb structure. Don't sweat the meter. Just hear the general length. Call the first sentence the in-sentence; call the second the out-sentence:

(In) *The daffodils have bloomed.* (Out) *The peepers smell them.*

Nothing fancy for now. Then, you can add an and, but, or or to link the in-sentence with the out, the inhalation with the exhalation:

(In) *The daffodils have bloomed,* (Out) *and the peepers smell them.*

Again, we're not striving for linguistic acrobatics, yet. We just want some comfort with the syntax of things. Try to write at least ten same-breath sentences. Then, try to expand your breath's length and your sentence's length to a count of five, maybe six, or seven. Here's a student's example of a slow count to six:

(In) *An afternoon in Abigail's alley gave me all I need to know about beauty.*
(Out) *Truth or not, in that shadowed beauty was where I yearned to live.*

Although writers like Emily Dickinson and Robert Creeley seem content with tight breaths, some writers—like Walt Whitman, Faulkner, and Norman Mailer—seem to inhale to a count of ninety (I think Mailer inhales once a page and Faulkner once every two pages).

Once you have a paragraph of same-length sentences and one or more longer ones, you have material to manipulate. Break it up if need be. For instance, divide or shorten the fourth sentence for emphasis. Maybe the fifth one too. Get used to playing with lengths just as you get accustomed to playing with your breath's lengths. Try the next practice to help you become even more adept at breaking the rhythm.

$\mathcal{T}$AKE A BREATH #2:
RETAIN YOUR BREATH AND MIX IT UP

INTENTION:

This practice builds upon the first one and helps you alter your customary syntactical patterns. Use the draft you started in the previous practice, or take another draft whose syntax flops like a swimming dog paddling for air.

The first breath practice (bahya kumbhuka sama vrtti), *reducing central nervous activity, is useful for writers who experience anxiety attacks, cannot shut off the writer's chatter, or cannot fall asleep. For the dormant minded or sluggish among us, the second breath practice* (antarā kumbhaka sama vrtti) *incidentally increases synaptic activity and arouses the sympathetic nervous system. A useful alternative to caffeine, it also helps writers whose blues or depression make them stuporous.*

FRIENDLY WARNING:
Be cautious with breath retention. If you have untreated high blood pressure or heart disease, then forgo these practices until you've consulted a physician. Also, only practice retaining your breath on the inhalation after you feel sufficiently comfortable with retaining your breath on the exhalation.

With the above cautions observed, come into a comfortable seated position, take two full breaths, and remind yourself, "What am I writing for?" After you feel the reply sufficiently in your body, clarify that you intend to hear how the rhythms of your writing subject need to be varied. When ready, breathe in to a count of four, breathe out to a count of four, and retain your breath to a count of four: In-4, Out-4, Hold-4 (five to ten times). Take pleasure in this breath.

Repeat the above pattern, except this time breathe in to four, hold for four more after the exhalation, and breathe out to four: In-4, Hold-4, Out-4. Be cautious if you attempt it. Notice the palpable sensations in your skull, your neck, elsewhere in your body.

Now, the variations. Not unlike riffs on a 4/4 melody, inhale to a count of six or eight and extend your out-breath to a count of four: In-6, Out-4. Or try extending how long you hold your breath to the following count: In-4, Hold-6, Out-4. The idea is to become versatile in your breath control and awareness so you can note what alterations best serve your mind and imagination.

Then, once you feel fairly adept at playing with your breath's structure, take a section of an existing draft and try to breathe to your sentences' lengths—just as you did with Kumin's poem. Doing so will help you hear whether or not your sentences together drip like water from a leaky faucet or whether they flow like water down a mountain stream. You may want the leaky faucet effect. It depends on what you want your sentences to do. Take this student example of three sentences: "The clients, the meetings, the conference calls, the e-mails—everything about her job seemed to add weight to an imaginary board on her chest. She needed a break. A wake." These three sentences' pace follows roughly a 10-3-1 count to reflect the character's near breathless exhaustion. Begin to hear how your own sentences flow. For a section full of monotonous sentence lengths, mix it up. Follow three long sentences with a pithy one. Or begin with pith. Then follow brevity with sentences whose phrases and clauses, their grammatical compliance notwithstanding, rollick and ramble down hills of your own devising. Play. Note which rhythm feels right in your body, for your subject, and for emphasis. When you've rewritten the passage, let a friend read it and breathe to see if she has the response you intended.

Once you feel comfortable mixing it up with an existing draft, you may grow more at ease mixing it up while you write. See if as you write you can deliberately stretch your sentences' lengths, intuitively adding and elaborating where you sense such tricks fit. Really roll with the way words unfold one by one or three by three or four by four like planks of wood cut just right for certain purposes and effects. Then cut it short. Enjoy building. Relish the feel of a hammer or an ax fitted in your palm. Love the craft.

Faulkner said he drafted As I Lay Dying in six weeks. During that time, he spent most of his days doing manual labor—sawing and hammering, lifting and loading—for eight, ten hours. Then, he'd come home and write into the night. No wonder that book flows like the Yoknapatawpha River (not to mention that it begins with the character Cash hammering): Faulkner enjoyed building, loved the syntax of things, plank by plank, nail by nail. From the foundation up, he felt it in his bones and breath and blood, and his readers, if they listen, have been, with each rereading, wholly, wholly kissed time and time again.

CHAPTER TWELVE

Straight from the Mouth: Artful Dialogue as Revelation

Reporter and radio essayist Jack Hitt interviewed inmates and explored the stories behind a professional production of *Hamlet* performed by hardened criminals at a high security prison near St. Louis. When Danny, a forty-four-year-old criminal, had the chance to perform, he chose the part of Hamlet's father—the ghost. He said he had never been so moved as when he read such lines as

> *I am thy father's spirit,*
> *Doomed for a certain term to walk the night*
> *And for the day confined to fast in fires,*
> *Till the foul crimes done in my days of nature*
> *Are burnt and purged away. But that I am forbid*
> *To tell the secrets of my prison house,*
> *I could a tale unfold whose lightest word*
> *Would harrow up thy soul, freeze thy young blood.*
>
> (ACT I, SC. V, 9–16)

Hitt asked Danny, "Who's speaking those words when you're onstage?" Danny paused, then said "I'm the body up there, but the words are coming from mostly, uh, uh, William Pride, the man that I, uh, killed. He, uh, he's mostly the one talking."[1] This prisoner's fragmented words are almost as compelling as Shakespeare's ghost's eloquent speech.

With the radio's advantage, Hitt let this prisoner and others speak "in their own words." How did Hitt get these criminals to unveil their own stories and their own ghosts as they worked on *Hamlet*? He inadvertently gave away his secret to good dialogue early in the piece. He said he had wondered—after having studied *Hamlet* and having seen a dozen professional and famous productions—

what else he could learn about the play. Then he realized that this play about murder and its consequences was going to be performed by criminals who know firsthand about violence and who are living out those consequences. "After hanging out with this group of convicted criminals for six months, I did discover something," Hitt admitted. "I didn't know anything about *Hamlet*."[2] Such humility and a willing suspension of judgment made Hitt a nonhostile source for these prisoners to speak to openly.

Like Hitt, many writers of artful dialogue have a certain disposition toward speech's broad potential to reveal wisdom. They recognize that *any* speech can be illuminating. Shakespeare's clowns, fools, and gravediggers sometimes speak, after all, with more wisdom than a king and his attendants. Similarly, yogis in several nondualistic schools of yoga, such as Vajrayana Tantra, recognize that any act of speech from any source can be a spiritual tool. I'm not interested, for instance, in branding "vulgarity" as somehow less truthful than a sermon, or in tagging a guru's words as "higher" revelations than those of the woman who operates the Library Laundromat down the road. This yogic openness to wisdom's myriad voices, coupled with a good ear and a keen understanding of why we humans talk in the first place, can help us craft artful dialogue in fiction, nonfiction, and drama.

Why do we talk? We ask questions. We share stories. We share facts. We warn. We want. We compete. We control. We defend. We talk to one another for any number of reasons, but most of these reasons can be pared down to one: to learn. In talking, you learn about your uncle's views of the President, what's happening in Liberia or in your ex-lover's heart. In all of this talk, intentionally or not, you learn about yourself—how your childhood experiences compare to your new friend's, how your opinions on hybrid cars compare to the deli owner's, how your handling of anger compares to your sister's.

When characters talk, we also listen to learn. Dialogue informs us about the speaker, the plot, the subject, other characters. Without being didactic, their dialogue teaches us, too, how people talk about themselves, others, and their notions of reality and truth. When we see on the page those floating eyelashes " " framed around someone's words, our inner ear perks as we sense an immediate and accurate source speaks. Even in fiction, dialogue somehow sucks us into thinking we're hearing it directly from the character's mouth, the illusion of speech unmediated by a biased narrator. Those curly punctuation marks grant a story credibility, which is why journalists scramble for the right quotation. If we can keep in mind these basic reasons why we talk and why we read dialogue, we can be more adept and artful with our characters' conversations in fiction and nonfiction.

Dialogue reveals. Dialogue can reveal plot information and geographical locale. It also tells us a character's thoughts, tone, age, the discrepancy between a character's thoughts and speech, conflict between characters, and a character's values. Understanding dialogue's basic function to reveal, we can intuit how *not* to write dialogue: Refrain from babbling. To prattle is to speak indiscriminately and without intention. Some schools of yoga contend that in a yogi's path, prattling (*prajalpa*) impedes a yogi's progress because it wastes a yogi's time and dissipates mental energy. It's not a bad principle for writing dialogue so you don't waste your readers' time. Consider the following example:

"Hey! How's it going?" Michelle said to Wendy.

"Hi!" Wendy said. "Fine, although I've been running a lot of errands, and I'm exhausted. How are you?"

"Good, I guess. A bit bushed and busy myself."

The dialogue reveals almost nothing and neither advances the story nor teases us enough to keep us guessing. Contrast that exchange with the following dialogue from the opening of Charles Baxter's clever fablelike story "The Cliff":

"I used to smoke Camels unfiltered," [the old man] told the boy. . . . "But I switched brands. Camels interfered with my eating. I couldn't taste what the Duchess cooked up. Meat, salad, Jell-O: it all tasted the same. So I went to low tar. You don't smoke, do you, boy?"

The boy stared at the road and shook his head.

"Not after what I've taught you, I hope not. You got to keep the body pure for the stuff we're doing."

"You don't keep it pure," the boy said.

"I don't have to. It's *been* pure. And, like I say, nobody is ever pure twice."[3]

In that short exchange, his voice conjures an image of a gruff man full of contradictions. The dialogue also veils enough to goad our questions. Who is this old man in relation to the boy? A teacher of some sort, we can infer. We also can guess that the boy is not enamored of his teacher, since he doesn't make eye contact with him and he challenges the old man on principle. The slight revelation contained in his reference to "the stuff we're doing" also teases us. What stuff? What's this talk of purity? Plot, conflict between the two characters, and theme are mixing it up in the dialogue.

Your character's speech often betrays more about himself than he intends. In John Cheever's short story "Reunion," a boy sees his father for the first—and, we find out, the last—time since his parents divorced. His father, a busy businessman, wants to take his son to a fancy restaurant in New York City to make a good impression. The father does just the opposite, primarily through his speech. Throughout the story, the boy is quoted maybe twice, whereas the father is quoted constantly—a revealing detail itself. As the father gets irate and impatient with one waiter after another, the story's simple structure follows the two characters from restaurant to restaurant. Here's a typical exchange at a restaurant where, the boy tells us, the waiters wear "pink jackets like hunting coats, and there was a lot of horse tack on the walls":

> "Master of the hounds! Tallyhoo and all that sort of thing. We'd like a little something in the way of a stirrup cup. Namely, two Bibson Geefeaters."
>
> "Two Bibson Geefeaters?" the waiter asked, smiling.
>
> "You know damned well what I want," my father said angrily. "I want two Beefeater Gibsons, and make it snappy. Things have changed in jolly old England. So my friend the duke tells me. Let's see what England can produce in the way of a cocktail."
>
> "This isn't England," the waiter said.
>
> "Don't argue with me," my father said. "Just do as you're told."[4]

These one-sided dialogues drive the story's tension and escalate with each new restaurant. Although we hear the father's condescension, impatience, and bullying, Cheever's masterful touch is not to let the boy, the story's narrator, comment on his father's behavior. The boy, like the reader, is an observer—privately embar-rassed, mortified, if not repulsed—as the father, allowed to talk all he wants, implicates himself.

When you select and place seemingly simple "small talk" ex-changes in a story, speech can become charged with undertones of emotion and meaning. Simon Ortiz once told me that the basis for a story is the basis for how he begins a conversation with someone he meets at a bar: "Where are you coming from?" and "Where are you going?" Those two questions are loaded, given certain contexts. Imagine: A man and woman stand in a kitchen. The woman, exas-perated, grabs the car keys. "Where are you going?" he asks. "Home!" she yells, and slams the kitchen door. A middle-aged woman driv-ing down the highway stops to pick up a hitchhiker, a young man, haggard but handsome. He leans in the window and asks with an Italian accent, "Where are you going?" "Home," she smiles, and opens the car door. A middle-aged woman crawls out of a motel bed, where a young man still sleeps. After she dresses, she takes her purse, leaves money on the nightstand, and, once she's opened the door, turns toward the bed. She extends a lonely grin and faint wave. The young man, groggy eyed, asks with an Italian accent, "Where are you going?" "Home," she says, and shuts the motel door.

With this understanding of how dialogue can function in sto-ries, how do you begin as a writer? Talk to people—or, better, get them to talk while you listen. To honor the myriad voices in this world worthy of being rendered in artful dialogue, consider this fun-damental yoga practice from Patanjali's *Yoga-Sutra*: "When a person is rooted in nonviolent speech, thought, and action, others relin-quish their hostility and defensiveness" (II.35). *Ahimsā*, nonvio-lence, is a fundamental tenet of yoga that encompasses everything from diet to thought to speech to action. I don't intend to simplify this practice; rather, I'm suggesting that as writers we can begin our practice of nonviolence as we talk to other people—a practice that can allow you, like Jack Hitt, to be tuned to all of us prisoners' sto-ries. If you meet someone on the bus, at a convention, or at a deli, practice being completely open, nonjudgmental, and nonaggres-sive. Catch your prejudgments, and suspend them. If you're genu-inely interested in hearing a person's story, begin with "Where are you coming from?" or "Where are you going?" A person will sense whether or not you're genuine, whether you're listening, or whether you're judging. As the person speaks, listen for the colorful phrases, the verbal tics, the broken syntax, or the overly stilted diction that reveals something about the person's character and spirit. If you're judging the person for his views, his grammar, or his accent, you'll likely never garner the person's trust.

Which leads me to the next point: Get out and talk. There's great value in silence and in restraining ourselves from babbling, but I don't advocate a purely ascetic approach to yoga or to writing. If you stay hobbled in your writing hole as if it were a Himalayan cave and hear how people talk only through television and books, then you may never capture the wonderful and real ways speech unfolds. Consider a passage from Nathaniel Hawthorne's *The Scarlet Letter*. As Hester Prynne walks through the Puritan village with her scarlet-dressed daughter Pearl, a Puritan child spies the pair, and says to the brood of other children: "Behold, verily, there is the woman of the scarlet letter; and, of a truth, moreover, there is the likeness of the scarlet letter running along by her side! Come, therefore, and let us fling mud at them!"[5] Oh, my. Verily, indeed. For all of his elegant phrasing and insight into the human heart that makes this novel a richly textured tale, Hawthorne needed to get out more often and talk among the villagers.

According to an ancient text, the *Ganapati Atharva Shirsha Upanishad*, the voice of daily talk, the chitter-chatter, is called *vaikhari*. The text warns against speaking only from *vaikhari*, the coarsest and most audible of four levels of sound, without other forms of truthful sound frequently mediating. Given to *vaikhari*'s own prattle, our speech gets distorted. Hear what's going down only from television, radio, popular music, escape literature, your friends, and you may write with a pastiche of catchphrases, clichés, colloquialisms, and the news's half-truths.

Still, with discipline, we'd be wise to listen to the world's chatter and to popular culture's babel. Writers often catch phrases and rhythms from the *Zeitgeist Vaikhari* and spin them from the air to the page in such a way that we can hear more clearly how daily talk betrays people's concerns and feelings. Like conceptual artist Barbara Kruger, writers listen to the muses of Madison Avenue as they sample commercialese and billboard-speak, radio talk and everyday chatter. Tom Wolfe has made a career of eavesdropping, cataloging, and imitating dialogues in subways, honkey tonks, art galleries, and penthouse parties. He can imitate the voices and syntax of a museum curator as accurately as a stock car race driver. With equal facility, young Scottish novelist Duncan McLean can capture the rhythms of a butcher's voice in Edinburgh or the waves of a waitress's voice in Buda, Texas. He told a group of students a few years ago, "You have to get inside your own head, but you also have to get out of your head and listen to all the voices around you—down your streets, in clubs and restaurants, at gas stations. Just listen."

You never know where a rich piece of dialogue will be given to you. While driving through Arkansas a couple of years ago, I stopped for dinner at a cheap chain cantina next to a Days Inn. The fluorescent lights brightened the *queso*-colored walls and the plastic daisies bunched in a plastic vase on each table. In a booth across the white-tiled aisle, a girl-woman around twenty or twenty-one and two boy-men, all three white and restless and trying to impress each other, chatted about reading and religion.

"I don't think Jesus was black," the girl announced. "I think he was extremely tanned." The boy-men looked dazed, their chips deposited like coins in a parking meter, their eyes glancing about the restaurant for different company, maybe wondering if she was really religious or just used it as a distraction from what the boys were really interested in.

"J'you see the game last night?" one guy said to the other.

"Nope. Wanted to, but had to work."

Despite their half-interest, or perhaps because of it, the girl's voice pushed its way to be heard, often forced to repeat itself as if the repetition would at last get through. She must have looked over at me, as she seemed to have changed subjects. "I never go to a restaurant alone. I never eat alone. Even at the Wal-Mart—even at the Wal-Mart—even at the Wal-Mart I don't eat alone. If I have to, I have something to read like *The Good News*. It helps me understand the Bible because people don't talk the same as they did when they wrote the King James Version. J'you ever read it?" She seemed pleased she'd got the subject back to the Lord, so she could perhaps get through to these guys a message or two about the Word.

"Nope. Wanted to, but never got around to it," one of them said. The other one shook his head.

"With *The Good News* I can understand the Bible, all the stories I remember, even with all the *thees* and *thous* and stuff. It's in my car. It's in my car right now."

"J'you see *American Pie?* Oh, God, that was funny," one guy asked the other.

"Nope. Wanted to."

"It's in my car. Listen. *The Good News's* in the backseat of my car. Listen to me." Her moment of witnessing seemed to be slipping as the two boy-men washed the chips down with Coke and kept shifting the subject to watching football and to sex scenes in a movie they'd seen.

Her voice and this scene became the basis of a short story titled "Good News" about a girl and two guys traveling across the South. She's seeking love and Jesus; they're seeking sex. Just listening without judgment let me capture the urgency in her manic repetition and in her pleas to be heard, to be listened to. The guys' voices, laconic and lackluster, seemed the comic foil. "Listen to me" becomes the story's refrain of desperation.

So, eavesdrop. You may think this practice unethical, but if you want to hear how people speak without self-consciousness, then listen to a dialogue in a public place—a grocery store, a restaurant, a gas station, a town board meeting (my favorite place to record speech patterns). Note the speech's cadence and texture, half-starts and repetitions. If you make this practice a habit, you may hear how people in ordinary circumstances struggle to communicate ideas and feelings. When you write dialogue for a story or nonfiction piece, try to create dialogue whose rhythms and content may reveal more about the person than the person realizes.

In workshops and classes, I often break up writers into groups of three. I'll give two of the people a topic to discuss while the third person listens in the background and takes notes. The recorder then shares with them bits of noted dialogue and speech traits—accents, dialects, fillers ("Uh" "hmm"), broken syntax, repeated words or phrases. The objective is to honor each person's unique speaking voice without judgment.

You also can listen to the electronic *vaikhari*. Try it. For at least a day, record the catchphrases, clichés, and telling homilies you hear from electronic sources—radio, television, and automated answering services. By day's or week's end, you may recognize patterns of our culture's flotsam that may give you fodder for creating a fiction or nonfiction scene. Weaving in and twisting these speech bits also can give a poem texture as it comments on the nature of our daily language. One student wrote a short story in which one of the characters spoke almost entirely in commercial jingles and sound bites.

Try combining dialogues with voices of popular culture for irony. Irony is a way of looking at life and saying, "There's much more to truth than we say, think we know, or expect." The main action that readers are noting is the foreground. Something else, though, can happen in the background that subtly "comments" on, highlights, reflects, or counters the foreground activity. In *The Great Gatsby* Fitzgerald weaves in numerous song lyrics and references to popular culture that comment on the characters' situations. In the novel's most heated scene, which happens in New York's Plaza Hotel, the cuckolded husband Tom strips Gatsby of all his glamour in front of his wife Daisy's eyes. From the hotel's lobby, "Mendelssohn's Wedding March" is playing from a wedding party.

In Elizabeth Tallent's short story "No One's a Mystery," popular culture's background meets dead-on with the story's foreground, even providing its title. The short short story revolves around a girl who's just turned eighteen and Jack, a middle-aged man with whom she's having an affair and who has just given her a diary for her birthday. The whole story, mostly dialogue, happens over an hour or so as they drive in his pickup. As the man's wife drives by, the girl ducks and looks at the pickup floor. As she's studying his beat-up boots and the floor crowded with pop tops, Rosanne Cash sings on the tape deck, "Nobody's into me, no one's a mystery." The song doesn't get much direct attention in the dialogue, yet it perfectly reflects the story's theme and the predictable outcome, given the almost clichéd nature of their relationship. So, as you create a scene for fiction or nonfiction, notice how the voices of popular culture in a scene's background can play upon your characters' dialogue and situation.

The next time you talk with somebody, try to listen with every part of your body, not just with your intellect. Let your breath be slow and full as you take in whatever that person has to say, however she needs to say it. Try not to compete, to prove wrong, to dominate, or to redirect. Savor the person's unique pitch and rhythm. Listen for what's being revealed and for what's being veiled.

CHAPTER THIRTEEN

The Art of Wandering
in First Drafts

When writers ask me for tips about first drafts, I tell them to get lost. In their drafting, that is. We have a stigma about getting lost. Some people view it as a sign of weakness. Parents dread the thought of their children getting lost. Some of our religions and fables teach us the hazards of straying from the path. One definition of *wander* is, after all, "to deviate in conduct or belief; to err; go astray." Rooted in *wind*, to "wander" sounds like being "wanton," to have no discipline. Yet, there is a discipline and an art to being able to wander well as writers.

If we fear getting lost, we might draft like an overscheduled tourist. I used to meet once a week with a writer to help him with his first novel. Although the storyline was potentially complex with intricate subplots and ideas about time bending, the characters felt flat and the scenes sketchy. Reading the draft unnerved me, as if I were taking an hour-long tour that shuttled me through Manhattan's highlights. So I asked him what he enjoyed about the process of writing itself. He squirmed and said he liked the ideas, getting the ideas out, but he didn't like wasting time with a lot of description, character development, or subtle suspense. He just wanted to get "through" the story, he said. When we draft like taskmasters, we're prone to stay "on track" and "on schedule." We know where we want to get to—the story's ending or punch line, the points we want to make—and we use language to "get there" as efficiently as possible. Staying safely on subject while drafting can be helpful for report makers and journalists but hazardous for novelists, poets, or creative nonfiction writers. We often remember surprises, novelty, revelation, and we encounter such things more often not when staying on schedule but when taking time to stray. No wonder that a former student once told me that she and her family had traveled around the world—always by packaged tours—yet, she confessed that when someone asks her what she recalls about Italy, Ireland, or Iran, she says, "I don't know. Not much. It all went by so quickly." You don't want your writing to fly by your readers.

As a writer, you want to be able to trust your faculties, to discover your innate traveling tools, to be so versatile in your writing that you learn how to navigate tricky terrain and find your way out of dense thickets. You want, in short, the ability to draft with confidence.

Poet and translator Andrew Schelling of Naropa University once told me what he viewed as the core distinctions between touring and journeying. When we tour, he said, we accumulate and take from a culture and return with more stuff—plastic knickknacks, ashtrays painted with "Tahiti is Smokin'," and jewelry we'll never wear once back in the States. When we journey, we open ourselves up to the place and to the moment and perhaps return transformed or at least slightly different. We have a fresh perspective and stronger wits instead of more trinkets and photographs.

So it can be with how we draft. Slow down. Get lost. Drafting is a time for journeying, for uncovering your story's unexpected plot twists, for delving more deeply into an image that keeps bugging your imagination, for discovering a character's disturbing blemish. When you get lost in your drafting, you often realize your real subject, something you wouldn't have found had you stuck with your original writing "plan."

Starting a fresh draft is one of the most exhilarating—and excruciating—parts of writing. When I sit down to write a first draft, I usually have no clue where I'll end up or even what my main point is. I follow some dim hum of an idea or an image that, I trust, gradually will reveal to me what I have to say or what story needs to be told. I come to so many dead ends that for every twenty pages I write, I usually keep maybe five pages in a final draft. And it's often when most stuck in the middle of a draft's thick forest that I know the writing is taking me somewhere I most need to go. When writing an essay on the role of myth in a yoga practice, I finally got to the place of feeling lost; it was then that I knew I had taken myself to the essay's core, complex ideas. This uncertainty drives some writers crazy. But you have to trust that feeling uncertain may mean you're on the right path (otherwise, you may be writing what you already know and, thus, what your readers already know, too). I don't have many moments when angels tap their feet to keep the beat of my sentences, but I do enjoy creating new paths, one word at a time. When drafting, I don't care how I look because I'm the only one watching: I overwrite, digress, strike the wrong chord with a word choice. I know later I must return and clean up, but without this unbridled process I wouldn't be able to start anywhere. I'd be stuck with frozen fingers, worrying what and how I should write.

I know. You don't have time to get lost, you might say. You feel lost enough as it is with the rest of your life, like it or not, and when you sit down to write, you don't want to dawdle or daydream. Dawdling isn't what I'm getting at, but slowing down is. We can "slow draft." Most of us have enough speed in our way of life; drafting can be a subversive act of sorts that resists our speed-driven culture. "Slow drafting" calms the analytical, taskmaster mind and awakens the fertile, intuitive reservoir of images stored in our embodied imagination. When we write without concern for speed and efficiency, we also may sharpen our wits and hone our navigating skills for the next time we write. Not that writing becomes any easier with each trip. But perhaps the more we challenge ourselves as we draft, the more versatile we will become and more able to move toward more difficult writing. We become trackers, sojourners, peregrinators. Not tourists. My safety measures are setting an intention and practicing yoga before I write. Doing so lets me wander safely within the bounds of time, deadlines, and energy. This process works for me. Remember, try things out for yourself. Experiment. A first draft is a place to explore ideas, images, and premonitions. You draft to discover. Later, you can go back to revision, revise, rewrite.

So once you've set a writing intention, you can begin a first draft not knowing where you're going. Forget everything you think you know about your subject, story, or image. If you can begin without preconceptions about your subject, you often leave yourself open to trusting your wits along the way. There are three basic suggestions I offer to writers when learning the art of drafting: 1) Begin with the concrete. 2) Heed your breath. 3) Be open to surprise and be willing to get lost.

If writing a first sentence daunts you, start with something concrete. Take an image. Maybe it's one that haunts you, a woman pacing a room. Describe the red chiffon dress with an orange leather belt she wore or the fresh scratch on the side of her cheek. See where describing that image's surfaces in detail takes you. Another similar way to begin is by describing a character's quirky action. For example, a story draft might start with "Alison reads dictionaries backwards. She tries to read a letter's worth of words a week. This afternoon, she's on 'u.' Umbilical." If as a writer you're intrigued enough, you'll ask yourself about your own character, "Why does she read dictionaries backwards? Why this discipline? Why is she reading the definition of umbilical when this story starts?" The same process works when writing nonfiction. If I'm writing about my mother, I might begin a personal essay with, "When I was ten, my mother tried out belly dancing." Now, I have no idea why at that time, in 1975, she came home with finger cymbals, a fringed purple and gold outfit, and a record with music reminiscent of Sinbad the Sailor, but I'm sure if I trusted my wits enough to recall such remote memories that some answers would avail themselves. If not, then this memory likely would lead to other related memories, and soon after writing to discover for two or three hours, I would be deep into some fresh territory. If you start someplace that beguiles your imagination, then you'll have a desire to draft to discover. Writing this way can produce a draft that might pique readers' curiosity as well.

Starting with details and images can also anchor your imagination (and your potential readers' imaginations) in this physical world, and because writing description stimulates the brain's more intuitive visual cortex and parietal lobe, your drafting often bypasses the more abstract and analytical voice that wants to figure things out and explain them away for writer and reader.

Another way to start your story, essay, or poem concretely is in the middle of a conversation. Dialogue creates immediacy in the writer's imagination and can, therefore, help you hear the piece's voices. Follow where remembering or creating the conversation leads you. "What's the story with your obsession with red pansies?" Benny asked his sister-in-law. Indeed, you the writer say to yourself.

What is her obsession with pansies? Who is Benny? You won't know until you draft some more. Sometimes writers start with a tango of topics. A novelist might start with an itch to explore the relationship between botany and desire. An essayist may wonder how myths of goats relate to notions of masculinity. A poet might set out to see in a series of couplets how the idea of origins and eggs relate. Characters, situations, anecdotes, and images—all the concrete aspects of writing imaginatively—become intuitive ways to explore these ideas.

As you draft, check in with your breath. Most of us hold our breath when we write. Holding the breath deliberately is an advanced yoga practice, but doing so unconsciously can create tension in our bodies and arouse the sympathetic nervous system, which may induce unconscious anxiety. Writing while periodically noting your breath, on the other hand, helps you write with a bit more ease (although it won't make writing easy). Your slow exhalations dissipate the chatter while you write, and breath awareness reminds you, too, that your source of drafting encompasses other parts of your body besides your head.

You release physical tension so you can be open to imaginative tension. So, if you feel compelled, let yourself detour. As in "untour." For instance, listen to a word's sound and let it rebound throughout your inner ear until by association another word suggests another path of words to take. Let's say you're writing about a time when you picked apples. The word *apple* in the first line of poetry or the first scene of a story might tickle the word *garden* or *Eden* or *Snow White*. Recurring images and sounds not only thread a series of lines or scenes together. An impression of a word—its connotation, its music—may prompt a memory, an analogy to a film or anecdote, another word, image, or metaphor. When we let our inner ear and eye follow these feathery associations, we let each word and sentence guide the next word and sentence. The piece's inner logic of interrelated words guides you as much as the outer logic of ideas and plot. I'm not suggesting a random, disjointed stream-of-consciousness. Instead, you follow a thread and follow your breath and at some point, any point, an image or word may beckon you to digress. Keith Abbott describes his writing process as a jazz improvisation: In the moment of writing itself, you let the music play you. Either way, you'll have perhaps a new, even richer story to tell. Read Arundhati Roy's *The God of Small Things* or a novel by Milan Kundera, Salman Rushdie, or Tom Robbins to sense how prose's current can charge fiction.

But cut yourself a little slack, because not all sounds are musical and not all ideas are worth keeping and sharing, just as not all food is piquant. Permit yourself to write crap. Pull out the leftovers, old worn-out drafts from ten years ago, if reworking them gives your imagination something palpable to sink its teeth into. Even if what you start to write sounds as if you've been writing the same thing for years, write it. Some writers have only one idea their whole life, on which each novel or set of poems they publish simply plays a variation. If you insist on drafting only when you feel each word must be recherché to avoid your words tasting like a rechauffé, then you might actually starve your muse. You'll have time later to clean up the mess—the excesses, the overwriting, the creative indul-gences, the melodrama—that you made. For now, enjoy the trek. Drafting, like cooking, can be messy.

To let yourself get lost while drafting is to go blind, to let go of seeing and figuring out so much. It's to stop seeking so much light and instead to be content at times with being in the dark where seeds germinate. A friend of mine used to write in the dark to free himself from his common reliance upon sight. Writer Kent Haruf pulls the wool over his eyes—literally a wool cap—when he dives into his first drafts so he won't be worried about hitting the right keys on his keyboard. He explains in the essay "To See Your Story Clearly, Start by Pulling the Wool Over Your Eyes" that he writes sections of stories loosely to quell his analytical mind and "to stay in touch with subliminal, subconscious impulses and to get the story down in some spontaneous way."[1] He's trying to follow his third eye. It can work. I've tried it. My imagination's engine, with this new-found freedom, happily chugs along on and off the track. This prac-tice works best, though, if you can type comfortably (although I've had writers try it hand writing in their notebooks too). You might close your eyes or turn out the lights, clarify an intention that is no more specific than to receive whatever your intuition has to give you and, with your eyes still closed, let go and write in the dark.

Yoga can help us let go of control and follow our imagination and intuition. To most yogis, intuition is "inborn knowledge" (*sahaja-jnāna*) or "inner knowledge" (*antar-jnāna*). It can grant us immediate knowledge about our essential nature. We don't need to mystify the third eye, the center for intuition that resides between our eyebrows. You might simply close your eyes and direct your eyeballs up and toward one another. Your eyeballs' nerves will feel tense, but if you can hold this position for one minute, you may be able to direct and pay attention to the inner images. Become comfortable with this space and acknowledge that you can consciously access what we call the unconscious, the intuitive, and the imaginative. The third eye, for most yogis, is in charge. It is often called the *ājnā-cakra*. The word *ājnā* means "command," hence *ājnā-cakra* translates as "command center" or "command wheel."

The third eye is believed to be activated when the pituitary gland and the pineal gland are stimulated. The pea-sized pituitary gland, located at the base of the brain and connected to the hypothalamus, is made up of two lobes with complementary functions. Because its frontal lobe is thought to regulate intuitive and emotional thoughts while the anterior lobe is thought to help us form concrete thoughts and abstract concepts, it's often called "the seat of the mind." The cone-shaped pineal gland, situated just behind the pituitary, can inhibit thoughts moving into action, thus encouraging our thoughts' inward turn. The pituitary gland, which secretes hormones that in turn moderate several of our other glands and organs' functions, is captain of our endocrine system and co-captain of our subtle body and imagination, that realm of the unconscious accessed by breath, emotion, and intellect.

By regularly stimulating the intuitive center, you can grow more comfortable with uncertainty and ambiguity while you draft.

*T*AKE A BREATH: UNBOX YOUR THIRD EYE

INTENTION:
The following practice can help you access your third eye center as you venture on a new piece of writing. You also can try it when you're stuck in the middle of a piece and need a way to get "off-track."

Open your laptop to a blank screen or your notebook to a blank sheet. The whiteness, vast and endless like sky, daunts some people. Rather than willing your way through the clouds, step back and unbox your third eye.

Come into a comfortable seated position with your sitting bones evenly planted on a blanket, floor, or chair's edge. As your spine extends in both directions, close your eyes and focus on your breath. Let it originate from your belly-cave about three fingertips below your navel, the inhalation inflating the belly, and the exhalation drawing the belly back. After at least two full breaths, remind yourself, "What am I writing for?" Once you've heard a subtle response, recall the subject of the piece you wish to draft. Maybe it's a story idea. Perhaps you have a title or character. Seems like not much to go on, but it's more than enough if you learn to unbox your third eye. If you have no subject and instead wish to keep the sky completely open, so be it. Your intention is to trust some other faculty besides your will and analytical mind to help you start a piece.

Connect your breath to your third eye. With each of the next five exhalations, contract your perineum—the muscle at your torso's base between your anus and your genitals. The lock you're creating in your perineum naturally directs your exhalation's energy back up your spine to your third eye. Let the inhalation draw energy down from your third eye along your spine to your perineum. The inhalation spreads the third eye's influence throughout your spinal column and through all of its nerve connections that branch out to the rest of your body; the exhalation reverses the energy back to your third eye.

Then, with eyes closed or slightly open, gaze up and between your eyes toward your third eye. You may be able to hold this gaze for a minute or two. If you feel a headache surface, return your eyes to a normal position, close them for a moment, and try again. This practice (shimbhava) can help you slow down some of the brain activity aroused when eyes are in their normal position—even with closed eyelids—to receive sensory input. It also helps you direct your thoughts toward the pituitary and pineal glands and may alter your vision temporarily. For at least five breaths, follow your inhalation from your third eye between your eyebrow to your belly's base, about three fingertips below your navel.

On the exhalation through your nose, hum lightly as you follow your breath from the pit of your gut up your spine to your third eye above and between your eyebrows.

With your writing subject circling within your breath and with eyes closed, draw your eyeballs up toward your third eye. Take a full breath to concentrate on stimulating the right eye and the brain's left hemisphere. Take a second full breath to stimulate the left eye and the brain's right side. On the third inhalation, draw the energy down from both eyes to your perineum, and on the third exhalation imagine that a lid on your third eye opens. Either it's a dominant image, expected or not, large or small, that relates to your subject, or it's a piece of dialogue germane to your story or idea. Heed whatever it is for only a few seconds, a minute at most, once it surfaces.

Then begin drafting. Don't worry where it's taking you. Follow your breath. Trust your wits and words to lay out a gravel path. Later, you can always retrace your steps and, if need be, erase your tracks. For now, the journey's the thing.

III.
FACING
EMOTIONAL CRAGS

CHAPTER FOURTEEN

Dogs, Lovers, and Other Things That Bite: Writing the Truth

"Truth'll nip you in the butt, and you may not be any wiser for the teeth marks in your cheeks." That gem came from Lynne, a widow who used to live next door to me before I moved from Texas. Sixty-something, she'd have me over occasionally to bring in her groceries, to clip her hedges, and to "sit a spell." That particular day we were talking about relationships: her marriage that could be rather sweet and nutty, and my relationship at the time that, if adapted to a play, would've rivaled *Who's Afraid of Virginia Woolf?* for sheer bizarreness. She told me about her son's wife, an ambitious lawyer who color-coded her sweaters, went into rages when a bath towel wasn't folded properly, and insisted upon throwing out any leftover food for fear it might get bacteria in the refrigerator. While my guffaws sent me into fits, I suddenly grimaced and stopped. Lynne must've seen the pang of recognition of my own crazy relationship. It was then that she offered me her Texas brand of wisdom. "Just hope when it bites," she added, "it doesn't have rabies." I never was sure how to interpret truth as a rabid dog. It's moments like that, though, that make me miss the Lone Star State.

Truth in writing can bite, or at least it can provoke a physical response. Emily Dickinson has that line about how true poetry takes her head off (no wonder she wrote, "Tell all the Truth but tell it slant"), and Kafka supposedly said that "we ought to read only the kind of books that wound and stab us." I called a writer friend of mine one recent morning and asked her a light question to chew on over breakfast: "What's the most truthful writing you've ever read?"

She paused, stumbled around the names of Tolstoy and Whitman, and said, "I'm really not sure, but I know it when I feel it. It can punch me in the gut while caressing the back of my neck." So, truth's a rabid dog, a murderer, and a seductive sadist. I know the feeling. While reading certain passages from, say, Salman Rushdie's *Midnight's Children* or Faulkner's *Go Down, Moses*, I've had to put the book down, catch my breath, and utter something profound, like "Holy shit." My temple throbs; my heart pounds. Truth can be sublime, at once beautiful and terrifying.

"So how do we write such neck-breaking, butt-biting truth?" a student once asked. We're all susceptible to being spin doctors of our own emotions, experiences, and images. We can drum up hack-neyed happy endings that would make John Hughes roll his eyes; we can go to the other extreme and rant like Al Sharpton without the rhetorical flair or one-liner wit; or we can dilute our genuine anger or passion into Hallmark homilies as if to put our prose on Prozac. And when we do so, we can hear our words' tinny quality that evokes no visceral response except a wince. Yes, how do we know when we're kidding ourselves, pretending to write the truth? Sometimes, I think anyone's guess is as good as mine, that we're all writing in the dark and hoping against hope that some word will at least light a votive to get us down the next corridor without our bumping a toe and blurting an invective. Yet, my yoga practice has given me a candle's worth of clarity on how to intuit truth as I write and read what I write. Yoga can awaken within us a deeper, more abiding sense of how our words can, in fact and in body, "ring true."

First, we have to agree upon what truth is—or at least what it is not—in writing. Truth in writing has less to do with factual honesty and more to do with emotional and imaginative honesty. Anyone who demands to know of a fiction writer, "Did this really happen?" misses the point about truth in writing. Truth in writing is some-thing more intuitive that has to do with a work's ability to become timeless in its timeliness and universal in its particularity. Stein-beck's *The Grapes of Wrath*, for instance, centers upon the plight of migrant farmers during the Dust Bowl of the 1930s. Steinbeck, the ever-ready journalist, traveled among the farmers, "immersed" himself in his subject, and rendered with precision the details of

Route 66, of families' social dynamics, and of the Southwest's terrain. Yet, he sensed something more significant in the people's plight than just the sum of details and facts, something that reflected the history of dispossessed people from the Hebrews onward. To feed this sense of something grand looming in their story, the agnostic author referenced the Old and New Testaments for guidance to rewrite the novel and to structure such an epic story. His venturous reflections upon humanity's perseverance he weaves throughout the novel, and its structure reflects a shift in the characters' humanity from being selfish and competitive to selfless and cooperative. Following his sense and not sticking with the facts led him to write a novel laden with truth.

There are a few paradoxes in writing with truth. Call them the Tao of Writing. One is if you *think* you're writing the truth, you're probably not. If you sense you're writing something that's driving you along more than you're driving it, then you might be getting there. Similarly, don't focus on the universals as much as on the particulars. If you try too hard to write Universal Truths, your writing may slip into clichéd "themes," and a priest or rabbi may invade your voice as you pontificate upon love and beauty or the world's injustices. I have a "big Truth" voice with a booming tone like Charlton Heston as Moses that, usually, if I recognize it in time, can be halted before I subject my readers to its admonitions.

So to render universals, begin with particulars. It's through the details of dialogue, character, setting, situation, and story that your fiction will unveil—surprisingly to you and to your readers—some inevitable sense of truth. Let's say you're writing a story about a demure, repressed character, Brian, and his spunky fiancée, Pamela. So over the dinner Brian has prepared, Pamela announces that she needs to "have some space to think about the future" and wants to travel for a few days with Mike, a guy she met at work and who has a charming summer home in Colorado where she and Mike can hang out, talk, help her sort through some things, you know. Brian, so utterly miffed, probably won't say much as he takes a bite of his stir-fry tatsoi. He may respond with "Maybe it needs more ginger or cloves. There's definitely something missing." If you have him break into a monologue or tirade about the misery of relationships and the fiasco of marriage as he flings his plate across the dining room, you're being emotionally dramatic but probably not emotionally honest with these particular characters, situation, dialogue, and story. (Although, granted, I know a guy whose mother kept the frying pan that his father flung against the wall in the plaster for two months so her husband could remember the one time he lost his cool.) From an honest attention to details, truth can emerge. Let it surprise you.

"You'll feel it. You'll hear it," I say to my students, knowing this response doesn't appease all of them because they're thirsty, and they want to feel and hear it now, but this response gets us going in the right direction. We can feel truth. Truth in yoga resonates at the cellular level. Many-named in Sanskrit, the most common tag for truth is *satya*, worldly truth, the truth we manifest in our everyday life. In *Yoga-Sutra* II.36, Patanjali notes that when a yogi embodies *satya* "his words become so potent that whatever he says comes to realization."[1] *Satya* can pervade each breath, sound, word, gesture, and decision. "It is not our mind, but the inner voice of our cells which has the power to implement our intentions," yogi B.K.S. Iyengar notes.[2] So when our writing correlates directly with our body's deepest intentions as well as with an intuitive sense that our writing's particulars relate to something honest and universal, when we indisputably feel something "in our bones," we write toward truth.

This is a good time to revisit the act of setting an intention. The question "What am I writing for?" can connect us with a source beyond reason where truth originates. Called "inborn knowledge" (*sahaja-jnāna*), intuition is that unmediated— indisputable—knowledge of truth. It's that quality that lets us feel truth in our gut. So when we ask ourselves, "What am I writing for?" the answer often is vague, a fleeting apparition, a breeze. Still, we aim to absorb the answer in every cell. We tune in our cells and trust that our actions, our writing, will line up accordingly. It'll take a while—years, maybe—to know what your truth is that you need to write. Even if you've been writing and publishing for years, it may take more time. No one wants to hear that. But it's the truth. Be patient.

Begin with the throat. I've been experimenting with how this word tunnel—which links our fiery, willful belly to our mouth—helps me and my students hear the truth. The throat in part is metaphorical for the channel through which words pass. With too much clutter and obstruction, our words become distorted, our intentions detracted. We write muck. The throat center, called the *vishuddi cakra*, houses energy for clear communication, courageous words, sacred speech. *Shuddi* means "to purify," specifically poisons, and if we purify our throat center, we can train our cells to register truth's notes.

The first Hatha-Yogis intuited the throat's power, for the throat's thyroid is an antitoxin. When stimulated, the thyroid gland secretes the hormone thyroxine, which moderates our metabolism. The thyroid helps the parasympathetic nervous system's functioning, which in turn keeps our vital organs operating while also calming down our thoughts. With increased inner quietude, we're more open to hear within. The thyroid also moderates the rate of our cells' death and replenishment as well as muscle tissues' aging. Slow cell turnover and slow tissue decay lead to longevity. A natural elixir exists in our throat. A healthy, open throat, then, helps clear the body's channels and gives us clarity, that open certainty, that unhesitating indisputability that we feel when we hear, feel, and write truth.

The **THROAT LOCK** (*kantha-bandha* or *jālandhara-bandha*) is a good starting place to appreciate the throat's importance for writing with truth. In a seated or standing position (mountain pose), you lengthen your spine and take at least two full breaths. As you inhale, you draw in your chin toward your collarbone notch and above your breastbone, and let the back of your neck lift upward as your shoulder blades drop, giving your cervical spine and throat's back side a good stretch. The lock position stimulates the thyroid and releases thyroxine, the "elixir." On the exhalation, you return your chin to its normal position. Repeat two more times to heighten your awareness of this area.

Some yogic lore contends that we have a *bindu* center at the top and back of our skull, a slight opening through which we receive the universe's answers to our queries about our existence, destiny, and so forth. It's a cosmic antenna. The **THROAT LOCK** is believed to adjust this antenna. If that idea is a bit out there for you, just consider that the throat lock, if practiced consistently, does help your body listen to and respond to something more than your typical daily chitchat.

Another easy way to quicken this center is through **VICTORIOUS BREATH** (*ujjayī-prāṇāyāma*). This breath keeps your glottis and epiglottis healthy and clears the throat's channels. It also soothes your nerves and boosts energy by aerating the lungs and increasing cerebral blood flow. With calmness and alertness, we're in a position to write with truth. The crudest way to practice **VICTORIOUS BREATH** is by contracting the glottis and breathing from the throat instead of from the nostrils. You may hear a hissing "sa" as you inhale and a raspy "ha" as you exhale. To take the practice a step farther, incorporate the **THROAT LOCK** by drawing in the chin as you inhale and exhale. The lock should help you feel breath caressing your throat's back and your mouth's roof, and it should help you hear your breath's "ocean voice" as it imitates the sounds of ocean waves. It also can heighten our ability to hear what's happening internally—essential for getting to the truth in our writing.

The throat center can be an ally when writing difficult sections of fiction or nonfiction. When poet and novelist Terry Wolverton rewrote a section of her memoir *Insurgent Muse: Life and Art at the Woman's Building* (City Lights, 2002), she knew she had to be truthful. The memoir includes not only historical background of the artists and writers with whom she worked while directing the Los Angeles Woman's Building during the 1970s; it also delves into stories about people she has loved and left, people she has hurt and who have hurt her. There was a lot of room for the book to offend, to hurt, to misrepresent. She told me in an interview, "I really wanted to make sure that my articulation was as open and clear as it possibly could be, and I needed to be a very clear channel in order to be honest and fair to the people that I was writing about." For forty mornings Wolverton, also a certified Kundalini Yoga teacher, practiced a Kundalini Yoga cleansing process called *kantha padma kriyā* (or, loosely, "the cleansing of the throat lotus")—a series of *āsanas*, visualizations, chants, and breathing that cleared her throat center. The process helped her check in with and act upon her intention, which was to tell the truth as accurately as she could present it. The energy and clarity she felt in her throat transferred to writing her memoir's especially difficult sections. When she found herself pausing for fear of hurting someone's feelings, she clarified her intention, heard what needed to be said, and got out of the way of the words that needed to emerge.

As mentioned earlier, truth in writing registers something universal and timeless. Many of us likewise sense an abiding force that keeps this world from spiraling out of control and keeps the planet from spinning off its axis. We sense a greater truth, maybe even an order to the cosmos beyond human perception. One name for this universal truth is *rita*. Because this truth is beyond human perception, we're given the faculty of intuition, *antar-jñāna* ("inner knowledge"), which helps us sense and "remember" the nature of everything as being inherently interconnected. Our reasoning alone—using the left hemispheric functions of breaking things down and dividing—won't help us feel this truth.

Your body is a tuning fork that helps you sound out the truth from your throat center. Deep listening helps us hear truth's vibrations. "When people are speaking truth," poet Olga Broumas once told me, "there are different vibrations than when they are spinning their wheels. That's also something very audibly perceptual if someone brings their attention to it." To tune in to these vibrations requires us to hear our body's internal vibrations, the vibrations from which language emanates. Sound vibrations travel to the outer ear's tympanic membrane, which sends them to the middle ear's three bones called ossicles, which in turn amplify the sound vibrations so the inner ear can pick them up and convert them into electrical signals that travel to the brain.[3] But we can't hear everything the universe has to offer, as human ears on average pick up sound frequencies from twenty to twenty thousand or maybe thirty thousand hertz. Your dog, though, can hear frequencies as high as forty thousand, and that bat circling the trees out back in the dark can hear hums as high as a hundred thousand hertz. The simple fact that human ears have a limited capacity to pick up the universe's rhythms as compared even to certain animals should suggest that there is much more to reality and truth than what we can know with our cognitive senses.[4] Despite our outer ear's limitations, physicists are confirming that everything in the universe is held together with pulsing "strings." The "seers" of the Rg Veda intuited these universal vibrations centuries ago, well before the mechanistic tools of science could confirm their existence, so some mechanism in the inner ear's deep recesses helps us sense this truth's vibrations.

When we write with truthfulness, we harmonize our words with these deep vibrations. Our words emanate from the universe's pulse, according to the Kundali-Upanishad. When you pause to imagine the origins of the sounds you've inherited, the sounds your mind and body and imagination somehow combine into words, which string into sentences, you likely recall the wonder of language itself. I know this explanation risks mystifying writing, but such is not my intent. Don't expect—or even seek out—"mystic visions" of beatitude. Doing so can distort your sense of what really needs to be written. It also can distort your sense of what writing, yoga, and meditation are about. They're more about awakening and transforming than about having mystic moments. If you have them, fine. I suggest, though, that you avoid attaching yourself to such experiences and feeling that you can only write something meaningful and truthful when you do have them. Nonetheless, my intention is to acknowledge that the source of what we write when we write from truth is often beyond the rational mind, even though it exists in some form within our body's cells.

So sound out the truth with your throat and mouth-organ. In her poem "Artemis," Olga Broumas says her work with "tonguelike forms that curve round a throat" begins with "O, the O-/mega, horseshoe, the cave of sound." It begins with O indeed. The shape of the womb, the shape of lips as they let that O sound pass through "the cave of sound," O is also a combination of A and U, considered in Sanskrit as manifestations of the universe's most supreme sounds. Some songs, hymns, and mantras remind us of words' potency. When writing or when listening to what we've written, hum an "Amen," a verse of "Amazing Grace," "Atman" ("Self"), or "AUM"—all of which begin with the beginning sounds. When these words hum through your word tunnel, your vishuddi cakra, they can remind us of the truth we embody. The vibrations, especially the humming m sound, rouse the right hemisphere and calm your thoughts. A few bars of one of these chants can clear your throat of the muck. Revere your words. They can be truth's midwives.

Truthful writing is our gift. In India I heard a story about truth and the goddess Vāc. In a time before "beforeness," a young goddess named Vāc, possessor of sacred speech, desired to give us mortals divinely charged language, but the Himalayan gods—not unlike their Olympian Greek neighbors who argued with the populist Prometheus—didn't want humans to have sacred speech. Vāc, distraught from the divine spat, fled to a forest, where she found refuge among the trees. The trees refused to extradite the sweet-sounding goddess unless the gods agreed that Vāc could endow humans with her linguistic gift. The gods gave in. So the "seers" of the *Rig-Veda* attribute Vāc with *inspiring* them, and now musicians remember that their lutes and flutes carved from trees' bodies must be played with the breath of sacred speech, and writers create words published on trees' flesh and with words that also emanate from Vāc's defiant truthfulness (even when doing so defies popular opinion).

It's a gift with a cost, then, always my next-to-last bit of warning to my students. In facing the struggle to write the truth, we in turn give this gift to others to persevere in expressing their own truth. Eugene O'Neill was tormented by the demons of his crazed-acting family until he exorcised them by writing in the mid-twentieth century *A Long Day's Journey Into Night*, one of this country's first plays to unveil truths about manipulative parents, addictions, and the yearning for transcendence through art. O'Neill's courage emboldened the likes of Arthur Miller, who went on to write similarly unsettling plays such as *Death of a Salesman* and *All My Sons*, plays that disrupted the 1950s ideal of perfect nuclear families and the pursuit of our untainted American dreams. Miller's willingness to tell the truth encouraged the likes of Edward Albee, whose *Who's Afraid of Virginia Woolf?* shows how cruel and destructive relationships and language can be. Memoirists likewise have had to face authentic struggles to tell the truth about themselves, their families, and being human. Arabian poets such as Nizar Qabbani have ventured for decades to tell the truth about being human under state oppression. Even before feminism came into vogue, Qabbani used his role as popular poet to unveil the social stigmas imposed upon erotic relationships. His daring helped a generation of other Middle Eastern poets, men and women, write truthfully about desire and love. Writers risk exile, if not from their countries then from their religious and social communities as well as from their families. Their struggle, though, inspires us to face the truth and to speak out.

You're probably going to offend some people. Get ready. Writing truth isn't always kind or pleasant. A friend of mine grew nauseous over several days while writing the most difficult parts of her memoir. She kept using metaphors of "getting something out" and "purging" to describe what the process felt like. Which is not to say you *have* to offend people or have to walk around with a knotted stomach to write truthfully. It's just chances are that if your writing is coasting along your consciousness's bay without a rock or wave, without a single idea that challenges your own or any of your readers' sensibilities or notions, without an image that causes them to pause and reconsider their surroundings or language itself—in short, without much of an effect on you or them—then you're probably not writing your truth. You have to write your truth. You have to write what simmers in the early morning hours in your imagination's background, waiting to be heard, and then what clamps you like a gila monster and makes you bowl over until you pay attention to it. Sound out the words, or let them sound you out. Stick with the honesty of details, first. The universe will follow.

Stand firm in the truth you write. Gandhi's specific form of political and spiritual resistance came to be tagged "firmness in truth," *satyagraha.*[5] Such whole-bodied resistance to complacency, to cliché, to simplistic writing, might be called the same.

My final bit of wisdom about truth is to laugh. All of this talk of truth can make us take ourselves too seriously. I don't know which god or goddess gave us this gift, but I love humor that bites me with the truth too. I agree with Saint John that in the Beginning was the Word, but sometimes I have this queasy feeling in my gut that the Creator, being a clever writer, made the Word a Pun and that sometimes we just don't get it. Dogs and gods, they'll both sneak up on you.

$\mathcal{T}$AKE A BREATH

INTENTION:

Try this practice to tune your body into an abiding source of truth for your writing. Engage it when you need to tap into a deeper source for emotional honesty, especially when writing an emotionally charged scene. It also can help you tune in to the current of truth as manifested in language. As with most practices in this book, its effects won't be immediate and it requires an authentic intention and persistent practice.

Choose a seated pose with your palms resting on the knees. With sitting bones weighted in the ground and spine lengthened, focus on your breath and make space for your intention. When you feel openness, ask yourself quietly, "What am I writing for?" Tend to whatever words or images surface in response and let that response spread throughout your throat and into your body. Be with that response. Then, clarify that you intend to write a piece on whatever your subject that stems from your own truth. Inhale, hearing your breath's hissing "sa," and exhale hearing your breath's raspy "ha." Then, repeat this way of breathing with your lips closed. Close your eyes and on the next slow inhalation, retain your breath and bring the chin to the chest or collarbone. Hold your breath for four seconds at first (longer with more practice). Then raise the head, drop the shoulders, and exhale slowly. Practice five times. This **THROAT LOCK** *practice (jālandhara-bandha), some yogis claim, can alleviate people's stuttering. It clears the throat's sky so you can hear Vāc's voice sing through your throat's reed.*

While you stimulate this level of sound, close your eyes and imagine how deeply words can register notes within you. Imagine your breath taking you to a place in your body where words' sounds originate. It's a source each of us possesses, a source innate in everything that creates. Draw your attention just above your outer ears, and imagine a blank screen in the back of your skull. This blank screen is the place of words' origin. Then, visualize how your words that you're going to employ need to sound—not the visual images you've written but the words' sounds themselves, their "visible sound." If the vibrations of what you want to write create a shape or picture, what would it look like? Rippling triangles, shivering parsnips, an elegant woman dressed in an eighteenth-century evening gown who waltzes while a mischievous boy dashes beneath her gown, an old man whittling a flute beneath an oak tree as the sun sets? Once the image or images feel right, imagine them bathing your inner body and vibrating in your cells.

Then begin to write. Write with a firm, resolved sense of truth. Keep breathing with the raspy **VICTORIOUS BREATH** *by contracting your glottis (at the back of your throat) if it helps keep things clear and blows away the Heckler. You won't be fooled by the emotional spin doctor who tries, for instance, either to end every conflict with a bouquet of flowers or to render a scene so utterly dismally that your characters' theme song must be the Stones' "Paint It Black." You'll be wary of hiding the truth with disingenuous humor or of dragging the truth through muddy moroseness. Once you've drafted, you can delete or change those parts whose tone seems insincere, whose mood seems maudlin or melodramatic.*

CHAPTER FIFTEEN

The Inner Heckler
Laughs Even at Sages:
Facing Fear

Abby, a writer in Woodstock who attends my workshops, had a feature article about Alzheimer's due to a major health magazine in less than two days. A freelance writer for eight years, she felt good about her interviews with specialists and people with the disease; the article, her third feature for this magazine, had the right angle to boost her reputation; and her relationship with the magazine's editor had solidified enough that Abby thought this article could lead to a permanent position on the staff. But then her Heckler showed up. *Do you really think you have a unique angle? Hasn't this topic been overdone?* The questions became relentless. *Aren't you really hacking your way through this "career"?* Suddenly, the interviews seemed superficial. The article's tone sounded all wrong. *That personal aside about your own memory loss makes you look self-indulgent, which you are, you know?* The voice undid her confidence, she later told me, and for much of the next day, her neck, shoulders, and right hand ached with doubt and fear that she wouldn't complete the assignment.

Then Abby remembered some ideas we had discussed in a workshop about these very topics. She pulled out some of Patanjali's sutras I had copied for the group: "Fear, subtle and arising from its own origin, visits even the wisest among us" (II.9) and "When doubt disturbs your thoughts, counter it with the opposite frame of mind" (II.33). She later told me that just rereading those sayings, written some eighteen hundred years ago and derived from at least another thousand years of previous yogic wisdom, started to ease

her body and to quell her Heckler. She practiced a couple of strategies I had shown her and caught the Heckler off guard by laughing
back at it and saying, "Yeah, so what if you're right? What's the
worst that could happen?" When she reread her article, she realized
that in a few places the tone was indeed off, but overall the piece
felt right. She knew it. What then, she wondered, was this voice's
origin? Maybe she had let too much ride on the article—her reputation, the prospect of a permanent position. Instead of just focusing
on the subject and writing, she was giving way too much attention
to the piece's possible success or failure.

With a few controlled breaths coupled with a concentration
practice, Abby soon heard another voice: the Inner Confidant(e).
The voice, with no false hope, simply said, "Trust yourself. Keep
writing. The ground's not going to fall out and drop you into a vast
ocean because of this article. And even if it did, you know how to
laugh, and your laugh will keep you afloat." Within a day, she finished and submitted the article, one that received numerous favor-
able reader replies. Although she doesn't yet have a permanent
position with the magazine, Abby says the experience of handling
this sudden attack of doubt gave her more confidence, and she's negotiating with another magazine editor for a position.

Doubt wracks the best of writers. So, too, its twin, fear. No matter our level of previous success or failure, the Inner Heckler's dual
voices surface with different irritations for each of us. Yet, by understanding the Inner Heckler's nature, we can ready ourselves to recognize its subtle forms and employ yoga's tools that consistently
help diverse writers muzzle it.

One of the Inner Heckler's voices is fear. It usually stems from
protecting the ego self, the "I." This sense of I-ness makes us aware
of life and, thus, of death. We cling to what comforts the ego self
and avoid what threatens and potentially could "kill" our sense of
self. Our fear of somebody else's criticism, then, and our fear of failure is at least metaphorically a fear of death—a death of part of our
ego self. These metaphors and hyperboles in our everyday language
suggest as much: "Her criticism *pierced* me." "His criticism *slaugh-
tered* me." "It *killed* me when my business went bankrupt." "When
they laughed at me, I could've *died*." Our Inner Heckler speaks

directly to our ego's desire for self-preservation. This desire, this clinging to the safe and familiar, is *abhinivesha*, and it ironically is not life affirming. It feeds the ego and starves our authentic self. The authentic self conversely feeds on exactly what starves the ego: risk, challenge, uncertainty.

Consider the myth of Apollo and Daphne.[1] I ask writers to review this story in light of being a writer and to explore with which character they as a writer identify. The Greek god Apollo tried to woo the nymph Daphne out of the woods with his achievements. Inventor of music, god of healing, voice of reasoning, source of light and harmony, the brilliant god with a luminary's vita tried everything to win her heart. But she fled. The introverted nymph didn't desire the illustrious world of laurels; instead, she sought the mysterious, dark realms of the woods where she (she thought) could be forever free and unattached. With the sun god fast on her heels, Daphne called for help to her river god father, who changed her form into that of a laurel tree. Although Apollo never caught Daphne's bodily figure, now he actually could stroke her grainy-barked torso, hang from her limbs, and lounge beneath her shade. With a telling gesture, his artful, love-hungry hands clipped her branches and wove them into a crown—the symbol of victory. Ironically, although Daphne fled from worldly recognition, a part of her transubstantiated body—the laurel leaves artfully woven into a crown—comes to represent artistic and civic accomplishment.

A part of us, like Apollo, seeks outward accomplishment. To create beautiful writing that others may enjoy, to get our art in public venues, praise, recognition, that laurel crown of publication, these are our Apollo yearnings. Yet, another part of us shuns the public hoopla. True, we may just naturally incline toward being alone, unbothered by the demands that readers and the publishing world make on writers. But fear and doubt also lead us to retreat like Daphne. As writers we may try to deny fear and doubt, to suppress and stomp them like unwelcome snakes. We claim we like to write in our own dark woods, not showing our work to anyone else and shying away from Apollo's lures of exposure and prominence. Many writers fear exposing their writing to the light and risking failure or—as one writer pointed out to me—risking success. For failure and success alike can change a person's life, fatally disrupting some of the ego's former patterns. Whether fear's origin be of failure, criticism, or success's laurels, the effect often is the same: We hide. And we don't change.

The Heckler's other voice is doubt. Doubt's nature in yoga is expressed as that state of mind in which we have conflicting thoughts (*samshaya*). Perhaps no story from yoga better illustrates a writer's doubt than that of Arjuna in the *Bhagavad-Gita*. This beautiful poem, composed probably in the third or fourth century BCE, occurs at the onset of a war between two clans of the same royal family. Arjuna, a member of the "virtuous" clan, has for his charioteer none other than Krishna, the god of love. Just as the war is about to begin, Arjuna asks Krishna to lead him to the battlefield's center so he can see the faces and features of the cousins, uncles, and brothers who are about to kill one another. Overwhelmed with grief and compassion, Arjuna collapses, weeps, and wails, for, full of doubt, he's torn between his love for his whole family and his duty to his clan. Time stops. Soldiers freeze. Arjuna, though animate, remains paralyzed with inaction.

Arjuna's indecisiveness reflects our own inaction as writers when doubt sets in. *While your partner and the rest of the world are working their tails off, you're floating in a world of words and imagination. Shouldn't you be spending your time on something that will pay for your kid's tuition? Shouldn't you be spending your time on something more practical? Fixing the fence? Going on a peace march? Humph. At least clean the bathroom.* Doubt divides us. We're torn between doing what our authentic self needs us to do (write!) and doing what we think we *should* do (be practical and profitable). So as soon as we make time to get to the desk, the Heckler shows up, and we find ourselves sprawled on the battlefield, unable to do the authentic work we know we were born to do.

Fear and doubt can inhabit and take over our bodies like obnoxious houseguests whom, after a few years, we've unintentionally allowed to move in for the long haul. Pretty soon, they're inviting over friends and relatives. In *Yoga-Sutra* I.30, Patanjali lists these relatives' names, so to speak, as the most common impediments to a yogi's path. What's related to doubt? Lack of progress on a spiritual path and delusion, for starters. Sluggishness and excitability, sloth, and illness come next. And as Sutra I.31 reminds us, such an open house invites other unwanted relatives: disturbed breathing, physical agitation and trembling, depression, and general suffering (*dukha*). Before we know it, a veritable clan of cousins whose names we barely know has taken over our home.

I know writers who somehow still write in such a home. Like a kid with six siblings, they learn to tune out the noise and ignore the house's state of increasing disrepair. One of my friends, who writes features for a major newspaper and who has published six novels, says (despite his frequent influenza and colds) he likes his body-mind the way it is: crowded, loud, and broken down. But he's also told me frequently that he often thinks he'd rather write a different kind of novel than the modern Western mysteries for which he has become known. Yet, whenever he starts one of his fantasy short stories, what does he hear? *If you're going to write fantasy, you'd better change your name, or else your fans and friends are going to laugh at you. Don't you think you should focus more on your feature or your novel that's a sure sell?* Success as a writer won't necessarily clean your house of the Heckler and its clan. In fact, success can breed more attachment to the fruits of our writing—the praise, the money, the recognition. Such attachment can become another room for the Heckler.

If we try to ignore doubt and fear over several years, we can unconsciously live in a fight-or-flight response. When fear and doubt heighten, our brain may sense danger, which triggers our heart rate to rise, and the endocrine system starts releasing excess amounts of adrenaline (the adrenaline rush) and cortisol. Although healthy in moderate amounts, too much cortisol can debilitate the immune system and exacerbate a cycle of stress. Our breath quickens, and our digestive system virtually stops functioning. If our fears escalate to anxiety or panic, our abdomen can become distressed, and our heart palpitates. Few of us may have panic attacks when we write, but the point is that fear and doubt can override our writing spirit and wreak havoc on our bodies.

We don't have to write this way. Yoga can help us shape our fear and doubt. Not just face them and definitely not suppress them. But transform them. Fear is not something to be "overcome," nor is it a "moral blemish" as some classical yoga texts suggest. When we write from a yogic place in our body and approach fear and doubt as something to be acknowledged, expressed, and tempered, we often can channel doubt and fear's fire one line at a time, one sentence at a time.

Given the above explanation of the fight-or-flight response, it should be no surprise that Patanjali recommends in Sutra I.34 we take a deep breath and retain our breath after the exhalation (*bahya kumbhaka*). Doing so calms the sympathetic nervous system and thereby quiets brain activity. Even just lengthening the exhalation to be twice as long as your inhalation without retaining your breath can quiet the Heckler. I suggest students imagine their out-breath as blowing out those annoying cousins.

A recent study has demonstrated that students with mixed backgrounds in practicing yoga had significantly reduced levels of cortisol after only one yoga class,[2] thereby alleviating some of the body's chemistry of fear. One way that yoga may reduce fear is through its work on what I call the "psoas constrictor." A sixteen-inch serpent called the psoas muscle potentially constricts our courage and contains much of our body and imagination's fear. Imagine a long, snakelike muscle attached near the middle of your spine (at the thoracic vertebra T12, to be exact) that connects to each of the five lower lumbar vertebrae (the lower back), through the pelvis, over the hip's ball and socket, and tails off at the thighbone's (femur's) lesser trochanter, not far from where your leg joins your hip. Physiologically, the psoas supports the internal organs and helps secure the pelvis. Its sleek body resting at our own body's central core, this muscle also literally connects our upper and lower halves. The psoas's head at the midspinal area resides near the central diaphragm—a muscular structure that moderates our breathing. Embedded in the psoas's "body" along the lower (lumbar) spine are several nerves that work with the diaphragm.

Place one hand's index, middle, and ring fingers horizontally beneath your navel. Take a deep inhalation, letting your belly expand like a balloon. On the exhalation, draw your navel and the area where your fingers rest back toward your spine. The nerve network along your lower back's spine and the region where your fingers reside—at the pit of your gut—is often called your abdominal brain. Why? A lot happens here. The psoas meets the diaphragm, which moderates our respiration, and here much of our digestion occurs. Two thirds of our body's blood flows here. This area is the solar plexus, the *manipura cakra*, the city-of-jewel center, the energetic area of personal power, balanced will, and control of intense feelings. Here we have guts or have a weak stomach for confrontation; we "have a spine" and stand up to fear and doubt, or we get nauseous and bend over like Arjuna or Daphne. It's what the Japanese call the *hara*, literally "gut." Zen master Daiun Sogaku Harada said, "You have to realize that the center of the universe is your belly-cave."

So, this massive muscle called the psoas—the body's longest one, in fact—plays a pivotal role in the rhythms of our breathing, of our blood circulation, and, thus, of our body and imagination's responses to fear. With practice we can uncoil the psoas and change a potential psoas constrictor into a psoas elixir, a muscle that can work with us to release or at least direct the energy of our fears of writing, of exposing ourselves, of giving ourselves the freedom to create, of mustering what Rollo May called "the courage to create." Poses such as warrior II (*viribridāsana II*), side-angle pose (*parsvakonāsana*), and some forward bends such as extended east-stretch pose (*paschimāttanāsana*) help lengthen the psoas and give us room to breathe and move (all illustrated in the Appendix). We literally can create space in our bodies to breathe and for our cells to live so they don't, in a sense, suffer claustrophobia from living in a cramped, balled-up house.

I also encourage students to get to the root of fear's origins. Patanjali notes that fear has its own *rasa*, its own quintessence, marrow (I.9). Transformation requires authentic movement toward and with that quality. So, as writers, if we genuinely wish to shape our fears, then we can view it as a natural serpent that coils in our psyche, one that can be lured out of its basket and perchance taught to dance on cue rather than to strike unconsciously. My work with a writer named Lori illustrates how we can get to fear's roots. A talented dancer, technical writer, and fiction writer, Lori came to me as a writing coach for help. Writing mysteries, she told me, had been her dream, and now she sensed at last that this mystery novel—complete with sympathetic characters and intricate plot twists and fantastic settings—was ready for publication. For eight years she had worked on this novel, had attended writing conferences, pored over "the-craft-of-mystery-writing" articles and books, and had been a dedicated member of a writing group. I reviewed her preface and instantly noticed her ability to corrall antsy words into beautifully choreographed sentences and plot lines. She is a writer, no doubt. So why does she need help?

"I'm afraid to send it off to an agent or publisher," Lori said, looking down at the floor like a little girl. Performance anxiety. All writers, even after publishing six books, get it. Like Daphne, Lori had been content to dwell for years in her dark lair, but the thought of offering her cherished manuscript to an agent mortified her. I assured her I could never help her overcome her fears, but possibly we could find ways to transform them. She was open to the idea of writing into her body as a way to identify and shift the flow of her fears. We spread out a couple of yoga mats and blankets and got to work. We worked with the Apollo-Daphne myth to unearth the archetypal patterns of her fear, we brainstormed different personal fears, and then we coaxed her snakes.

And we got to the roots. In the process of our work through dialogue, visualization, bodywork, and writing, we discovered Lori's patterns of fear that stem from her lifelong need for approval as well as patterns of qualified praise. A sister to six gifted brothers, many of them older, she soon learned that all of her accomplishments— winning academic awards and scholarships, becoming a successful dancer, becoming a successful technical writer, having a happy marriage and charming son—were rarely good enough compared to those of her older siblings.

During our bodywork, Lori kept seeing a dancer standing in a rapidly flowing stream. Her feet stuck in the mud, the water flowed more quickly and grew higher, so she resorted to flailing her arms like a crazy whooping crane sending out an emergency call and a mating call in one, and for a while she found her peace in dancing from her hips up until gradually her winged embrace of empty space wedged her feet so she could dance both with and against the stream's current. After she sketched the images, I suggested she write a prose meditation upon these images, the liberation of her body from fear. "Analyze less," I suggested. "Feel more. Imagine more. As you write, follow one image at a time." Our intellect, in its mighty efforts to render fears impotent and invisible, often harms more than helps us. Imagination and intuition, however, frequently let us tame and transform fears.

Several months later, I ran into Lori. Not only had she mustered the courage to submit some of her short stories for publication, but two of three also had been accepted, and upon receiving another writer's advice about her novel she had decided to divide the long book into two shorter ones. She also had found an agent for it. The work we had done together, she said, had shifted her attitude and shifted energy in her body.

One intuitive way to inquire into your fear's origins is to list sayings, colloquialisms, quotations, and titles of works you've heard about or related to fear. "We have nothing to fear but fear itself" and *"Who's Afraid of Virginia Woolf?"* will get you started. After listing fifteen or more, see if any patterns, such as common images or common attitudes, surface. Take one or more of these sayings or quotations and write a prose piece in which you offer fresh insight into how to contend with fear. In your writing, avoid the word *fear*. Or list everything you fear about writing and everything your Heckler tells you to avoid writing. Everything. Then, from the second-person point of view, write a playful list piece called "Ten Ways to Avoid Writing."

Sometimes we just need Krishna, literature's first writing coach, to kick us in the rear. When Arjuna wept on the battlefield, Krishna's first response was essentially "Stop crying. Get up. Face the music, and live in dignity, not doubt." While time stood still, Krishna, though, also had infinite patience for Arjuna's deepest, most distressing questions about attachment, desire, conflicted feelings, and yoga. Krishna became for Arjuna his Heckler's antagonist: his Confidant. The Confidant embodies the Heckler's most daunting antagonist: *shraddhā*. The usual translation as "faith" is misleading; the word encompasses in English qualities such as "confidence" and "mental repose." Our Inner Confidant(e), the force of *shraddhā*, supports us unconditionally yet lures us from our comforting safety spots to new places, possible clearings where we may even receive recognition for our work. The Confidant inspires and guides us and doesn't let us get away with whining. We have work to do, and it's work that even our dearest loved ones often don't understand. With courage, steadfastness, and centeredness, we can face the battle that, we soon discover, is really no battle at all. We realize, too, that there's really nothing and no one to conquer. "When doubt disturbs your thoughts," Patanjali reminds us, "counter it with the opposite frame of mind" (II.33). We can convert the same energy that brings stifling doubt into invigorating confidence so we can face risk and uncertainty. The Heckler's opponent and opposite thought is the Confidant. Listen to it. Inhale confidence; exhale doubt.

Before fiction writer Andre Dubus died, he learned how to drive into fear. A fortuitous coincidence helped him move out of his comfortable mode of writing fiction and face the demons he had embodied for ten years after a crippling automobile accident. One night while helping a stranded driver on the side of a busy freeway, Dubus was struck by a car and lost the use of a leg. Although the driver never stopped, someone else did and called for help. Despite his daily agony in a wheelchair, he never wrote about his own situation. Too painful to face, he said, and so he stayed with fiction until ten years later some new neighbors moved in across the street. The woman, it turns out, was the one, the witness, who stopped to call for aid. Within a few weeks of getting to know her and her husband, Dubus finally faced his body, his pain, all of the demons he had embodied for ten years, and wrote his memoir. He said he suddenly felt "so possessed" to write about his experience—not to forget about or be done with it, because writing, he said, didn't rid him of anything. Instead, he just wanted "to go there" and "see if in that place there was any light."[3] Writing won't rid you of your fears. It can give you, though, ways to work with them.

We don't have to send fear back down more deeply into its hole; we can coax it out with our flute, let it spread its terrifyingly beautiful body before us, and see what it has to teach us. Sometimes, the best advice I can offer students about fear of writing is simple: Write. Drive into it. Fear is usually not a brick wall as much as a large mound of snow. It seems daunting and impassable, but if you keep your hands on the steering wheel, your wits alert, you can drive right through it. The best way I know how to keep driving is just to drive with little knowledge of what exactly is around the next bend.

Arjuna's driver, Krishna, gave Arjuna the best driving instructions I've ever read: "Self-possessed, resolute, act/without any thought of results,/open to success or failure./This equanimity is yoga" (2.48).[4] Replace the word *act* with *write*. And the next time you hear the Heckler tell you that you *should* be doing something more profitable or practical, reverse that voice with this pearl from Arjuna's Confidant: "It is better to perform your own duty poorly, than to perform someone else's duty perfectly; when you do what you should be doing, no pain will come to you" (3.35). The trick is to know that to act authentically is to act on your own authority and that writing is your duty to your authentic self.

*T*AKE A BREATH:
LAUGH AT THE HECKLER AND EMBODY CONFIDENCE

INTENTION:
When you work with your lower body in harmony with your upper body and heart, you can become an adept who frightens fear into obeisance. To embody confidence and faith (*shraddhā*) and to fend off the Heckler, try this practice for at least fifteen writing sessions.

Come into **MOUNTAIN POSE** *(tadāsana), focusing upon your feet first. Drop your weight so forcefully into your heels that no one could pick you up. If you can name one of your fears related to writing, do so. With eyes closed, take two full breaths and ask yourself, "What am I writing for?" Let that question pervade your whole body, knowing there's a core motive for your writing. Allow the response to surface without force and to guide you like a Confidant. Then clarify that your specific intention is to keep the Heckler at bay and to write with confidence.*

Keeping full energy in your legs, bring your right foot back three to four feet and pivot your right foot forward toward your left leg at least forty-five degrees. Let your pelvis be open so that one sitting bone is almost behind the other. Adjust the width between your feet so you can maintain weight in the back heel without collapsing into your back arch. Draw your attention from heels to hips and bend your front knee.

Let your knee line up over your ankle, neither in front of nor to one side of it. Bring your arms straight up so your left arm should be in front of you, your right behind, both palms down. Gaze over your left middle finger. This position is the skeletal form of **WARRIOR II POSE** (vira-bhadrāsana II). The pose stretches your psoas, tones your abdominals, and increases respiration. If this pose strains you, keep your hands at your hips. It's imperative that you find the variation of this pose that stretches your psoas and groins yet also gives you a strong sense of "root-edness." Nothing can knock you over.

Now, experience the internal form. Shrug your shoulders up and draw your shoulders back and down along your spine to let your heart open and support you in tandem with your lower body. On each of the next five inhalations, fill up your heart, and on each of the exhalations draw your attention to your belly. Close your eyes and imagine the in-breath, coming down from your heart, and the out-breath, coming up from your perineum, mix in your belly. Imagine your heart's force churn-ing your fear. The belly's fire converts fear into confident action. Be sure to repeat this practice on the other side.

Then move to the desk and start writing. Write for at least one hour, and anytime you hear the Heckler's voice, inhale confidence into your heart and laugh out loud at the Heckler as you keep writing. What's stop-ping you? Try to stay with this practice for at least seven to ten minutes a day before you write, for at least fifteen days or fifteen writing sessions. Fear is subtle. So, too, is changing fear's form. It's true that even sages get the blues and get laughed at, but they know how to laugh back and at themselves.

CHAPTER SIXTEEN

You Are Wide and Full of Contradictions: Writing Based on Your Self

W e love the first person, at least this country's current reading habits suggest so. Memoirs and personal essays have had a renaissance of sorts. So, too, autobiographical and confessional poems (even if the autobiographies and confessions be partially fictional) have resurfaced prominently in journals, collections, and anthologies during the past twelve years. Why? Maybe our socially and politically tumultuous times send us to read about what we know—personal experience, as one theory goes. Maybe we're increasingly "self" absorbed (witness shifts in television programming toward more lurid talk shows and "reality" TV) and thus choose to write primarily about ourselves and read primarily about people's personal experiences that mirror ours so we can project ourselves into a writer's world.

Possibly, though, we simply hunger to make and shape meaning. To essay (from the French *essayer*) is to attempt, to try out, to experiment. It is rarely to proselytize, to preach, to assert with absolute certainty. When writing personal essays—whether three pages or three hundred pages—we wander through the thick paths of our memories and of our current impressions that we might happen upon a clearing, some small truth or at least some intuitive pattern among experiences that grant life significance. Fiction allows us certain freedoms because our "characters" can explore our ideas and experiences at a personal distance, and poetry can play between the borders of nonfiction and fiction so that a speaker's experiences may or may not be literally the poet's any more than a fiction writer's. Each of these genres can be a vehicle for moving more deeply into the self's alleys and bays, its bistros and institutions.

Part of writing the truth includes exploring the truth of our self (or selves). Writing directly about the self or from our own experiences is tricky, though. A friend recently told me she wasn't sure her self merited so much attention in her writing. "How do I write about myself without being self-absorbed?" students often ask. Self-absorption, self-aggrandizement (an ugly-sounding word), and self-delusion, these are vines that can entangle some of us. It's possible that once you get cozy with "I," you'll regard it as so wise and important that you'll be certain everyone will want to hear whatever it's done, thought, or dreamed. Several writers I meet are more stifled, though, by self-negation and self-loathing. They'll either avoid writing about themselves altogether, or when they do write about themselves their text as mirror reflects themselves in one dimension. To keep free from being tripped up and to help us celebrate this multifarious thing called "self " as writers, yoga offers several useful concepts and practices.

Much of the advice I've offered writers over the years concerning writing about the self can be related to compassion. Cultivate compassion for your whole self, I implore them. Active compassion, *karunā* in Pali, may distinguish a self-absorbed writer—no matter how fine his or her craft—from an emotionally mature writer. In *The Art of Fiction*, John Gardner discusses aspiring writers' "errors of the soul" and "errors of character" such as "lack of due warmth" and "sentimentality." These qualities reflect a novice writer's inability to treat emotional scenes maturely. Gardner suggests that writing teachers cannot "correct" these errors. "Correct," no, yet I do think writing instructors can model how to write with active compassion that is neither cold nor saccharine sweet but authentic. Developing a writer's active compassion requires honesty with ourselves when writing memoirs, personal essays, or even fictional alter egos. Such honesty means that we can embrace the full spectrum of our self— or selves—as complex and contradictory, a genuine city of selves.

How do you have active compassion for yourself without being self-adoring? To cultivate compassion will not necessarily lead us to write sugary poetry appropriate for Mother's Day. Words of compassion often cut through obstructions and deliver truth with a prick, slice, slash, or slaying of a person's ego. Compassion requires identification with all parts of our self, so for starters, explore at least slight faults and limitations of what you consider your self—one of your past selves or present ones.

If you can't examine your foibles critically, your nonfiction will suffer. When one memoirist published her story in the early 1990s about being a morally lost teenager hooked on antidepressants, she came across to many readers as being self-obsessed and neurotic. She aimed her anger at the "social system" that pressured this girl on one hand to succeed and on the other hand to cast herself as a beauty doll whose worth rested only in pleasing boys. Her tone, mostly whining and blaming, marred what could have been a powerful story about girls' struggles with these real and often conflicting pressures. Casting oneself solely as a victim ironically does not garner many readers' sympathy and compassion. When we write about our own experience, we must occasionally slay—or at least laugh at—the ego. Having compassion for the self means that we also muster a complex perspective about the personal hardships our ego self has encountered. A complex perspective means that we don't let our self-portraits become socially constructed clichés of "victim" or even of "hero" or "survivor."

Consider, on the other hand, Penny Wolfson's personal essay "Moonrise" in her book *Moonrise: One Family, Genetic Identity, and Muscular Dystrophy* (New York: St. Martin's Press, 2003), about her relationship with her teenage son, a victim of the disease. What could have been a self-centered essay about a woman's despair toward her son's illness, about her anger toward fate's irrational pickings, about her martyrdom in sacrificing her wants for her son's well-being, instead reads as a poignant, realistic depiction of a mother who tries as best she may to understand both her son's brilliance and his condition. Prone to collapsing from decayed bones, the son in one scene falls in a grocery store parking lot. As he calls out to his mother between gritted teeth to help him, she admits to herself and to us that what she feels is not pity or despair, but anger and resentment. She acknowledges her "terrible impatience" and wonders if she's a witch, a bad mother who can't have patience.

Notes of such blemishing self-revelation register this essay's tone. Wolfson's neither pleased with nor condoning her anger; she's simply admitting it, and by admitting and wondering about it invites us as readers at once to have compassion for her and to admit to our own anger and frustration in such difficult situations.

Or take Nancy Mairs's revelatory memoir *Remembering the Bone House: An Erotics of Place and Space.* In her 1989 preface she acknowledges how her upbringing to be a polite young lady who remains silent on certain subjects—particularly of the body and things erotic—could easily lead her to self-censorship. She notes that such social conventions imposed on a woman can "foster feelings of shame that lead her to trivialize her own experience and prevent her from discovering the depth and complexity of her life." Mairs isn't silent or polite. For as she notes in the next sentence, "I've spoken as plainly and truthfully as the squirms and wriggles of the human psyche will permit."[1] F. Scott Fitzgerald's most illuminating writing may have been not his fiction but his nonfiction personal essays collected as *The Crack-Up.* Written during the 1930s, they offer a startlingly self-disclosing analysis of his self-absorbed mental breakdown. He reveals not only how every act toward another human being ultimately was motivated by self-preservation but also how he loathed people of various races, backgrounds, and classes. "All rather inhuman and undernourished, isn't it?" he writes at one point of his own condition. "Well, that, children, is the true sign of cracking up."[2] This way of writing about oneself so forthrightly, of course, also transfers to fiction. Updike's alter ego Henry Bech or Philip Roth's Portnoy are full of failings and inner contradictions. As discussed earlier in this book, writing the truth can make you uncomfortable, especially when you're writing about yourself. But identifying and accepting our blemishes is an essential step to portraying ourselves or our semiautobiographical protagonists with any real flesh that our readers would want to see more of.

Now, you may have no problem poking fun at yourself. Lately, it's become almost expected for writers to assume an ironic, if not cynical, persona as they lampoon themselves, their family, and every facet of society the writer observes. An ironic persona indeed can be used in a striking way to expose just how absurd our lives can be, but it also can become a shield, a convenient dodge to avoid exploring our lives' gravitas. One writer, recently graduated from college and well steeped in all things ironic, attended one of my workshops and said her greatest breakthrough in the workshop was her ability for the first time to write seriously about herself and her family.

How do we come to such a place of self-acceptance that when depicting ourselves in writing we can admit our uncomfortable feelings in sensitive situations, can admit our faults and errors, without making ourselves seem pitiful and without falling into the traps of cynicism? In this case, we become aware of how we view and feel about ourselves both at the desk and away from the desk.

This complex yet individuated self in several yoga texts is called *jiva* or *jīva-ātman*. It's described as being "bound," as being entwined, as a capricious animal. Although most yogis in nondualistic Hatha-Yoga traditions ultimately seek to liberate the self in this world (*jivan-mukta*), as writers (and as yogis) we would be wise, first, simply to acknowledge this self's complex nature before trying to leap into liberation. The self *is* fickle. Its mercurial nature, connected to the flickering psyche, often evades even the most astute seeker's net. Desire, fear, courage, love, vitriol, adoration, spite, pride, these emotions and attributes drive much of the *jīva-ātman's* activity. Being bound or entangled in this twine of pain and pleasure is a central cause of the self's suffering.

The extent to which you or a character feels bound or boundless may drive you to write, as might these related questions: "What is the nature and source of this character's suffering?" "What's unique about her existence in this entanglement of pleasure and pain?" "How does he uniquely cope with his own brand of suffering?" Camus's Meursault in the novel *L'Etranger* has a peculiarly detached way of coping, and his utter lack of emotion offers us an ambiguous glimpse into the heart of a character who, while trying to be authentic with his emotions, comes off as being emotionally stunted. Solzhenitsyn's Ivan Denisovich controls his psyche's attachments during a day of his life in a concentration camp so that while being trapped in a prison, his mind doesn't trap him. The heart of your story—fiction or nonfiction—similarly might explore these questions related to the *jīva-ātman's* restlessness: "What does she think she lacks that she thinks she deeply wants?" "How will she set about getting it?" "What will get in her way?" "In the end will she get it?" Such questions can form the basis of your story's conflict, plot, and resolution.

Thoughts make up a considerable part of the self. So track some of them for five minutes. Set a timer. Don't try to record them in detail—you'll never keep up with the whirl. Just note bits of the good, the bad, and the ugly. You want a brownie, you notice your back hurts, you want to glimpse God, the kids yelling on the sidewalk outside get on your nerves, then you think they're cute. Five minutes could produce just that much randomness. Now, you won't put all of those thoughts (I hope) into a piece related to your present situation, but if you're not already acknowledging and accepting how quirky, idiosyncratic, and unpredictable your thoughts are, then start.

Actions also make up part of the self. Everything we think and do contributes to the path we take or are given. Such is a basic premise of *karman*—translated to "action." It also refers to the moral force of one's actions or thoughts. By moral force, I mean the consequences—preferable or not—from our thoughts and actions. The *Bhagavad-Gita* identifies three types of actions according to the self's intentions: those selfless actions that are aligned with noble intentions but have no attachment to outcome, those ego actions motivated by a search for a pleasurable outcome, and those careless actions performed without regard for the harm that could come from them. My guess is each of us acts upon all three, especially the first two categories (although I know a few reckless writers whose actions occasionally fall into the latter).

So when writing about a past event or experience, explore your motives. Likewise, what makes writing fiction so compelling for some authors is the opportunity to explore their protagonist's motives. For instance, let's say you're writing a short story about a character based on yourself who volunteers his time to offer free art lessons at a homeless shelter downtown. The character would like to think he's motivated by that Kantian ideal of goodwill, and you, the writer, find out that indeed the character is partly driven by a deep desire to help others find an avenue to express themselves through painting and drawing. But as the story unfolds, you discover that the character also wants to compensate for his otherwise self-absorbed life (as he views it). You also discover that he's trying to beef up his vita so he can apply for a grant that pays artists to offer "socially progressive" workshops. Clearly, the lines between the first two categories of *karman*—selfless and ego driven—are obscured. Now, if he started trying to seduce one of the women, it wouldn't be difficult to put that action into the latter category unless, of course, you present the characters as possibly "in love" (which might only serve to make the story overly dramatic instead of interesting).

You don't need to psychoanalyze your actions or confess your (or your protagonist's) debauchery. Your job as a writer is to explore actions and their consequences as honestly as you can, and through such an exploration perhaps your piece of fiction or true essay implies a worldview or even a moral view without preaching to your readers, asking forgiveness of your readers, or simply shocking your readers' sensibilities. There's a danger, too, in oversimplifying a story—whether fiction or nonfiction—by simplistically stating that the artist, for example, just wanted to boost his vita. A story gets interesting (for you and for readers) when motives get mixed.

So examine your motives. Identify three to five things you did today for other people. What was your motive? Selfish? Selfless? Both? Are you really a martyr? Are you really that manipulative? Then, list three things you said today to someone else. What did each comment reveal about you, your character, your motives? Was there a discrepancy between what you intended and thought and what you said? You'll discover that you're large and wide and full of contradictions. When you write about yourself, past or present, be attentive to portraying actions with mixed or conflicting motives.

Appreciate your self's smallness as well. It's tiny, really, made of minuscule, subatomic elements and of a series of wee moments. I heard a writing teacher of some repute tell a student that her writing would improve once she "went out into the world and had more experiences." This advice not only negated this woman's life, but it seems misdirected. We don't have to travel to Africa to hunt tigers or descend into a moral morass and take heroin in order to have a life worth writing about. If we focus only on exotica such as going to an ashram in India or on the common "big" life events such as getting married or divorced, or losing a parent, then their scale may tempt us as writers to examine the obvious external details of "what happened." Yet, any piece of fiction or nonfiction worth reading and rereading is always more than a recount of what happened. Forget for now the cataclysmic earthquakes that we narrowly escaped—those "big" moments we think are "life defining"; the greater challenge of writing about yourself, in nonfiction or fiction, is to divine meaning in mundane moments.

To do so, my students and I each create a simple chart of our life's map by making rows on a piece of paper that designate times in our lives labeled, for instance, 1–6 (years old), 7–12, 13–19, 20–29, 30–39, 40–49, et cetera. Then we jot down brief notes about moments that we experienced during these life periods. The notes can be as brief as "met hobo near train tracks," "fell out of tree," or "hummingbird moth landed on my foot." Your writing about a "small" moment prompts you to consider how subtly impressions are made upon your psyche and character.

Then, form a sutra self. A "sutra" is a thread. It's also an aphoristic bit of wisdom that is part of a series of aphorisms "threaded together." Hence, the *Yoga-Sutra*. In mapping such moments as described above, you'll probably notice patterns between or among them. One student realized how frequently she had listed times when she had met a stranger—from when she was eight to when she was forty. That observation led her to write a compelling essay titled "Talk to Strangers: A Mother's Advice." Someone else noticed his obsession with Patsy Cline's and Ani di Franco's music (an odd pair that didn't appear on anyone else's map) and used that observation to form an essay, and another student recognized how different kinds of cheeses played a part in his remembering romantic moments (which could've been, uh, cheesy, but he handled the connection well in a short story). In her memoir *Sleeping with Cats*, Marge Piercy loosely held together different parts of her delightfully crazy life according to the cats she owned, or that owned her, at different phases. Such a memoir's, personal essay's, or short story's structure, then, may be seemingly fragmented as the writer threads a series of related anecdotes with commentary. The sutras' wisdom often surfaces for the writers while they're writing, threading, and rearranging the moments.

Similarly, honor your obsessions (or your protagonist's obsessions). You don't need to perpetuate the idea that all writers are neurotic and obsessive-compulsive, but surely your thoughts latch on to some crazed set of thoughts, habits, even trends, that no writer yet has explored fully. Nicholson Baker wrote a book-length essay not about his obsession with John Updike but about his feeling anxiously influenced by the senior writer. It's a wonderful study in quirky connections and threads, threads which often offer (but not always) some glimmer of self-understanding. Granted, much of yoga is about quieting the inner chatter, which means that some writers might be out of a job—or at least completely "out of character"—but yoga also is about accepting those thoughts. This is compassion for the self of the highest order: not to yell at ourselves for talking so loud inside our heads, but to acknowledge these thoughts and their oft-beguiling patterns.

Finally, get a different perspective on yourself. Switch persons. The standard rule for memoir writing and personal essay writing has been to write in the first-person singular ("I," "me," "my," "mine."). Colson Whitehead's series of thirteen essays that comprise *The Colossus of New York* frequently shifts among first-person, second-person, and third-person points of view. When writing poetry, I especially experiment with second- and third-person for a couple of reasons: It frees me from feeling restricted to talking about the "facts" of what I think about myself, and doing so grants me distance, as if I'm looking at myself through an alter ego's eyes. Updike had his own character, his alter ego Henry Bech, interview him in an essay a few years ago. Jorge Luis Borges, always toying with notions of authorship, wrote a story called "Borges and I" in which the narrator sits down next to Borges and converses with him.

In Adrienne Rich's poem "Integrity," she offers us a thoughtful model for exploring the whole, complex self. Her self has come back to a shore, so to speak, with sun-scalded arms and with a beautiful understanding: that she has "selves." It's such a simple yet startling realization for her after so many years. Two selves she acknowledges especially, anger and tenderness that she says "breathe" in her "as angels, not polarities" woven from the same spider's body.[3] Rich acknowledges her complex self, her integral self (or selves). Images in the poem appear to surface from both the poet's memories and from her subtle imagination. Writers in my workshops similarly have explored surprising and seemingly contradictory facets of themselves. "There is an ocean in me," one writer's piece begins. She then explores how she feels trapped in her mind's pond, unwilling to venture too far beyond the unknown. Another writer was surprised to explore two concepts that defined parts of her selves: teacher and whore. The word *whore*, even more surprising, shares similar roots with *charity*, so her whore self may be a teacher, and her teacher self a whore.

When exploring the self, we often have to trick or try to bypass the ego. It'll get in the way of your cultivating compassion for your whole, contradictory self. It often won't let you see the self's subtle shades. Several students, though, have had remarkable success in gleaning surprising insight into the self by engaging yogic breath work and *āsana* while visualizing with the subtle imagination. The breath work, in tandem with certain body movements, stimulates both of the brain's hemispheres so that the right hemisphere, for instance, surfaces more imagery from the physical and subtle imagination. The following TAKE A BREATH exercise can further your self-exploration and your celebration of the self's myriad faces and shapes. This simple yet effective sequence makes it easy to practice on a regular basis. Every time you come back to this practice, the results may differ. After participating in a workshop, a theater artist named Dianne continued to practice the following sequence and turned the focus upon her mother. She created a vivid, embodied portrait in which distinctions between Dianne and her mother often dissolved. She now practices this sequence regularly before writing.

As you acknowledge complex facets of the *jīva-ātman*, you extend compassion to it all—the good, the bad, the sweet, the sour, the thin and fat. What a piece of work you are.

$\mathcal{T}$AKE A BREATH:
COMPASSION FOR THE INTEGRAL SELF

INTENTION:
Try this practice to gain fresh ideas for portraying the complexities of your seemingly contradictory self. You can use the insight gained for exploring facets of your self in a personal essay, memoir, short story, novel, or poem.

I suggest you read through and try the following sequence one to three times before combining the movements with the inner concentration and visualization. You can review the sequence for this chapter in the Appendix, which also includes two optional poses—OPEN-HEARTED STANDING FORWARD BEND (hridaya-uttanāsana) and AWKWARD CHAIR POSE (utkatāsana). *Use the sequence as a starting point for you to stimulate your subtle imagination when trying to explore your self in fresh ways.*

To prepare for this practice, come into MOUNTAIN POSE (tadā-sana) *and for at least five breaths try to empty your thoughts and prepare to receive. Let go of preconceptions about yourself. With palms together at your heart, quietly ask yourself, "What am I writing for?" Inhale the response and let it circulate throughout your body. Let the response inform your self's actions. When ready, specify that you intend to gain fresh insight into the nature of your self's essential contradictions without self-censorship.*

Once you feel clarity about your intention, bend your elbows and hold your palms in front of you, elbow-height. Gaze at your dominant palm and fingers. See your palm as a mirror that reflects back to you images of yourself you consciously present to the rest of the world, the part of you that you hope others see. Take it all in. When ready, gaze at your other palm. This palm reflects those parts of yourself you don't always acknowledge, that you often try to hide from yourself and from others. Take it all in.

Bring your hands to your sides and close your eyes. What two words or images suddenly surface that each represents the right side and the left side of your self or selves? Let go of controlling what arises. Be open to surprise, and let your body take in the words or images. With eyes still closed, inhale and extend your arms straight in front of you, palms facing away. In this OFFERING MOUNTAIN POSE (pushpa tadāsana), *you extend both selves to the world. Your hands' and selves' back sides face you. How do these selves appear to others? When was a small moment that one or both of them appeared to others? Take it in for a few breaths.*

On an exhalation, open your arms straight to the side, shoulder-height into EVEN-HEARTED MOUNTAIN POSE (sama-hridaya-tādāsana). *Inhale, filling your heart space. Exhale, turn your head to the right hand, and breathe compassion from the heart through parted lips to* this part of your self. Inhale, head to center, and exhale, repeating on the other side, noticing how it feels to extend compassion to each side.

Exhale and bring your hands behind you, fingers interlaced, into **OPEN-HEARTED MOUNTAIN POSE** (hridaya-tādāsana). Open your heart as you lift your hands, arms straight. Observe how the images or words come back together and play with one another behind your back. Perhaps parts of a memory surface in which these halves emerged within the same action or moment. Let pertinent details well up without analysis. Inhale fully and as you exhale bring together your hands, your selves, at your heart. Observe how these images relate again and perchance unite. Avoid forcing any reconciliation, though.

Many writers continue this sequence one to three more times until ready to write. Once you have received information from your body, breath, and subtle imagination, draft a piece—either a prose piece, poem, or interior monologue—in which you explore at least two seemingly contradictory facets, two "angels," of your embodied self. You might situate your self in a specific memory and recount an incident in which these two selves emerged, or you might begin a reflective prose piece in which you poetically explore two seemingly contradictory facets of your self for fiction or nonfiction.

While you write, the journey's not over. See what writing itself unveils. You can begin with a palpable image, and weave in particular details. Heed the rhythms of your heart and of your breath as you write. Metaphors should unfold naturally and subtly. If you're writing fiction, project the images and insight into a character or protagonist's body and perspective. Finally, avoid trying to reconcile the two parts too easily.

CHAPTER SEVENTEEN

Stories of Scars
and Deep Memories:
Writing Beyond Trauma

My third eye is scarred. Dented. Or at least the skin region where my third eye resides has been rent. I don't remember exactly what happened, but one summer night, when I was seventeen and drank too much whiskey, I nodded asleep while driving, veered to the left on a quiet street, and crashed into someone's parked Cadillac. My forehead smashed into and cracked the windshield, and a piece of broken glass lodged itself between my eyebrows. My car—my old Toyota Corolla, the first and last car my father bought me—was to-taled. Luckily, my friend Jodie had followed my car on the way home. He had tried to wrest my car keys from my hands, but I had refused. A lot of whiskey combined with my stubborn seventeen-year-old self made for an intolerable friend, but Jodie stayed by my side. "Listen, you have to wake up your father," he had told me. It was after two in the morning. He told me the name of the road and the neighborhood where we had left my wrecked car and asked if I knew how to get back there. I nodded, hugged my friend, and apologized for being such a jerk.

My father—sprawled, crashed, on his bed—looked like a hiber-nating bear. Sobering up quickly, I pulled the sympathy card by stooping to his eye level as I shook him so that when he would open his eyes he'd see my face caked with blood. Even drunk and dazed from a car crash, I could be manipulative. It worked for a mo-ment. At first, I whimpered; then, I confessed.

Terror and anger must have rushed through my father. He must have seen himself. Not only a spawn of himself but himself twenty-six years younger and just as lost and uncontrollable in a drunken forest. He likely had been trying to sleep off his own meeting with Jack Daniel and his cronies. At that moment, standing before an irresponsible and ungrateful teenage son, he probably didn't remember teaching me at nine years old how to mix his whiskey-and-waters during his all-night poker games and praising me with a chuckle when I lay heavy on the whiskey. Eight years after that first bartending lesson, I genuinely thought that being a man in part meant drinking a lot and keeping your wits. I had mastered the drinking part but had failed the wits bit of the formula. I'm not sure which of these facts—that I drank a great deal or that I had lost control of the steering wheel or that I mirrored him so clearly—angered him most. He would punish me mostly by not letting me have another car and by insisting that I learn to handle my liquor. When I rub that spot now I still remember the reckless spirit I have inherited and have domesticated that I not end up lost and alone on a dead-end road. But this dent at my third eye also reminds me of my uniquely fractured imagination, that I often see reality through a shattered windshield, a windshield that at once distorts vision like a kaleidoscope and distills light's reflections like a snowflake. Where some people see ugliness, I often see a story.

We all have scars and bodily oddities. Bunions that stick out the insides of my feet look like sixth toes. My ring finger's knuckle still swells from an argument several years ago when a friend (still a friend) yanked my finger back and out of joint. And skin still scabs on my belly button from a bad picking habit started when I was four years old. Whether inherited or accumulated, our bodies' scars, scabs, and beautiful irregularities harbor stories rich for the telling. Our scars remind us of foibles and fights, of accidents and adventures. Our "irregularities"—our nose that others call a ski slope, our feet petite and narrow like a geisha's, our birthmark on our thigh that looks like a profile of Lincoln—bespeak our unique brand of being in our bodies. We're all scarred. No need to pack on the concealer to hide our wrinkles. Another aspect of extending compassion to the self is to explore this physical body itself—the blood and guts and especially the wounds, the scars, and anything anyone else might call a "physical oddity."

Yet when writing about our or our characters' literal wounds and scars, our ways of making meaning of such experiences can fall into cultural clichés, again, of "victim," "hero," or "survivor." Authentic writing moves us beyond such conditioned responses and demands we explore our unique experiences with unique insight, that we move beyond viewing our experiences solely as traumatic and entertain possibly the tragic if not mythic dimensions of such experiences. By discovering the complex patterns of how and why we each are uniquely scarred or shaped, we can reimagine our bodies as guiding reservoirs of creativity.

Several students and writers grow uncomfortable with this kind of exploration. They've become accustomed to forgetting this physical body with aching joints, swollen ankles, a scarred cheek, an untrustworthy uterus, a gimp eye. But yoga and authentic writing are not about denying or transcending the body. You come to yoga and to writing from where you are. If your neck is stiff, it's stiff. If your back aches from a ski accident in 1983, so be it. Yoga and authentic writing each ask us to accept where we are, and where we are has largely to do with where our physical bodies are. Our physical bodies are part and parcel of who we are and of who our characters are. So taking a journey into the physical body is a journey into the self's most palpable map.

Our flesh's marks—our divets, birthmarks, pimple potholes, skin tracks, and "irregularities"—belie our memories of mishaps and bed stories of who we are and who we've been. Sensory data itself traveling along our spine often leaves traces. When we hit our heads or jam our thumbs, the sensory stimulation that registers pain reaches the interior part of the brain called the thalamus and along the way makes subtle imprints on parts of the body. The sensory stimuli that help us determine where we are and how we move in space reach the cerebral cortex and leave distinct impressions on parts of the body. It's as if our "accidents" leave internal scars—or at least internal tracks of memory.

When our neck whips in a car crash or our skin welts from wasp stings or our ankle twists on soft grass, then our instincts heighten, our breath quickens. Our altering breath imprints our cellular structure slightly, subtly. Less dramatic breaths—as you watch your cat lap milk or feathery snowflakes float to the ground—still impress.

At each cell's center, a nucleus contains forty-six chromosomes that map part of the body's genetic code and a part of who we are or how we view our self. Since at each cell's nucleus or center reside some of our genetic stuff, it's as if each breath potentially plays with who we are and who we will become. These stimuli in turn register with our body's previous sensory experiences, so that our body's memory in part shapes our perceptions of any present experience. Mindful movement, breath work, and visualization can bring some of these impressions out of storage.

As writers we can find much fodder for our writing if we delve into our scars, wounds, and other bodily oddities. Doing so can grant us wisdom about our own or our characters' histories and motivations, their physical reality in relation to their psychic reality. Ugliness, scars, and bodily oddities often drive the fates of fictional characters. Cyrano de Bergerac's nose, we likely know, helped him foster a quick wit and a sharp tongue that at once could pierce the hearts of his enemies and pluck the heart of his unrequited love. There's also Hugo's Quasimodo, who despite or because of his humbling hunchback, swings for Esmerelda's love. Essayists have found their scars and bodily oddities to be deep fodder for digging too: Esmerelda Santiago maps her skin marks and dots ("Skin"), Floyd Skloot offers startling revelations about having "an insult to the brain" ("Gray Area: Thinking with a Damaged Brain"), and Phillip Lopate exposes several parts of himself including his eyebrows that grow together, his various scars, and even his penis, which has two peeing holes and "has the personality of a cat" ("Portrait of My Body"). None of these essayists' work I would describe, incidentally, as solipsistic or pure navel-gazing. Their respective idiosyncratic "irregularities" become springboards for reflecting universally upon identity, appearance, memory, love, self.

Authentic writing moves beyond the traumatic into the tragic, the comic, and/or the mythic. Avoid falling into conditioned ruts when making meaning of being scarred or appearing odd. Years of watching made-for-television movies, despite good intentions, may perpetuate the simplistic categories of trauma: "victim" or "survivor." Trauma is not tragedy. It's not enough as a writer only to render the facts that something bad happened to your or a character's body (and psyche). Authentic writing is more than retelling what happened. In trauma writing, a writer may see only one cause. The cause may be something outside of one's self (an automobile accident, an abusive parent or spouse, a natural disaster), or it may be some single point of self-blame (carelessness, cowardice, stubbornness). A tragic view mixes both and more. So explore complexly how a person's fate stems from a mix of personal decisions and personal dominant qualities as well as outside forces of other people's and society's influence. Even venture to wonder about larger factors perhaps of "divine plan" or of chance (depending on your beliefs and still avoiding being preachy). In such a complex account, when a protagonist constantly faces mishap, sorrow, and ultimately ruin—in light of, if not despite, seemingly noble personal atttributes—then your story may be a tragedy, a complex worldview of self and world.

But complexity can be comic too. So you might mix the comic with the tragic. Shakespeare brings in his fools to remind us of our absurdities and frailties. If something ridiculous happened simultaneously or in relation to the event you're recounting (or inventing), include it. In Mark Twain's bleak novella *The Tragedy of Pudd'nhead Wilson*, a plantation owner's baby is born on the same day as his light-skinned slave's baby. The slave switches the babies' beds, an act that propels a series of comic and mostly tragic consequences. The slave's baby, treated as a plantation owner's son (even by his mother), grows up to be a morally wretched and wounded individual who loses his inheritance to gambling and drinking and who sells his mother down the river for some money. Yet, Twain's dark sense of humor, especially through the witticisms of the title character "Pudd'nhead Wilson," keeps the novel from being weighted with too much gravity. Francine Prose's self-deprecating sense of humor also provides comic relief in her essay "The Nose" in which she recalls the first time she realized in sixth grade she was tagged "the kid with the big nose." Similarly, a student explored, with initial discomfort, how one of her breasts is notably smaller than the other. Recounting with horror and amusement how a former boyfriend used to ridicule her, she gave her readers a glimpse into one person's ability to celebrate her unique form. Not every scar, wound, or oddity may lend itself to wit, but a light tone and self-revelation, without becoming solely therapeutic and overly self-analytical, can make your writing both delightful and insightful.

And explore the mythic. Each of us lives a mythic life. When the meaning of our lives exceeds rational cause-effect explanations and enters the realm of story and of patterns, of coincidence and chance and fate and synchronicity, of symbol and of metaphor, scars become more than sore spots of resentment or embarrassment; they become wellsprings of meaning and of magic. Visit a museum, for instance, and make notes on how various parts of the body are represented in different sections. Oriental, African, and American Indian art portray the human body in mysterious and mythic ways. Venture your own interpretations of this body's significance. As you make notes or sketches of these human forms, wonder how you can reimagine your character's physical body more dynamically, more mythically. Review an anthology of mythology. Joseph Campbell's series *The Masks of God* might be a good start. Campbell spans the gamut from Oriental to Occidental to what he called Primitive Mythology. These tales remind us that our bodies are repositories of ancient stories that link us as human beings on a level beyond the rational and analytical. We can go back to Achilles' famous heel, accidentally not dipped in the River Lethe (the River of Forgetfulness), to recall how physical wounds can shape our fate, but your own character's body also contains a symbolic and mythic dimension.

A surgeon and essayist, Renee Rossi, wrote this sketch called "Soft Spots" during a Yoga as Muse workshop:

When I was a child playing hide and seek, I hid behind the couch below a large, framed Maurice Utrillo canvas—an impressionistic blend of Europeans walking down some cobblestone street lined with brownstones. I think it was late autumn. The frame came down on the centerpiece of my head with a crunch, the crunch of a depressed skull fracture. I might have said, "Look now, Mother, I've reopened my fontanelle," as I now bore the prescient knowledge of all those Europeans. My dent proved itself a font for new ideas, the flat spot to balance a book bag on the way home from school, obviating the need for study, and later, the vent of the volcano of my body at puberty.

A few years back I flew in the air in a rollover accident. When the car hit the ground, my skull was compressed like an accordion between earth and floorboards. I was glad for my vent hole; shedding the hair in clumps right over it to make room for the new stream of molten lava issuing forth from the pain of my mother's death a few days before. I was reborn out of the spout in my crown, Athena, the wisdom-warrior, strong woman-child of Zeus, alone to face the world without my mother.

Her seemingly detached tone and her playful use of a surgeon's diction grants her a perspective that doesn't reduce the piece to emotional trauma. The connections between these two memories didn't surface in Renee until she moved through some yoga poses and heeded her subtle imagination. While working with her breath and imagination, the allusion to Athena suddenly surfaced and, blending with the fact of her mother's death, fits the piece's tone and focus.

Artist Frida Kahlo suffered a life-altering, body-impairing trolley accident when she was a young woman. In the film *Frida*, as Frida and her soon-to-be husband Diego Rivera begin to make love for the first time, she stops him. "I have a scar," she says. "Let's see." He slides her dress down and looks along her lower back, where a six-inch scar from her trolley accident makes tracks on her back and spine. "You're perfect," he says, and kisses her back and its tracks. Sure, the accident traumatized her body and her psyche and ultimately shaped her rage, her art, and her early death. But her story wasn't all trauma. She created a life rich with love and pain, of pleasure and revelation, and from her life she created a series of dreamlike canvases that give us glimpses into humanity's mythic body.

We can begin our own journey into our character's physical body by kissing it and acknowledging its unique perfection.

*T*AKE A BREATH: HONOR YOUR CHARACTER'S SCARS AND ODDITIES

INTENTION:

This practice will help you get started in stimulating your cellular memory and your subtle imagination to explore either your or a character's physical body. I use *character* instead of *you* not only for fiction writers but also for nonfiction writers who need some artistic distance even if they're writing about themselves.

From **ADAMANTINE POSE** (vajrāsana) *or a seated pose of your choice, lengthen your spine and take at least two full breaths. When you've calmed some of your chatter, ask yourself, "What am I writing for?" The answer will circulate throughout your cellular body and inform how you explore your character's physical and mythic body. Then, clarify that you intend to pursue the nature and significance of a character's scar, wound, or oddity.*

Keep your eyes closed, and come onto your hands and knees into **CAT POSE** (marjarāsana). *Exhale and arch your upper back as your tailbone drops toward the ground. Inhale and bring your back into a straight table back. Repeat this movement between exhaling and arching with inhaling and straightening four more times. Then exhale as you curve your spine sideways to the left by looking back toward your right hip. Then repeat on the other side. This movement rouses the stored sensory stimuli and impressions along your central nervous system.*

When ready, come into **CORPSE POSE** (savāsana) *by resting on your back, your knees bent if you wish, elbows toward your torso, your palms for now toward the ceiling. Breathe steadily. Using either your physical imagination or one hand, scan your body for scars, wounds, or irregularities: train-track ridges in your skin from a surgery, that healed yet still visible scar that forms a kiva in the skin below your left eye, or that one earlobe that hangs lower than the other. Rather than being ashamed of this place in your body, honor it. With your imagination, notice this place's shape, texture, hue. Move over it from every possible angle, and notice with appreciation every tiny ridge, mound, valley, or creek.*

Then begin to extend your exhalations. As you extend your exhala-

tion for four to six slow seconds, imagine the breath illuminating your body's hallways. Walk your breath along your spine and to the place you're exploring. As you continue to breathe deeply, ask your imagination and body the following: What happened that led to the scar? How old was the character? Where was he or she? Who else was involved? How did the character carry her or his body at the time? Consider consequences: What happened as a result of this scar or as a result of the incident that rendered the scar? What other incidents in the character's life before or after this scar might relate to this incident? How did elements of society, of nature, of chance, play into this event? What prevalent trait of the self might have led to this event? *Don't force answers. Just let them surface. These questions help you approach a story's storage room, but answering them alone may not give you a full story.*

Then begin to imagine this physical body in a larger context. As you continue with your deep breathing, imagine this body in a sea of human bodies. Each body floats like a boat—a ship, canoe, paddleboat, sailboat—across this vast sea. This one body's unique shape links in some mythic way to this sea. These questions might help you imagine the body in the context of human beings' beautiful mythic struggle (or dance) with their own and others' vulnerabilities, clashes, disappointments, and mistakes: How does this scar and this incident define part of the character's uniqueness? What does it look like—a shield? a bridge?—that could symbolize the self or the self's journey? What other stories from literature, fairy tales, mythologies, or legends might give light to your story's meaning? What does the scar and its story or stories reveal about the tenuous nature of being human?

When you've allowed some impressions to surface sufficiently, begin writing. You can begin with description. Locate its unique hues. Aim for particularity. Don't settle for "red" or "purple." Precise descriptive diction grants your body part its deserved uniqueness. Then, explore its metaphorical reality. Fashion its shape in words by letting loose your childlike mind of associations and metaphors. Does it look like an animal? A thing? A place in nature or in a city? A type of building? A temple? A passageway? Sketch the scar—as it is or metaphorically. Find the shape in your subtle imagination that shows how the scar and its metaphor are one.

Starting with description lets you journal into your body without much emotional or intellectual complication. Your senses and imagination help you concentrate on your character's body as it is in the present. Then, you can move more comfortably into the trickier terrain of telling the stories related to the scar or body part.

Being open to wonder as you draft, heed any unexpected connections or telling images that might stand in for explicit analysis. You need not overanalyze. Be subtle by describing another story, artwork, fairy tale, or myth that might connect. If it applies unevenly, all the better. The comparison will potentially be even more particular. As you explore the story, be patient. Authentic writing and active compassion do not lead to simplistic forgiveness. They lead to acknowledging an incident in all of its complexities and trying to portray those complexities as truthfully as possible. Refrain from easy answers; aim for truthfulness.

CHAPTER EIGHTEEN

Compassion for Your Characters— the Good, the Bad, and the Downright Depraved

Some writers are goddesses and gods. Maybe I'm overstating the point. Granted, no photo of Balzac or Faulkner sits on my altar. It's not their aura or their magnum opus that inspires my awe. It's their capacity to characterize that makes them divine. Their ability to form authentic characters whose hearts and minds and bodies I otherwise would never inhabit puts them in the company of the androgynous figure Avalokiteshvara, which translates to "He (or She) Who Hears the Outcries (Sounds) of the World." So struck and moved by hearing and seeing humanity's cacophony of suffering, this essential Buddhist figure sprouted a thousand arms and hands—with an eye in each palm—to help not only hurting humans caught in their own hells, but suffering animals as well. You don't have to be Mother Teresa to write authentically (no doubt that a writer can appear gracious and loving in her pages and near depraved and loathsome in her daily interactions). Yet, ultimately, to sustain your practice of writing authentic fiction, nonfiction, or poetry, you can work to develop active compassion, *karunā*, for other beings, especially—and here's the kicker—for those "characters" who don't reciprocate your feelings, for those wholesome ones who just flat out get on your nerves, and for those characters whose very existence challenges your patience and desire to contain your judgment.

Ten years ago, I may not have understood how yoga could improve not only a writer's relationships with her mother but also her novel. But now I'm not surprised. One writer I met in a Yoga as

Muse workshop recently told me how she doesn't dread talking on the telephone to her mother anymore. "I actually try to listen to her." Dorie even tries to imagine what her mother is doing on the other end of the line—rubbing her stiff wrists, staring at the muted daily news that only heightens her fear of the world. Especially whenever Dorie's mother begins her harping song with the refrains about Dorie's failed marriage, her dead-end job, or her "wayward" twenty-something children, Dorie tries to feel the sensations in her mother's aching back from forty years of living on a farm in Maine with her husband, now dead, and her four sons and one daughter— or the algetic wrist and hip, broken from a recent fall off the front porch when a squirrel startled her. "Little my mother complains about really gets to me much anymore," Dorie said, "except when she starts in about how much weight I'm gaining. Then, I'm just ready to hang up." She laughs. "But I'm practicing, and it's helping me write my novel." The protagonist of Dorie's novel is based partially upon her mother.

Dorie trains her body and imagination to embody compassion while writing by harnessing her breath, setting an intention to nurture her compassion as a novelist, and moving through a series of simple poses designed to energize the heart region. "It's a way of training my unconscious while I write," she told me, a training she says helps her "crawl into the skin" of her often miserable yet endearing protagonist. As a result of Dorie's practice, several of her characters have become more rounded, her narrator's point of view more complicated, even unreliable in a way that has deepened the plot. She even feels more at ease when moving into emotionally charged scenes. The habit sounds simple—practice compassion— but any writer who has tried to extend compassion toward a character of fiction or nonfiction whom she deems difficult, even reprehensible, knows it's far from easy.

But a yoga practice has helped me, Dorie, and numerous other writers feel more versatile when portraying characters of any shade of personality. Patanjali's *Yoga-Sutra* I.33 speaks directly to this practice: "When you're friendly toward those who are happier than you, compassionate toward those who have so much pain they cannot extend compassion to you, joy toward those whose accomplishments exceed yours, and indifference to those who make mistakes, your mind becomes tranquil." Yes, and you merit sainthood, too, you're probably thinking. Yet if we wish to write authentic fiction, nonfiction, and poetry that informs our hearts of what it means to be human, we need to extend compassion not just to ourselves and to our own physical bodies—as we explored in previous chapters— but also toward those characters who live in suffering. Just as working with the heart region helps us view ourselves more complexly and with compassion, so our heart region and our imagination can guide us in literally embodying compassion for our characters, corrupt or charismatic.

Allow me a brief explanation. Our heart's power for us as writers may exceed the power of its metaphors and symbols, for current science validates yoga's ancient wisdom. Our hearts are wired with neural networks so complex that some people call the heart another brain.[1] Our nerve-charged hearts emit an electromagnetic field of energy—a literal domain of energy produced from and surrounding the heart. What's unusual about the heart's electromagnetic field is how far it reaches—fifteen feet or more. For instance, the heartbeat's waves can be graphed on a machine called an ECG (electrocardiograph) similar to how our brain's waves can be graphed on a machine called an EEG (electroencephalograph). Its charge apparently is so strong that an ECG placed within three feet of you can measure your heart's waves and energy field without being directly hooked up to your physical body. That is, your charged heart casts off energy around you. Literally. Your body inhabits that field. Literally.

The work of HeartMath Institute—a research center in Boulder Creek, California—has been verifying what yogis have been teaching for centuries: that when our thoughts correlate with our physical heart, we shift our physical energy. After thirty years of research, scientists at HeartMath have been helping people especially who suffer from anxiety by taking them through a simple process: When a person recognizes anxious thoughts surfacing, she shifts her mind's focus to the heart region, slows down her exhalations, and imagines a peaceful scene. Not only do such a person's brain waves, as measured by an EEG, slow down to the alpha-wave rhythms—the rhythms of one-pointed concentration as discussed earlier in this book—but the brain waves' graph also mirrors with startling similarity the heart waves' graph as measured on an ECG. The brain and the heart synchronize, and the person's anxiety dissipates as she or he feels not only more at ease but also more connected with all around her or him. It's no wonder that texts such as the *Shiva-Sutra* advise us that "when a person shifts her thoughts to the heart, she experiences unity" (1.15). In yogic terms, we take our attention as writers to the essential heart center, the *anāhata-cakra*.

So, it takes practice, but as writers we have the stuff of compassion and of powerful writing both within us and around us. I have met liberal-minded child beaters and women haters, conservative-minded pedophiles and prostitutes, corporate crooks and petty thieves, warmhearted hunters and cold-blooded vegans, heroin addicts and sex addicts, hypocritical priests and abusive gurus. They live in Dallas. They live in Woodstock. They live on Texas prairies, the Himalayan nooks, the Australian outback. Money-centered cities or art-centered towns, it doesn't matter. The human heart's shades and shadows live and move everywhere. And such is the stuff of good (or at least memorable and enlightening, though not necessarily enlightened) characters.

I agree with Faulkner: Give me a drunk, unreliable, unrepentant woman over a chaste one anytime. At least in literature. Faulkner says in his *Writers at Work* interview with *The Paris Review* that one of his favorite characters is Dickens's Sarah Gamp: "a drunkard, an opportunist, unreliable," he says, "most of her character was bad, but at least it was character." Indeed. So much so we call a person of such ill repute a "gamp" now in her honor. Think of the most powerful characters you've ever encountered. They're often ones who challenge your heart's boundaries. I prefer to read about corrupt characters over unblemished saints and gurus, not because I hover over the carcasses of the depraved but because literature, with less-than-perfect protagonists, often slyly expands my heart's walls to let these social orphans in to rest and chat a spell. Dostoyevsky's Raskolnikov, Nabokov's Humbert Humbert, Joyce Carol Oates's maniacal, sadistic surburban mothers, or Truman Capote's cold-blooded murderers—these characters' interior monologues and sordid acts take me into the oft-ignored crags of humanity's caves. While wedged like a spelunker in a writer's discomforting pages, I may have no choice but to see myself in the sharp-toothed stalagmites of a character's heinous deeds.

A couple of years ago, I was reading aloud to my wife Toni Morrison's first published novel, *The Bluest Eye*. The novel's opening descriptions prompt pity for the little girl Pecola, who desires to be everything that she is not: white and blond with blue eyes. The perspective of the novel's second section shifts, though, as we follow her father Cholly Breedlove's upbringing as he drifts from home to home, as white men humiliate him in his first sexual experience, as he attempts, despite his hard boyhood, to live as an adult in a romantically musical rhythm, and as he loses his music to marriage, daily drudgery, and drink. Once the reader has accepted Cholly into his heart, the story returns to his life as a father. As I read aloud to my wife the beginning of a pivotal scene between Cholly and Pecola in their kitchen, I paused and said, "I don't think I can read the next part aloud. I'm afraid I know what's about to happen." I had recalled a vague, brief reference in the book's opening pages to Pecola having her father's baby. Now, over 150 pages and a widened heart later, I read the next two pages, put the book and my head down, and just sighed, not knowing how I felt. Cholly raped his daughter. "He fucked her," Morrison writes. Anger, pity, confusion, swirled in my reader's heart. Pecola had entered my heart from the beginning, but by this scene so had Cholly. And he stayed there. The bastard stayed there.

Many characters enter and dwell in my heart not because I see myself as them, nor because I aspire to be like them, but simply because they are human, all too human.

Forget being a guru. Writers aren't gurus or preachers. *Guru* means "remover of darkness," whereas writers often bring us into the darkness of the human condition. Novelist Hubert Selby (author of *Last Exit to Brooklyn*) once told me that writers *must* embrace the darkness of their own hearts and of others' hearts. And once you move characters into the darkness, you don't necessarily lift them out of the inferno with some miraculous visit by an angel. Novelist Rosellen Brown has written about her bemusement not just with readers but with critics as well who expect some of her morally messy and confused characters to "lift themselves up" from their morass and make a tidy fablelike ending. About the characters she creates, Brown writes that, rather than make smooth-edged dolls, "if I let their texture stay rough and their responses danger-ously lifelike, I dare to think I might have resonant characters pocked and shadowed with complexity."[2] Without a willing under-standing of the human heart's frailties and complexities, we'll weave thin characters better left for Lifetime movies.

Of course, even good characters need our full compassion. If we're portraying otherwise noble characters, we must be willing to render their mistakes and wicked thoughts with as much compas-sion as when we handle their kindness and generosity. Too much goodness is as unbelievable as too much evil. Arthur Miller once said that we like characters such as the flawed John Proctor (the protagonist in his play *The Crucible*) because we can more readily identify with a blemished character than with a seemingly perfect one. Not to allow an otherwise admirable character to fail or have flaws is like insisting a spouse or child not have a misstep. If you're working with a character you like, you'll find out soon enough the nature, if not the names, of his blemishes. It's like falling in love with somebody. With time, he'll start irritating you with his limited perception of women or how trapped he is in identifying himself with his job or how he can't seem to follow an idea to its logical conclusion.

How do we come to this place of compassion in our bodies? How do we extend compassion to our characters? Practicing yoga can alter our writer's heart indelibly. By quietly awakening within us ancient memories of being unified with the universe, yoga gradu-ally rearranges how we view ourselves in relation to other people.

For the sake of contrast, try this. In a seated position, cross your arms and crouch forward, your midback arched. Note what it feels like to protect and to close your heart. Note what singular word or image surfaces that describes how writing from this position would feel. Then bring your arms out and either to the sides or all of the way behind you. What one word or image surfaces to describe how writing from this position would feel? Students often respond with words such as "locked versus free" or "crowded versus open" respec-tively. But others will respond with "safe versus vulnerable" or "pro-tected versus dangerous" to describe the same positions. Either response, of course, is valid, but it's a quick way to assess how you feel about living and writing with an open heart.

Another approach is to levy the judgment. Come into CRAMPED HEART POSITION again by crossing your arms and crouching forward, your midback arched. Note what it feels like to protect and to close your heart. Staying hunched over, close your eyes and imagine your heart as a shrinking room with walls closing in like a medieval dungeon. Feel the sensations of your heart shrinking. Is your breath skipping and constricting? Does your head hurt? Do you feel safe? Strong? Weak? See and feel the character or person enter this closed-in room, and notice how it feels when he or she enters. View the character through a one-way window as you preside over him or her like a chief judge. Let the walls continue to close enough to restrict most of her or his movement. As if through a sound system, levy all of your criticism and judgments on this character. Let loose your litany of admonitions and accusations. Don't hold back. When you're ready, write your judgment addressed to the character. Do you feel relief or even more tension in your body, mind, heart, and imagination? This practice usually brings mixed responses from writers. Some of them feel relieved; others feel drained. Writing from this place can be exhausting because we're fighting our characters, and it takes far more energy to write a novel or memoir in which we're full of rage and judgment than full of clear compassion.

So begin by acknowledging that every character suffers—even the seemingly cheery ones whose successes get on your nerves as much as the depraved ones who challenge our morality. *Dukha*, suffering, is a condition of having a vitiated heart, Bernard Bouanchaud notes in his commentaries of the *Yoga-Sutra*. Check into your character's suffering. Why does she suffer? What does she lack or think she lacks? What has happened to her, and how has she responded in such a way as to induce her own suffering? What is she attached to? How does it physically feel to inhabit his suffering body? As you begin to play out your character's actions, thoughts, and scenes with an open heart, you almost accidentally develop compassion for him. You will find that you have to let him do things that you wouldn't want him to do but he nonetheless must do and learn for himself. When we can begin to inhabit the hearts of our characters nonjudgmentally, when we can inhabit their painful, knotted bodies, hear their thoughts, and hear the world through their clouded ears, we are practicing one of a writer's most remarkable gifts: compassion.

If you're writing a memoir, you might have a greater challenge with these practices than do some fiction writers I know and have worked with. The people—often a difficult parent, a spouse or former partner—are too "real" and close to be imagined richly. One traditional meditation practice that works for such writers is, first, to imagine a dear friend or mother figure, someone who has nurtured you or been a source of selfless support. You imagine that person in your heart for several minutes. Then, you imagine the difficult or corrupt character—the mother or father, the former lover, abusive stranger—as that friend or mother figure in your heart. This step won't be easy for most of us, which is why it requires *practice*. Alice Walker wrote in a recent essay that a variation of this meditation—called *metta* (lovingkindness) meditation—sustained her not only through a divorce but also through writing three novels, including *The Color Purple* (a novel that portrays corrupt characters with far more compassion and complexity, incidentally, than does the movie version). Embodying compassion requires consistent effort if we genuinely wish it to emanate from us as we write (and live). The practice can help you begin to hear how this person views life, and perchance how he or she does in fact sustain and nourish you and others—or at least has the potential to do so, buried though it may be beneath years of soiled actions and intentions. Your job as a writer, quite often, is to explore and to uncover that potential, however slight it may be.

The interior monologue may be the best literary form to support this practice for writers of all genres. Not always a stream-of-consciousness form, an interior monologue is told from the character's first-person point of view. We the reader are privy to the character's thoughts, perceptions, conceptions, secrets, and longings. We see her own corner of reality as she rails to us against her pregnant daughter and the rest of the corrupted world or as he confesses to us his desires for the young girl down the road. Interior monologues provide structure for Faulkner's *As I Lay Dying*, James Kelman's Booker Prize–winning *How Late it Was, How Late*, and Kingsolver's

Poisonwood Bible. We respectively enter the bodies and minds of poor, perplexed Mississippians, a down-and-out and blind alcoholic in Scotland, and four girls and a mother from Georgia uprooted to Africa. Sandra Cisneros uses the form throughout much of the short story collection *Woman Hollering Creek.* The form invites us into the neighborhood mostly of Hispanic girls and women whose varied background and travails Cisneros renders with equal compassion. German Romantic author Friedrich Schiller wrote in 1801 that the person who lacks a full education of humanity's complexities "never sees others in himself, but only himself in others." Writing in the first-person interior monologue can educate you to bring those difficult others into your self.

If writing nonfiction, you also can experiment with the interior monologue. Tammy, one writer with whom I worked in Connecticut, took a risk when she extended compassion (for the first time, she said) to her mother. Tammy's working on a series of personal essays related to her family and to her history in the healing arts, yet each time she tries to write about her mother she finds her tone strained and point of view limited. We went through a process that allowed her to explore her mother's perspective and body, as well as to hear her mother's voice distinctly. Here's an excerpt from the interior monologue she drafted at the workshop:

> He's coming to see me and this sweet newborn baby clutched to my breast. Orange light bleeds through the hospital blinds onto my blankets. "When he comes we mustn't tell him." The newborn bundle of soft, pink, mottled flesh squirms closer to the smell of a full breast but doesn't answer. "If he knows the truth he won't come back for us," I whisper. Its forehead so smooth, its wisps of fine, black hair too. Will he notice? Will he mind? What if he says, "This baby doesn't look like me?" What will I say to him? It's 1962. I'm an independent woman. I'll be OK without a husband. Won't I? Oh, my body aches. Oh, God, this C-section wound, a gaping, stitched hole from my pubis to navel. Such a hole in me. He'll never know. But maybe the doctor knows. I wonder if he knows I'm a nurse. And that my breasts were firm and beautiful before this baby, before they were filled to exploding with milk that threatens to pull them

down to my knees. What if no one wants me ever again? What if I miss my chance and am alone now with my sagging breasts and this screaming baby. Why is she screaming? I raise the pillows and press the button for the nurse. Please God, someone, come and take this baby. She won't stop crying and my belly hurts and my breasts are leaking and where is my husband. Is anyone coming to see me?

Tammy's knowledge of her own birth to a woman who committed adultery provides the setting and inspiration, but her imagination and heart fuel the monologue. Placing the mother character in a specific situation anchored Tammy's imaginative compassion and allowed her to begin viewing a crucial situation from someone else's body, mind, and heart.

If you need inspiration from people less close than your family, take your practice away from the desk and mat. During the next week, become aware of strangers. Zero in on one person. Without stalking, watch him or her. If you're at a restaurant, note how he eats and speaks and twitches and laughs. If you're on the subway, note what she's wearing, what he's reading, how she smells (if you're that close). Record in your mind all of the facts. Then, when no one's looking, record in your notebook the facts and imagine the character. That is, without giving way to stereotypical assumptions, imagine the person's name, her earliest memory, his deepest desire, her most relished secret, where he has a tattoo, her most reviled song, what he says when he talks to himself. The Lakota tribe has a saying that has kept me in good stead for years: Imagine your life richly. Give it a twist: Imagine a stranger's life richly. You could develop worse habits.

Sing the unloved's song. Rilke wrote a series of song-poems, each from the point of view of society's downtrodden—a fool, a drunkard, a prostitute. Like an Emile Zola novel, these songs of the destitute offer truthful, endearing glimpses of how certain members of our society might feel and think. Edgar Lee Masters's *Spoon River Anthology* is a more benign collection of poems, each told from the point of view of a town's deceased citizen looking back on his or her life. W. D. Snodgrass took a bold leap of compassion when in his book *Füehrer Bunker* he wrote a series of poems from the perspectives of various well-known Nazis, including Eva Braun, Hitler's mistress. So, try to sing the unloved's song. Whether the unloved be a misunderstood relative, a despised politician, or a mother who drowned her children, write a poem or prose piece from her or his perspective. Tell us about the objects that matter most to her, find and repeat the refrain that defines his way of life, reveal her deepest longings, expose her secrets that help us understand her. Avoid sentimentality. Be ruthless if you think the person may be ruthless with herself. Be actively compassionate, not sweet. Play with whether the person's "song" would be composed in rhyme, in couplets, in chaotic and uneven lines, or in a prose poem. Let the form, in other words, reflect the person. Such an act of writing is an act of *karunā*.

For the writer, isolated, self-consuming and self-consumed, her work can be imprisoned and imprisoning. When work flows, though, from a source of love, when it unites with what we love, when work *is* love, then our hands come together. They celebrate, reach out, and applaud humanity for all of its frailty, strength, and victory.

$\mathcal{T}$AKE A BREATH: REACH OUT

INTENTION:
This practice can increase awareness of your heart center so you can write from your heart (without being effusive or maudlin). It also can help you begin to pay attention to what subjects need your compassion as a writer.

Rest on your back in **CORPSE POSE** *(savāsana). Lift your arms straight overhead while keeping your shoulders secured in their joints. Spread your fingers and face your palms toward the ceiling. Let your in-breath fill your heart space and expand your rib cage's bars. Close your eyes and follow the exhalation from your heart and out your arms and fingers. Inhale as you cross your arms and bring your hands to the backs of the opposite shoulders so you hug yourself. From here, breathe into the back of your heart space and between your shoulder blades. Inhale, bringing your arms and palms up again toward the ceiling. As your breath* coats your heart, imagine the subjects you wish and need to reach out to in your writing. Is someone calling you to listen? To what creatures, person, or group of people do you need to open your writer's heart? Exhale as you bring your arms down their respective sides and let your heart space open. Note how receptive you are in this position, as if you could take in all that calls your heart to hear. If something or someone especially is calling, then respond in writing for a page or more.

$\mathcal{T}$AKE A BREATH:
MAKE ROOM FOR THE DIFFICULT

INTENTION:
This practice helps you imagine and embody
a difficult character.

If possible, kneel in ADAMANTINE POSE (vajrāsana), and let the tops of your feet and your shins sink toward the floor. Several writers prefer to place a folded blanket between their calves and thighs in this pose. Otherwise, review the Appendix to come to a seated pose of your choice. With a firm connection to the ground, take at least two full breaths. When ready, establish your twofold intention by asking yourself, "What am I writing for?" Inhale the response up into your heart space. Then, clarify your intention to imagine and to embody a difficult character.

Eyes closed, see this character or person in a situation (imagined or remembered). Take a few minutes to draw your attention to your heart space as you recall from your physical or subtle imagination the details of the scene as if they were recurring in your heart. See the room's surroundings if it's an interior space. Notice the air's texture. Scan the character's body from crown to feet. Notice what truly unique features this character's body possesses.

Keeping your eyes closed, inhale deeply into your heart space. With each inhalation, imagine your heart's walls begin to loosen. Move the walls back. On an inhalation, lift your arms straight out in front of you and then to the sides in EVEN-HEARTED MOUNTAIN POSE (sama-hyridaya-tādāsana). Feel the hands reach out as you discover what this character wants. Try to articulate what this deep want is and how his or her body reflects that want.

Move your arms into OPEN-HEARTED MOUNTAIN POSE (hridaya-tadasana) by bringing your arms behind your back and try to bring your palms toward one another and straighten your arms as you lift your hands toward the ceiling. Open your heart and face toward the ceiling. Take three to five full breaths and release. Repeat three times, each time imagining your heart's walls making room for this difficult character or person. On the third time, see your heart's walls open even as your heart's room expands three, four, or more feet beyond your body.

On an inhalation, cross your arms and hug yourself. In this pose, begin to embody this character and begin to see the scenery from the character's point of view. How does this body feel? How does it move in this scene? How does this body help or hinder the character in getting what he or she wants?

Come out of the pose and rest on your back in CORPSE POSE (savāsana). Then listen. What does she or he have to say? Let the unique timbre and music of the voice strike your heart's unstruck cord, your anāhata. What is she thinking? How do his thought patterns flow or skip? What images keep surfacing, haunting, or soothing?

Then, write. With sensuous imagery and particularity, describe the scene from the person or character's point of view. Try to capture his or her unique way of speaking, the colloquialisms, the rhythms, the favorite words. Don't let the character reveal everything to your readers all at once. What we explored about dialogue's ability to reveal earlier in this book applies as well to interior monologues. Continue to be surprised as you write, and refrain from betraying your own judgments of the character's actions or personality. Aim to take your reader somewhere new—into this character's head, heart, and body.

CHAPTER NINETEEN

Converting Anger into
Authentic Writing

Yogi and Buddhist Sylvia Boorstein once said that practicing compassion never means that we can't be angry. Since you're a human being and writer with convictions, surely there's some human behavior that rankles your skin and sends your sweetness bones packing for a while. My writing students are often angry. War rumbles on, jobs evaporate, Americans sleepwalk—these are common litanies I hear. Because I practice and teach yoga, students sometimes cower when I press them more on what ticks them off as if I think "anger is bad, bad, bad."

"Good for you for being mad," I tell them. "You have convictions. Something matters to you." Then they'll blush and mutter some neorelativist apology of "Well, I'm not perfect either, but, but." Of course you're not perfect, and it's just this falling short of perfection that so outrages us sometimes. So once they get over the common discomfort of actually acknowledging they're angry, we talk about satire. I spent, or misspent, my youth on *Mad* magazine, *Monty Python*, and Mark Twain. When I was sixteen, awakening to human beings' utter contradictions and hypocrisies, I thrived on sarcasm, puns, innuendoes, subtle put-downs, and sheer fabrications and distortions of the facts. Satire gave me and my friends soft armor to wear in a world we found increasingly strange, unreliable, and hostile.

Satire lets us convert anger into authentic writing. Some variation of anger—a feeling of injustice, righteous indignation, disgust, or contempt toward some facet of humanity—fans the fire of many inflammatory satirists. Satire is criticism driven most often by wit that can form a whole piece or can serve part of larger work. And hypocrisy and ignorance remain its two most common subjects (we seem to provide one another with endless amounts of material). Some of yoga's practices and principles not only can help you confront and convert that anger; they also can keep your satire from becoming mean-spirited sarcasm.

Before we explore satire, consider the other options of "working" with anger: letting it fly or ignoring it. You probably sense or know what anger does to your body. We tag habitually angry people as "tightly wound" for a reason. Anger signals the sympathetic nervous system to stimulate the adrenal gland, which releases adrenaline and cortisol, which in turn constrict muscles, especially in the stomach, shoulders, neck, and jaw—all places where our bodies prepare the troops for defense or attack. Our bodies, from our midriff to our neck, tighten. This hormone release and muscle constriction shortens our breath and flushes our flesh. No coincidence that the English word *anger* is kin to the Old English *enge*, "to narrow" and, more tellingly, to the Latin *angere*, "to strangle." Habitual anger narrows our arteries and chokes our voice. And the mind on anger? "The mind is its own place, and in itself/Can make a Heaven of Hell, a Hell of Heaven," John Milton wrote in *Paradise Lost*. No wonder, then, that numerous yogic texts deem anger (*krodha*) as one of hell's main gates (meaning one's mental hell and not a steamy underground club where the morally decadent are locked in and subjected to AC/DC perennially playing "Hell's Bells"). *Krodha*, anger, especially excessive and chronic anger, no doubt obstructs concentration and thus meditation. When boiling mad, we can't think straight. Or think at all. We become disoriented and confused. We lose our way.

Writing with rage, anger's most extreme mask, often leads to incoherent rants that, we usually hope, we don't have the foolhardiness to submit for publication even if to our loved one's collection of personal notes. Like fury, rage sends us over the top, over the edge, down into our darkest lair where who knows what creatures will come out in our full-moon midnights. We become traffic vigilantes. We toss our spouse's strewn dirty clothes into the street. We are "mad," indeed. With anger so deeply embedded, a writer likely will have difficulty breaking this broncolike emotion into artful writing.

But suppressing the demon altogether only irritates it. Left unattended, this volatile emotion can creep through the body like a dangerous imp, playing tricks in the house of the culprit's mind. You can stew and steam, releasing your frightful diatribes about the woes of humanity only occasionally as you drive your children to school. Or you may sense you're enraged at something or someone but cannot name the target, much less aim accurately. Writing done with repressed anger can become distorted and manipulative, the demon disguising the intention.

So, authentic writing isn't necessarily about just venting steam to make ourselves feel better while everyone else around us feels drenched and beaten from our hurricane release, nor is it about keeping our polite mouths shut when we know something's wrong and unjust, if not absurd. Authentic writing includes identifying the level of our anger, finding the broad target of our anger, and finding the most effective way to transform that anger into art.

Satire is a middle way between diatribe and repression.

With satire, there are no sacred cows—not even in India or in yoga. Yoga helps us embrace life's paradoxes. Indeed. "To create a new self, we must destroy an old one." "Soaring requires rootedness." "You have to heat up to enjoy cooling down." A shrewd yoga teacher I used to know was always espousing these kinds of aphorisms that, if he were on a roll, could lead to a brain-numbing homily. His hair casting an aniline sheen, he was noble in a creepy sort of way and so earnest, if not smarmy, that he could've moonlighted by selling stolen Bibles to widows (especially attractive widows). This guy had special powers, all right. He'd waltz into class wearing all white, waving his wand of incense, his supercilious eyes half-hidden by his eyelids, a gesture that assured us of his spiritually superior serenity.

Then, this New Age Elmer Gantry would wrap his legs in lotus, glance around the room, and land his eyes on a young female student dutifully clad in her minimalist yoga gear. ("Less is more," I think was another of his mantras. What a wit this guy was.) While the student would swoon and blush beneath his gaze, he would say, his voice echoing through the studio like that of Shiva himself, some pearls of wisdom such as "Yoga is about divine union, about the feminine and the masculine merging together in ecstasy." In the same breath in which he would pronounce to us the virtues of chaste thought and action, he would add that, however, if you just so happened to meet an advanced yogi, then you could take a leap of, say, seven years of spiritual training by making love to such a teacher. Seven years of spiritual training in a torrid hour—now, *there's* a salesman. By the end of class, he'd have the student's phone number for, I'm sure, a private session of spiritual leapfrog. He was always making generous gestures like that with his time and energy. You know, he doesn't *have* to give those privates, as one student reminded me when I suggested possible impropriety. Yeah, I'd never thought of it that way. What magnanimity.

So, here's where students become really uneasy when we talk about satire. They realize that not only are they going to acknowledge and convert their anger, but they're also going to offend someone (a usual sign of successful satire). Yet, once they get started on listing what bugs them in this world, their fears for a while disappear, and I have to interrupt the rants of those very students who previously seemed to be the most reticent mice before their red eyes pop out.

Satire's angry voices often rise out of irritation or indignation. Irritation scratches our back the wrong way. To be vexed or irked is more like "pre-anger," a prelude to the big acts. So during the next week, track what bugs you. Slow drivers, fast drivers, messy people, tidy people, weather changes that foil our plans and parades, smug people, shy people, misbehaving children (someone else's, of course), misbehaving computers (your own, of course), or anything that disrupts our creative flow can nettle us. List at least ten human behaviors or societal trends that irritate you. Refrain from limiting your focus to just one person—such as a roommate, family member, or politician. Instead, focus on the behavior that can be generalized. For instance, if your husband drives you bonkers when he circles a packed parking lot for five minutes to wait for a spot near the store to open, use your husband as an example of the larger human behavior (because your husband isn't the only one with this peculiar condition). From your list, choose a topic that really rouses your ire but also seems like fun to explore.

If you're not merely irritated but indignant, your target may supersede your personal irritations or neuroses. The rage is "out" of and beyond your self; it is outrage, not inrage. Emotions of injustice, unfairness, or shamefulness on a personal, social, or political level fuel this potent writing. Say, hypothetically, if when unwarranted war is on the brink of breaking out and only one lone bird among a democracy's senators sings out with eloquent indignation and only a few writers can muster the wits and time and wherewithal to be heard, then you may be alarmed and indignant. (Just to give a hypothetical.) A few students have a harder time with this list because they realize a moral judgment against one or another sort of behavior is inherent in the majority of these topics. Yet, most of us have a gnawing feeling that something is not right in the world, that some imbalance and injustice does exist that genuinely bothers us. All-too-human enough to be shaken from our own bliss, we're sensitive to others' suffering. We even grieve. For the English *anger* also comes from the Old Norse word *angr*, "grief." Don't be afraid to touch even what's most sacred to you and most taboo to others to criticize.

These topics aren't easy to acknowledge or to explore. Yoga *āsana* and *prāṇāyāma*, though, provide ways to do so. If you drop and circle your lower jaw, you'll probably notice by the degree of your jaw's tightness whether or not you clench your teeth, an indicator of unconscious anger and tension. Your neck muscles, directly influenced by the jaw, also betray where we ball up. Drop attention a little lower to your chest. There, around our heart, because of restricted breathing that anger induces, we store quite a bit of frustration. So, poses that help stretch and open up these areas can work like release valves that both relieve and frighten students because we don't always realize just how much anger inhabits our bodies. Yoga students have broken out in tears while practicing back bends—poses that, because of how they open the thoracic spine and chest area, could be called "heart openers." Often, these tears are mixed with anger, confusion, and relief. With an ongoing practice, though, of *āsana* and *prāṇāyāma*, you can learn to identify your anger and convert it into something else rather than let it dictate your thoughts and reactions. Your body becomes an ally in greater self-understanding, an aid in any writing but especially in a form as potentially tricky as satire.

Once you've acknowledged and chosen a subject, you then can choose an existing form to buttress your satire. Eulogies, for one. Or obituaries. Ellen Goodman writes a clever mock eulogy and mock obituary of "The Company Man," a generic EveryBusinessMan who forfeited everything else in his life—his marriage, his children, his friends—to be loyal to his company, which, in the end, merely saw him as a well-behaved cog. Goodman assumes the somber tone and journalistic format of an obituary so convincingly, peppering it with just the right details and fabricated dialogue, that she will fool any careless reader who may see merit in such corporate sacrifice. Imagine that an imaginary person who embodies your wrath's target has died. How would you sum up the quality of that life? What legacy? Have at it.

You also can don a mask. Assume the perspective of the very group of people whose behavior you loathe or at least deem morally repugnant. Crawl into the skin of one of them, and talk from that person's point of view (while, of course, revealing that point of view's inanity, as you see it). It's a frightening prospect, isn't it? Imagine how it would feel to spoof Hitler in his own words. Or the white guy in Texas who dragged the African-American man James Byrd behind his pickup. You can see the risk. Not only might your thought patterns, sentences, and images—in short, your "voice"— get confused with a bigot, serial killer, corporate bamboozler, war propandist, or whoever your target may be. Your greatest challenge is to strike the right tone that communicates to your audience your intent—namely to show the idiocy, absurdity, or moral depravity of whoever's belief system or worldview you're mimicking. With the wrong tone, your readers will think you're coarse, insensitive, or brutish (when in fact these may be the very qualities you're aiming to expose). So, take a risk, but you don't have to begin by crawling into the skin of the world's Louis Farrakhans or David Dukes.

Start with a group of people more benign. Like the jaded privileged youth who like to "slum" by doing "working-class" things. This group is loosely the focus of the persona monologue of "I'll Try Anything with a Detached Air of Superiority," written by the staff of the satirical magazine *The Onion*. The title sums up this twenty-something group's "philosophy." Beginning with "I'm a pretty

sophisticated, well-educated person," it details for us how she (I assume for some reason it's a she but could easily be a he) ventures to
bowling parties, professional football games, and even rummage
sales to whoop it up among the hoi polloi—but always with bemusement, as if the working class are a novelty, like someone from
another nationality on exhibit. Her attempts to analyze herself and
to poise herself as having a sophisticated sensibility are summed up
in these lines toward the end: "If you can do such things and still
maintain your sense of haughty superiority, you've done more than
merely lived. You've tasted the sickly sweet nectar that life has to
offer and said, 'I am above this. I am better than this. This is beneath me, but I will still do it because I'm open minded enough to
try anything and look down my nose at it at least once.' "[1] I can
hear a grating pseudo–Boston Brahmin tone trying to cover an
otherwise snotty little-girl voice that rationalizes and self-promotes
her daring "class adventures." People with this attitude may irk you,
but this piece at least may help you laugh, if only with scorn.

So your persona can be a caricature voice representative of a
loathsome group, or it can be a mockery of a single person's voice.
It can appear in your fiction, nonfiction, or poetry—no matter. Let's
say, hypothetically, there was a high public political figure whose
grammar and diction sounded embarrassingly like that of a fourth-
grader whose views on family, work, and foreign policy have been
steeped on Dynasty and The A-Team. Let's say that same figure tried
to deflect criticism of his (or her!) illiteracy. It wouldn't be difficult
for you to invent a line this person might say such as "I know there
are lots of people out there that value intellectuables and say I use
malapropoisms. But I really see, don't see, the connection between
having a big vocation—er, vacation, uh, vocabulary—and my job."
Can you imagine such a person?

Then try looking at yourself. Dave Eggers, Nick Hornby, Neal
Pollack, and possibly self-deprecating jokesters such as David
Sedaris and David Rakoff are Ironic Young Men (or Ironic Johns,
not to be confused with Robert Bly) who have roughed up this
country's pages and airwaves with their bald, edgy wit. Having mastered the personal narrative form in fiction and nonfiction, they take
as their targets their closest friends, relatives, and—a key trait—
themselves. If these writers are angry at anything, it's people who

take themselves too seriously. Dave Eggers—whose *A Heartbreaking Work of Staggering Genius* mocked almost every facet of the ever-popular memoir while still telling a story full of pathos—has a mission to slaughter every grazing sacred cow among the literati while still poking fun at his own ambitions. If uneasy with piercing others' egos, start with your own. Come on. You have at least a tad of self-importance worth pricking.

Your other risk in all satire—far more common, unfortunately, than a writer's misstep—is poor reading. Many readers, especially of the self-important sort, just don't get irony, wit, and satire. A high school teacher told me that some of her students still get up in arms over Jonathan Swift's "A Modest Proposal." One student wrote her a sincere note saying that, in essence, "during these times when reports of child abuse have risen, I don't think we should be reading something, no matter how historically relevant, that advocates eating babies." Such misreading cost a former Dallas newspaper columnist his job in the 1980s when he wrote a spoof on the song "We are the World," the popular song, most of whose proceeds went to help starving children, sung by a medley of rock stars. Among the do-good celebs were Michael Jackson, Cyndi Lauper, and Bob Dylan. The journalist's piece poked fun of the celebrities' personal quirks and pretensions, but several readers took umbrage because they considered the project too earnest. When the writer refused to apologize, since he was spoofing the song, not being serious, he resigned.

To avoid this sort of misreading, clue your readers in with your language. Sure, you can begin with the mock-formal tone of a scholar examining the cultural phenomenon of increasingly stupider television shows being viewed (and written) by people with college degrees, or of a scientist reviewing a study of a new epidemic of cultural amnesia, or of an anthropologist observing, say, a tribe of the CowHomeBoys, those white adolescent males from predominantly rural and suburban neighborhoods who feel like they're living on the edge by wearing hooded sweatshirts, putting a Band-Aid on their nose, and blurting lines to each other they've snagged from rap music. But then have some fun with your tongue. Exaggerate to the point of near-absurdity that pushes your readers almost to the point of disbelief. Pun if it fits. Mix in unabashed metaphors that zap the target with plain language, or pepper in words my mother would deem "from the sewer" with *le mot juste*. In satire, you can have a tossed salad of tones and diction levels, but be ready to give your readers more than a few leaves of iceberg lettuce and some tomato slices dressed in French. Trust that your readers will have more taste and will be surprisingly satiated by your tongue-tickling wordplay. Such play should remind most careful readers that at least to some extent, despite an authentic intention, your tongue is in your cheek.

When writing satire, it's essential to be clear about your intention. Satire, perhaps more than other kinds of writing, is distinguished by intention (although some of the young Ironist Johns love to mix intentions and keep you guessing at every sentence). Simple sarcasm intends to hurt, burn, or tear down a target rather than to provoke someone. Likewise, humor alone aims to entertain and not to provoke. Perhaps it helps you to consider how you want your readers to respond. If you wish them to wince at your words' force and then to loathe the target, then you may be writing something critical but not satirical. If you want your words to make your readers chuckle without the least bit of resistance or disturbance, then comedy may be your métier. But if you want your readers to laugh with a bit of dissonance, either from seeing themselves in your subject or from having their moral birdcage rattled, then your intent is satire. And what the self-deprecating Dorothy Parker says of wit applies to satire (which was her intended application): "Wit has truth in it; wisecracking is simply calisthenics with words." So when you sense something in your writing sounds cruel, remind yourself of your intention. Ask yourself what truth you're trying to reveal (and what falsehood to lay bare).

Hate alone doesn't drive satire, but don't discount its force. Now, you may think this talk of hatred very unyogilike. Not so. Remember our earlier discussion about paradox? Try this one: Intense hatred of God can liberate you. At least according to one interpretation of a legend from an ancient yoga text called the *Bhagavata-Purana*. According to one account of the legend, a king named Shushupala so despised the god Visnu that he ultimately merged with Visnu. His utter hatred for the god worked on his mind like a meditation; because he thought so much of Visnu in his hatred, he united with the divine. There is an obscure and controversial practice, then, called "yoga of hatred" (*dvesha-yoga*), in which a practitioner learns to fear the divine by having an impassioned hatred for the divine. The awe-inspiring emotions prompt a blissful union.

So be careful what you hate. You just might actually hate it enough to merge with it. For instance, a certain political figure toward whom I occasionally harbor animosity reappears in my dreams. In my waking life, my tongue can't stop lashing this easy target for my own "unresolved" hostility toward arrogant, ignorant people with too much power. At night, though, my unconscious is telling me something else. In one dream, the former governor ran into my house to warn me of an army of tornadoes headed my way. I was annoyed, yet surprised, even thankful. A year ago, I dreamt I worked for this same politician, who is now in a higher office, as one of his most respected writers and advisors. In the dream, I fell out of his favor although I deeply desired to please the head honcho. The big boss also recently helped me cross a street in New York City. Amid the city squalor, we chatted about the weather, our families, our mutual friends. The sunlight glowed behind his head. I smiled. I was quite sure that if he asked me to have a beer while we chatted about foreign policy, I'd join him. We'd become buddies. The dreams keep mixing up my feelings. In my waking life, he's my enemy; in my dream life, he's my ally. Do I detest him or love him? Is there something in him in me? If you can become what you hate, I expect to wake up one morning in his body in his bed beside his wife. I shall smile at her and recite a poem by Walt Whitman or Sam Hamill, and then I'll prepare for a press conference about bombs made of poems, poem-bombs that will explode with metaphors and music, will be dropped on the capital of a nation whose leader threatens to stifle his people's imaginative freedom. United we dream. There's an essay brewing there that I haven't dared to write yet.

What we writers hate and what we love with fervor are often the same. And most of us know that quite often the target of our love is also the target of our anger, as our lovers and spouses can attest. But becoming acquainted with our hatred and anger helps us as writers to know our intentions for writing pieces fueled by such fire. More than anger, hatred is easy to deny. Don't gloat in cruel hatred, but at least acknowledge what in this world you genuinely despise personally, politically, spiritually, socially. Words you abhor. Textures you hate. People's behavior. Kinds of people, if you dare admit it. Experiences. Trends. Films. Songs. Perhaps in the delight of writing about what you hate, you'll come to love some of it.

To dare to write satire is, finally, dare I say it, an act of compassion. It's better to acknowledge, shape, and communicate these feelings than to stay muzzled in a room all your own. Not just because writing satire's healthy for you. It's healthy for all of us. Writing satire implies you still have hope. You're putting it out there because you sense it might provoke people to think, maybe even change their attitudes or behavior. It implies you believe in your convictions, your voice, your wit, and wit helps us cope. When we express anger with wit, laughter relaxes tight jaws and necks as well as mutes anger's shout.

Throughout parts of India, yogis called "crazy adepts" engage the full spectrum of human beings' emotional life. On cue, they can weep or guffaw, act horny or prudish, tremble and cower or stand tall with puffed chest. As people—even gurus—try to continue with their serious business, these clowns mock them. At the most serious sacred ceremonies, people laugh. Such double-sided consciousness embodies the seriousness of laughter that satire prompts. These crazy adepts—not unlike Hopi clowns or Buddhist clowns or satirists—remind us of our foibles and foolishness.

Learn to be a crazy adept writer. Crazy adept writers understand the unwieldy nature of their emotional demons and learn how to shape these emotions artfully. Crazy adepts also risk looking like fools. Anne Sexton once wrote, "As a writer one has to take the chance of being a fool. That perhaps requires the greatest courage." I love that. And respect it.

ᴛAKE A BREATH

INTENTION:
Focus upon some human behavior that makes you irritated or indignant. This practice can help you raise your anger to the surface so you can move it to witty writing.

Begin in **MOUNTAIN POSE** (tadāsana). *Stand approximately six to eight inches away from a wall. Once you've taken at least two complete breaths, ask yourself, "What am I writing for?" The response can be revealing, particularly when working with satire for the first time. Then specify that for this session you aim to begin a draft of a satirical piece or section of a piece.*

When ready, inhale and lift your arms out to each side into **EVEN-HEARTED POSE** (sama-hridayāsana), *arms straight and with your fingers folded inward and your thumbs stretched up and back. Follow this movement: Exhale, thumbs forward. Inhale, thumbs up. Exhale, thumbs backward. Inhale, thumbs up. Repeat. And repeat. And repeat. For at least five minutes. Yes, five. You should feel irritation in your neck and shoulders. This variation of a practice common among kundalini practitioners I find remarkably irritating—which is part of its alchemical work.*

Then, still standing six to eight inches away from a wall, with a lengthened torso, inhale and stretch your arms straight overhead and back, arching your back and bringing your fingertips to the wall. Keep your hips forward. Exhale and return to **MOUNTAIN POSE**. *Repeat. As you bring your fingertips to the wall, keep your hips over your ankles so your midback will bend and your chest will open. If you're more flexible, you can move your heels farther away from the wall. If you're not feeling any pain, repeat three more times and then remain with your fingertips at the wall and lift your heart toward the ceiling.*

Finally, take your hands to your hips and keep your heart open. Take a deep inhalation, and on each of your next two exhalations, extend your tongue out toward your chin as far as it will reach, direct your eyes upward, and from your feet and root center upward roar out an "AHH" as loud as you can, letting your grief or irritation or anger vibrate through your body, across the room, and off of the nearest mountain. (See photograph of Soaring Lock pose front view in the Appendix). This isn't a variation of Reichian therapy. It's a way to rouse your throat center, to relieve your neck and jaws of tension, and to laugh at yourself. Did you look at yourself in the mirror? Did you hear yourself?

Write with your whole body. With vibrations still moving through your neck, chest, and back, begin writing when you're ready. Your narrator might begin with a description of physical sensations and then move outward to the subject of your ire. The words might lead your narrator to a memory, an incident, an image. Begin playfully describing someone behaving the way that irritates you. What you write may come from an actual memory or a hypothetical incident. Begin with the specific and then follow the specific to a general humorous essay about this irritation or indignation. Notice if with irritated jaws and shoulders your syntax seems jumpy, your imagination slightly skewed if not wicked. Have fun with this piece and assume, like a crazy adept, a different tone or persona if you're not accustomed to voicing your irritation. Gradually, you'll discover a point, a focus, maybe even a humorous solution that will help you revise the piece if you wish. But as you write, enjoy riding the passion of your contempt. Write with a strong spine.

IV.
LOOKING BACK AND LOOKING FORWARD

CHAPTER TWENTY

Eating Leaves and Other Ways to Re-vision for Form

When Dianne Ackerman describes her first flight lesson, she relates it to our human longing to step back and to see the earth as a whole, how rivers feed into oceans, how factories and mountains feed into rivers. The same is true for writers. You learn to dwell well in the details, but you also want to be able to step back and look at a whole piece of your writing as if looking at a meadow from a hilltop, to see how one section relates to, feeds into, plays off of, another and how a poem's stanzas, a story's scenes, a book's chapters, may need resequencing. This ability to envision a piece of writing as a whole and to rework it accordingly with both intuition and analysis is to re-vision, an awkward verb form I prefer to distinguish it from the more particular and minute steps of revising. To re-vision well, we should consider the nature of form. Without form, Flaubert said, there is no art.

Everything—be it a sonnet, a sonata, a sentence, a snowflake, a baseball pitch, a memorable kiss—has a form. Even oak tree leaves, each of which may come from the same tree, have a beautiful, distinct form. Generally, the leaves' shapes, like the shapes of human bodies, appear the same, uniform. Yet, within each leaf resides a slightly distinct pattern.

Such is true, too, of yoga *āsanas*—perhaps the most recognizable aspect of yoga in the West. In fact, when most people in the United States say they "practice yoga," they mean they practice the physical forms. Some of my yoga students come to class thinking that each pose has a Form, some Platonic ideal toward which each of us with a serious practice must and should strive. Undoubtedly certain universal principles exist for aligning the spine in each pose that help us practice with safety and depth, and undoubtedly it's beautiful to watch a veteran yogi flow from one exquisite pose to the next. Yet, we can deepen our experience with yoga if we realize that each person—whose physical temple has a different history, shape, and internal working—need not strike a pose exactly the same as everyone else's. We can appreciate tradition's forms without being stifled by uniformity or conformity.

A yoga pose is also a form, a *rūpa* in Sanskrit. *Rūpa* refers not only to the body and to physical beauty, but also to a physical "sign," that is, a sort of message from the gods. An authentic yoga pose stems from a yogi's genuine intention as well as from the yogi finding the organic variation of the pose that suits his or her body at the time of practice. By "organic," I mean that the pose may be fluid instead of static; it should feel natural and *com*posed, not *im*posed. There's also something beautiful in watching a beginner find her own variation of a pose that suits her body and spirit for any given time.

So it goes with writing and learning to re-vision. With a genuine intention, we let a form, at once fluid and organic, emerge from the needs of any given writing at any given time. For the form of a story, essay, or poem can be rigid, simplistic, and predictable, or it can be elegant, intricate, subtle, and unique. At a superficial glance, many complex texts may appear to possess similar external structures or no artful structure whatsoever; yet, they often embody unique shapes whose intricacies—whose *inner* form—escape the untrained eye, mind, and imagination.

If we've become lost in our first drafts (which, ideally, I think we should) and even in our second, third, fourth, and fifth drafts, at some point we need to step back and view our writing from afar. How do we see a piece as a whole, and how do we begin to re-vision? Since an organic form feels alive, not static, first, think about your piece's movement. In *The Essay: Theory and Pedagogy for an Active Form*, Paul Heilker of Virginia Tech reminds us of the authentic essay's "kinetic" form. To write an essay, Heilker notes, is to be in perpetual motion like that of a dancer or a golfer's swing (or, I should add, a yogi's flow): "[T]he essay is kineticism incarnate—the embodiment of perpetual mobility, motion, and movement."[1] The same is true, though, of a charged poem or story. Our ideas, images, and words carry us (and the reader) through the piece with some anticipation and exhilaration that we don't always know where we're going next, and yet we sense that when the piece is complete it is a beautiful whole, however rough or loose its edges.

One key to considering movement is the reader's experience. Although we sense what we like in what we read, sometimes we can't put our finger on why one book works magic on us and another flops. Much of the magic on the reader has to do with movement, how a piece shifts, progresses, shimmies, surprises, weaves, and destroys along the way. Form shapes much of how readers experience a text, and readers' experiences with texts—their surprises, their predictions, their connection making, their emotional shifts—often help determine whether or not a text is effective (that is, whether or not a text "affects" readers). How does a piece move a reader's intellect, heart, and/or imagination? Amateur writers rarely think about the reader's experience. Their writing is for themselves, and they think they'll tarnish some "pure experience" of writing by reworking it. Yet, it takes a lot of rewriting to make a piece appear natural. Several writers I know and respect draft for themselves and re-vision and revise for their readers' experience. This re-visioning, then, can be a joyous way of giving to our readers something exquisite and well crafted that still has the feel of being organic.

Take a piece of your writing and think about its beginning, middle, and end. With my students, we get out our drafts, reread them to ourselves, and then read them to one or two other people in class, and consider these matters.

Beginnings: A beginning should be an entryway at once compelling enough for the reader to enter and subtle enough for the careful reader later to learn just why that beginning was so appropriate. When Hemingway showed Fitzgerald one of his early drafts of what became *The Sun Also Rises*, Fitzgerald recommended he cut the first forty thousand words, which mostly provided exposition related to Jake Barnes's experiences in World War I, and begin the story in the fictional present in Paris. Hemingway took his advice, and the novel catapulted Hemingway into fame as literature's new golden boy of the 1920s. Notice if you're beginning in a safe and dull place, or if you're starting a poem, scene, or chapter with a reliable "trick" you learned years ago in a writing workshop. Maybe in your first two or four pages you're warming up your engine and don't get going until page five. Scrap the first four pages. A friend of mine poured out his soul to write his first novel, some six hundred–plus pages. His agent told him that in six hundred pages he basically had an excellent twelve-page short story. My friend pulled the best part of the manuscript and burned the rest.

Middles: Your middle shouldn't idle; it should keep your reader revved. A sign of a dull middle is if you're staying methodically on subject and on schedule. Notice if you're halfway through and you haven't been surprised once by anything that's surfaced in your imagination or language. If you're falling asleep as you read what you've written, imagine how your readers will respond. Or maybe you're holding your breath because you're writing so rapidly just to get finished. The other extreme may be that you've digressed so much and gotten so lost that the piece's energy and movement are too scattered to sustain even the most patient reader's attention.

Endings: Beware if you wrap up everything in floral designed paper, if you force your characters to make up, if the sun always comes out. Or maybe you don your philosopher-theologian hat with the equivalent of a two-page appendix that explains your clever symbolism. (I actually heard a writer at a reading take pains to interpret all of his poem's symbols.) Not every loose end has to be tied, not every symbol explicated. For the tragic-minded fiction writers, beware of killing your characters at the end or having them commit suicide unless you really mean it, that is, unless like Camus or Kate Chopin you consider suicide an important existential question. Otherwise, your readers may feel cheated.

I know these signs well. They're all bad habits I've had and that still hang around. Beginning writers get scared, so they rely on these things. Seasoned writers get lazy. In both cases, it's easier to travel down a reliable road clearly mapped and demarcated than to detour down a nameless gravel road. Yet, it is exactly at a dead end that you might find an unmarked entryway to a beautiful forest.

The "magical movement" inherent in several forms stems from their organic nature, something that *appears* at once natural and artfully, if not effortlessly, composed. There's an art to executing most yoga poses. It's why they seem somehow so natural and feel so right to the body. Yogis create poses in part by knowledge and by experimentation, trying out forms to see how each one affects the body-mind. When something works, they stay with the pose until they refine it without it becoming rigid. Similarly, in writing there are boundless organic shapes that can help us imagine and re-vision how parts of our writing can be reformed. So once we've picked up on and identified problems with our writing's form, I give writers ideas for "mapping" their stories and poems. I have them consider and imagine unconventional, organic maps that I hope will help them create their writing's unique form.

Take the letter *S*. Imagine the top of the *S* as your story's beginning, which employs a memorable image or anecdote. Then, you seem to curve away from the subject—down the back of the *S*—until your story's middle refers again to the opening image or anecdote and, then, slides down the story's belly in another apparent digression and, ultimately, closes with a renewed reference to the opening image or anecdote. Such structures demand the reader be patient and enjoy the storyteller's circuitous path as a sort of literary odyssey in which the reader is not going to return to Ithaca by the most efficient route. Odysseus, after all, was a journeyer, not a tourist. Something in the peregrination, the gods know, builds character—and delights writers and readers.

Then there's the DNA story form. A DNA strand is composed of three molecules that entwine around one another and, in their mutual individuality, form a single unit. Similarly, in Hatha-Yoga, we have an image of the subtle body that works as an analogy for this form. A single line of energy runs approximately up the spine while two other core and complementary lines of energy begin on opposite sides of the spine's base and spiral up either side of the spine. They intersect one another at certain key points near the midline until all three meet at the third eye. In DNA stories, two or three substories, themes, or images begin separately yet seem to be remotely related as they occasionally intersect. Two or more characters, in parallel storylines, may fatefully meet one another. In the introduction to Barry Lopez's *Arctic Dreams*, he begins with two compelling memories—one of bowing to a nest of plovers, the other of seeing the gravestone of an Arctic explorer while back in the United States. He explores the two memories at first independently; then, gradually, you sense how the two intersect and come together in Lopez's new dreams for the Arctic, his dreams of our be-ing humble enough to bow to the earth even while we explore new terrain. The two strands unite.

Past and present can flip-flop and meet too. The chapters in Margaret Atwood's novel *Cat's Eye* alternate between the protago-nist's past and her present. An artist, the protagonist is haunted by childhood memories of an older girl who bullied and tortured her while seemingly remaining her friend. Her past unites with her pre-sent life when her childhood "friend" appears at the protagonist's art opening. It makes for a compelling climax. This movement back and forth keeps readers—and you the writer—guessing how the parts may or may not come together. Atwood peppers in comments by the protagonist's physicist brother about physics and time bend-ing, to reflect, of course, upon the novel's exquisite form.

To sense how the movement of one of your stories affects your readers' imagination, film it. Imagine you were to film parts of the writing with a wide-angled, regular-angled, or zoom-in lens. The zoom-in lens applies to those parts of your story in which you hone in on the details, the filaments of Ella's eyelashes or the texture of tortillas cooked on an open stove. The zoom-in lens can be a writer's primary lens—as in the work of Proust or Nicholson Baker. The regular-angle lens applies to action and narration. The wide-angle lens applies to all of those scenes in which you offer some contextual perspective, such as describing a whole town in which a character lives or when your narrator gives historical or personal background information. The wide-angle also applies to those parts in which your narrator reflects upon "the big picture," the big ideas in your piece. For most stories and poems, these musings are woven amid the zoom-in details and regular-lens action. It's a visual cliché in movies for the camera, once the last words are spoken, the last human gesture made, to pull back and give us a bird's-eye view of the city in which our hapless or happy characters have been con-tending with life's drama. You don't need to overanalyze your piece's perspective, and I suggest you not color-code parts of your story ac-cording to zoom-in, regular-angle, and wide-angle sections, else you'll spend precious time coloring more than writing (and we don't need another excuse to avoid writing). My point is, though, that with a sensibility to "lenses" you, the writer, can play with and guide your reader's imagination.

The other way you build internal movement is through repeating or associating key words or images or incidents. These repetitions, like color strands in a tapestry, unify a complex text. They hold together an essay, story, or poem's parts more subtly than paragraphs or stanzas. Usually, you don't do this knowingly at first. A ladybug keeps appearing in certain scenes, and before you know it, the dotted bug has invaded several parts of your story or poem. Why is this insect or just the word *ladybug* bugging you to be repeated? That question propels you to re-vision. Readers enjoy piecing together these beads, although they don't have to amount to heavy symbolism. (And writers such as Thomas Pynchon and filmmakers such as David Lynch love to toy with our symbol-making minds.) So review your draft and note how some words and images have naturally been repeated or naturally associate with one another. You likely will have a medley of associated words. Your job now is to play with how best to emphasize these key words and images without being heavy handed.

Reread a story, essay, or poem whose movement you want to map—yours or someone else's (I like to map writers' works to figure out how the parts hold together). Note how it begins, how that first sentence or line invites you in to sit and listen, to be engaged, to be puzzled and delighted. Flip to the end. An editor of a journal I know says whenever he goes through his stack of short story submissions, he reads the first paragraph. If the first paragraph has made a compelling enough invitation to read further, then he moves directly to the last scene. If there's a compelling enough relationship and progression from beginning to end, then he'll bother to read the middle. So notice how the beginning and end relate. What's happened to the character? What similar words or images appear in both places, suggesting some subtle movement? John Cheever's short story "Reunion" begins with "The last time I saw my father was in Grand Central Station," which seems innocent enough until we compare it with the closing sentence: " 'Good-bye, Daddy,' I said, and I went down the stairs and got my train, and that was the last time I saw my father."[2] *Last* means final, not previous.

Similarly, Gary Soto's essay "The Pie," which recounts how as a boy he stole a slice of apple pie, begins, "I knew enough about hell to stop me from stealing," and ends with "I knew sin was what you take and didn't give back."[3] There's been a shift in the boy's thinking and in his knowledge—a key word in this clever contemporary morality tale that plays off of Eve taking from the Tree of Knowledge.

If you're really lost in your draft, try defining your piece's purpose. Ask yourself, *What are you trying to get at and explore in this piece? What do you intend for your readers to think, to feel, to reconsider, to experience by this work's end?* Granted, many of us aren't sure what the heck we're trying to do when drafting except dodge being clueless, and the intentions we set early in a writing project, of course, change by the time we finish a piece days, weeks, months later. But answering these two questions clearly can give you perspective on your piece's whole form because then you can assess how well or not your beginning, middle, and end meet that purpose. Some people may think that these questions should come earlier—maybe even during the drafting stage. I would agree if you're writing journalistic or strictly expository prose (and if you're on a looming deadline). But these questions, while vital, can short-circuit the more organic ways of finding a form.

If necessary, get out the scissors. Or their equivalent for long works—index cards. Cut up sections of a draft and rearrange its parts. See how one section might create more interesting tension when rubbed against another. See how a bit of fragmentation or disjointedness might suit the piece better than seamless fluidity. Omit a section, and see if the piece is better for the excision. Go directly to the part that you think is cutest, the most precious, even the most clever. Cut it. You'll be glad you did. Believe me. Index cards I use for longer essays and books. I write topics and tentative titles on the cards and flip-flop and rearrange, gauging which one is best for the beginning, the best sequencing of one to the next, and the best for the ending. In fact, I did this very thing for this chapter. After writing several drafts, I wrote fourteen topics on fourteen cards, laid them out on my worktable, and played with their order like puzzle pieces. My imagination likes the physical manipulation.

Finally, there's the very real need of incubation. While living in a cabin in the Berkshires last summer, I reached down to plug in my desk lamp and noticed what I thought were at first huge dust balls collected around the laptop's plug. Shaped like silken garlic cloves, two half-finger long rock-climber tents lay suspended from the precipice of the computer plug and outlet. Outdoors, any one of the thousands of trees might have made a suitable resting space for this caterpillar and his friend, but they chose instead to come indoors and wrap themselves where we humans have channeled virtual fire. I wanted to imagine then, without wrenching the moment of its overt symbolism, some reciprocal charge from the energy being stored in those cocoons and the energy being stored at the cord's other end.

On the main doorway's threshold, a half dozen or so cocoons were nestled too. Cocoons on the threshold. Inside these pupal caves, their jaws shift into long, curled tongues, their short antennanne grow longer, and from their backs emerge four large wings. One night, as I fed the woodstove old sheets of this manuscript, I imagined the converted words and leaves, the pulpy slivers, transmuting with my imagination and subtle body and spinning out of the small smokestack a billowy, silken cocoon that feeds down the roof, slithers over the windows, and wraps me in a satin oasis. There I would stay for as long as needed, in complete retreat with these strange images and impulses and ideas that often usurp my willful mind's and body's banana republic, their poem-grenades and story-bombs sabotaging my conscious desire to keep things orderly and logical. The window covers would give me just enough translucence to nourish me and just enough opacity to keep me looking in, looking in, looking in. What shape shifting could I perform, I wondered. Cristo (the artist of grand wrapping) couldn't make a better artist's studio.

A kids' book on bugs says that these worms probably have gone through three to five instars, stages of molting and transforming. Each time, they eat so much they literally grow too big for their skin, which busts at their backs' seams and gives them a new range of colors, bumps, and hair. They are horizontal pillars of patience.

In this way, caterpillars are a writer's insect. For after eating leaves for weeks, they inch their way with utter instinct in search of some warm, safe spot to settle for a few weeks, to spin themselves into a web, to retreat. And then they wait. They incubate. They eat up images and ideas until their bodies burst.

It seems worth pointing out here that musician, former surgeon, and founder of New York City's Polarity Therapy Institute John Beaulieu once showed me a diagram of where in the skull the pituitary gland, the gland the third eye stimulates, sits. It's housed in a groove of the sphenoid bone. The diagram, with no stretch of the imagination, clearly resembles a butterfly or moth, complete with four wings, spots on the wings, and eyes at the optic foramen. A butterfly imprint on our skull.

So incubate. Let your stories, images, ideas, and drafts sit for a while. John Gardner said he would place a drafted story in a drawer for a year, and if after a year the story merited more work, he'd consider revising it. Time gave him perspective on the manuscript's shape and the language's texture. Would that most of us had such patience and persistence. When Richard Ford realizes the muse isn't visiting, he doesn't fret; he watches *SportsCenter* and forgets about her. He advocates taking breaks so he can consider whether what he's written is worth keeping or scrapping and so he can reward himself for some grueling (but, he warns, not overly difficult) work. Too, the ritual of taking a break allows the writer to follow the example of his subject and live in the world. Similarly, Paul West has written about that dreamy place where writers float he calls "The Castle of Indolence." Give in to it, he says. Surrender to its lull. It's often in these moments of not working that the freshest ideas suddenly and surprisingly surface.

We need not escape to an island or lock ourselves up in a New England cabin to incubate. Instead, some tools of yoga help us withdraw from our external senses that we may attune ourselves to our inner ones. Deliberately withdrawing from the external senses is called *pratyahara*, what Patanjali calls the fifth limb of yoga. *Pratyahara* prepares yogis for concentration, meditation, and bliss. We can practice this limb for a few minutes in our own study or bedroom. Doing so may help us rest in the silky coat of those ideas we want to birth in a new form. Stepping back and reseeing our writing may require that, for a while at least, we stop looking at it so logically with our normal eyes.

A heightened intuition mixed with clarity of intention can

help us with all of these practices for re-vision—from mapping movement, to cutting up, to incubating. Intuitive insight occurs not when the brain is lazy but when certain parts of the defensive hind brain, responsible for our fight-or-flight response, quiets, and parts of the creative brain, such as the frontal lobe, are active. We can alter this brain activity by harnessing our outer senses as well as by shifting the body's position to increase cerebral blood flow. When we alter our body appropriately, we can shift our outer and inner vision so that we have the insight to re-vision.

One practice described and honored in the *Hatha-Yoga-Pradipika* helps yogis tune into their third eye. It helps me and several other writers quickly withdraw from our external senses, that we may have a fresh perspective on our writing. If you have untreated blood-pressure issues or heart problems, please do not try the breath retention part of this practice. You can practice closing all of the other "gates" except your nostrils. While in a comfortable seated position at or away from your desk, focus on your breath. Place each thumb in your ear, each index finger atop your eyelids, and each middle finger's tip along the outside of each nostril. Place each ring fingertip at the top of your lips and each pinkie fingertip at the bottom of your lips. Other students prefer to rest on their backs and use an eye pillow and earplugs. Take a deep inhalation, hold the inhalation, and let your middle fingers close your nostrils. Hold here for as long as you're comfortable. It may only be a few seconds at first. Repeat at least three times. As you do so, notice how shutting off light from your eyelids, closing your eyes, and even shutting off the sound of your breath heightens your stillness.

Then, rest your hands on your thighs and move your eyeballs up toward your third eye and try to imagine the shape of your story, essay, or poem in question. If a sudden image surprisingly surfaces, either stay with it, or open your eyes and note it or sketch it. If nothing surfaces, imagine you're taking a trip through your writing. How does the journey begin? How does the entry feel? What key image or concept designates the opening? How does the journey progress to the next part? And to the next? What key images or concepts keep recurring? How does one feed into the next? Follow the path that your writing has laid out or wants to lay out in your memory. If you have difficulty remembering certain parts, don't fret.

Take the forgetting as a possible sign for re-visioning something more memorable. Notice how it feels to arrive at the end of the path. As you look back, can you see the beginning? Have you looped back near where you started? Or is there no going back?

When ready, open your eyes and roughly sketch or jot down notes from this experience.

$\mathcal{T}$AKE A BREATH: INVERT YOUR VISION

Benefits: *The practice of* REVERSED ATTITUDE GESTURE (viparīta-karanī mudrā) *and its variations is not so much to turn your work upside down as it is to shift your body's regular flow and help you relax your senses, especially your eyes, so you can improve your inner vision. Options 2 and 3 below also increase cerebral blood flow and can slow down your brain waves— both physiological traits of creative activity. Each of these poses is believed to shift vital energy back toward the brain and is known to cool down the sympathetic nervous system as well, allowing the defensive part of our brains to rest and the creative parts of our brain to awaken.*

> **FRIENDLY WARNING:**
> Remember, the idea is to find the form that fits your body at any given time and not to force your body to fit a form. If none of these variations feels right for your body, then recline in CORPSE POSE (*savāsana*). If you've been practicing for a while and have some flexibility in your neck and cervical spine, see the Appendix and Chapter 23 for two more advanced variations using REVERSED ATTITUDE GESTURE or SHOULDER STAND. Variation #2 is not photographed.

INTENTION:

Move naturally into this pose when you feel it's time to withdraw and to gain some insight into your writing's form while not looking so hard.

Writer Dame Edith Sitwell, according to Diane Ackerman's A Natural History of the Senses, used to close herself up in a coffin for a few hours before writing. You try it. Wait for night. Draw the blinds. Take a notepad and pen and turn out the lights. Light a candle. Use earplugs if you have them. Then, find the variation of the form that suits your body at this moment.

Variation #1: CORPSE POSE (savāsana). *Rest on your back, knees bent or straight. Let your arms rest to the sides, palms face up. Breathe from your belly's base.*

Variation #2: LEGS UP THE WALL. *For this popular variation of* REVERSED ATTITUDE GESTURE, *come to a wall, rest on your left side, and push your tush against the wall while still on your side. Once you feel both buttocks against the wall, come onto your back as your legs climb the wall. If this position feels uncomfortable, then place a folded blanket with a three-foot length six inches away from the wall on which your back can rest, and let your buttocks hang off the edge of the blanket. Let your back body melt into the ground as your legs rest and your blood flow shifts.*

Once you've found the variation that feels most relaxing yet stimulating, close your eyes and keep your focus on your breath. Anytime you smell, hear, or even feel something, try to let go of paying too much attention to it and instead draw your eyeballs up toward your third eye as you guide your breath from your third eye and up and down your spine. As thoughts or images surface, also try to let go of them. Try doing so for at least two minutes. Then, breathe less and less distinctly. Don't worry about deep breathing. Aim for soft yet satisfying (not deep) breaths. Take breaths whose undulations are so indistinct you can't hear yourself breathe and can barely feel your body moving with your breath. Try doing so for another two minutes.

This practice is challenging at first and may not get any easier for a while. Here's a suggested schedule for using the practice fifteen times to let a draft incubate:

First–Fifth Sessions: *Get comfortable with the practice. Get comfortable with letting go of thinking about your draft and with focusing less and less on your senses and thoughts. You might do so for only five minutes at a time.*

Sixth–Tenth Sessions: *Try to lengthen the practice by five minutes. Notice if any sessions become easier for you. During this stage, observe any changes in the quality of your mind and body as you draft pieces* other than the one you're incubating. Are you less distracted? More receptive? If not, don't fret. Aim for a caterpillar's patience.

Eleventh–Fifteenth Sessions: *In these last sessions, your third eye may grant you some insight into the nature of what needs re-visioning in your draft. As you move deeply into withdrawing from your senses during these sessions, keep open to an image that may relate integrally to your draft.*

But remember this: Refrain from expecting anything, grand or small, to happen. In fact, the insight may come between sessions while you're planting cherry tomatoes in your garden, while you're sailing, or while you're walking your dog. Insight may actually come during the seventh session or even during the third one. But just try not to force the moth or butterfly to emerge too soon. Each practice can set the conditions for insight to surface.

CHAPTER TWENTY-ONE

Letting Go of
Delusion and Control:
Revise!

At last you've finished drafting your novel. You've even "re-visioned" parts of it into good shape and form. But you're not through yet. You still must revise. I meet writers in almost every class and workshop who harbor antipathy toward revising. Why? What keeps us from revising? Some beginning writers resist revising because of the "Tainting the Pristine Moment Syndrome." Based on the Jack Kerouac idea that real writing rolls onto the page in a transcendent, exalted moment when a writer levitates from her chair while draft-ing, this argument claims that to revise an otherwise "inspired" poem or story taints its authenticity. Legends of writers composing novels in six weeks in a frenzied flurry often feed this idea and ulti-mately starve beginning writers from understanding the years of crafting that may have preceded that six-weeks performance. This notion of the first draft as the final, authentic draft keeps writers who otherwise have talent from producing work worth reading and re-reading. My Texas friend has a more colorful name for this syn-drome: the "Whatever I Shit is Gold Syndrome."

Each part of the writing process, though, has its valuable place. In drafting, you create characters, get lost in fresh ideas, and dis-cover your story's heart. You are an artist. In re-visioning, you re-imagine your writing's structure, incubate on its shape, and make global changes. You are a designer. In revising, you hone in on, prune, double-check, and correct your manuscript's details. You are a caretaker. To revise and to edit your manuscript can be an act of respect for your creation and for your potential readers.

I say the following from experience: Much resistance to revising stems from delusion and refusal to let go of control. Delusion, of course, is when we have a false judgment or opinion about something—in this case, our writing. *Bhranti-darshana* in Sanskrit translates loosely to "living in delusion" or "having mistaken notions." Patanjali lists it in Sutra I.30 as being a major obstacle to a yogi's path of self-realization. I know this concept intimately because I've embodied its various forms for years and continue to do so. If you readily use any of the following defenses to yourself (all too familiar to me) or to someone editing your writing, beware of delusion:

- "X just doesn't understand my writing style." [X could be a trusted friend, editor, spouse/partner]
- "But that's the story's funniest/cleverest/most original line/image/example!"
- "I've been writing/publishing for ten years; I know what I'm doing."
- "I graduated from X; I know what I'm doing."
- "I was inspired when I wrote that; I can't touch it, or I'll taint it."

Directly related to delusion is demanding absolute control of our writing. "I am the author; thus, I am the authority" sums up this mentality.

Don't fret, though. Limited self-understanding and false self-conceptions simply are part of being human. Thankfully, we can reflect upon our writing's qualities, we can reassess our writing, and we can refine our craft. To let go of delusion and control requires in part cultivating discernment. In yoga, discernment is called *viveka*, the ability to separate what factors in one's life contribute to self-realization from those that do not. A yogi chooses and omits activities, habits, and external elements accordingly. A writer's discernment is less daunting, for it is a disciplined process of distinguishing which words, phrases, or sentences work and do not work in a piece of writing. Having discernment can exercise your intellect and sharpen your craft. As you grow more confident in handling your craft's finer details, you rely more on your own authority.

My writing process is not simply linear as in moving smoothly from drafting to re-visioning to revising, nor is it for most writers I know. Granted, I do prepare myself for a revising and editing session differently from a drafting session. In a drafting session, I'm wandering, sauntering, moving through forward bends or other poses that will induce my subtle imagination to open up some fresh ideas and images and metaphors. My open-minded drafting buddy goads me to do what I wish. My editing taskmaster, though, is a no-nonsense and rather persnickety female figure, a necessary foil to my frolicking drafting buddy. She knows we have work to do and not always much time in which to finish it. My drafting buddy generates ideas; my editing taskmaster helps me choose, cut, and replace. So when I revise, I want to be alert, not dreamy. I have a clear path and mission. Usually, because my drafts tend to be bloated and weedy, my mission is to slay, slice, and prune—slay my drafting ego that may wish to hold on to precious parts of my writing, slice the excess words and sentences, and prune the wordy phrases. I become a linguistic hunter and gardener.

Yet, as much as I would like to distinguish my drafting sessions from my revising sessions, they often overlap, and my process is more recursive than linear. Sometimes I write and rewrite several sentences as each one comes out—a series of steps and back steps, creations and erasures, on the word-processing screen—as if to steal the proper timbre or tone. My taskmaster nudges her way in with questions: This word or that word? Begin this sentence here? Place this phrase where? What are my options? I'm rewriting this very paragraph's sentences as I'm drafting them. My taskmaster wants to protect me from making a fool of myself, whereas my drafting buddy encourages me to do so, but I get nowhere without both of them.

I share with writers and students other things I do to develop a discerning attitude when revising is my mission. A few standing yoga poses, back bends, and particular breath work can increase cerebral blood flow and ensnare the wandering mind to stay on discernment's path. Refine, refine, refine often is my mantra. Once I get my body and mind in agreement with the task before me, I print out a draft (my taskmaster likes to mark things up). Sometimes I stand up and read a draft aloud. Whether sitting or standing, this practice of reading aloud can help you hear almost instantly the clunky sentence structures and inappropriate or imprecise word choices. You'll hear the foggy nonsense that you and your drafting buddy thought was, a week ago, the most brilliant thing ever written.

In the early stages of editing, you might recruit someone you trust just to listen without commenting. James Thurber, an avid reviser never satisfied with his first drafts, said his wife was his best editor. When reading his early drafts she would say, referring to his attempts at humor, something like "Thurber! This stuff is high school nonsense." When I begin editing, I don't want that kind of feedback yet, but having another attentive person present can make you more aware of a potential audience. It directs your writer's mind toward communicating with or affecting someone. Sometimes when I read aloud a sentence that I think is funny to my wife, she will release a near-inaudible groan. My taskmaster nods and makes a small x and ? in the margin, and I read on.

In these read-aloud sessions, you might feel like a happy weeder in a neglected garden, near giddy when drawing lines through rows of words and marking X's through paragraphs. I underline sentences whose structure needs revisiting. Next to paragraphs that need rewriting I draw vertical lines in the margins and make a brief note—more color, less color, more examples, fewer examples. A circled word tells me later I need to find a more precise or appropriate word or that I need to check its meaning. You have to find, of course, what works for you, but whatever you do, tend to the details.

Usually, the first point of business is words. Choose the right word. It helps to know a word's denotation—its literal, agreed-upon meaning—and its connotation. Connotations are a word's shades of meaning, the associations that readers register with words. Take the various synonyms for "thin": *skinny, gaunt, scrawny, svelte, slim, sleek, reedy, twiggy, stalky, lanky, puny, meager, cadaverous*. Each option's literal meaning hovers loosely around the field of "thin," yet nearly each option's shade of meaning can signal a completely different effect. If you want to suggest that a character appears like a walking corpse, then *cadaverous* is your word, but if you want your character's body frame to conjure the image of a feline form, graceful and elegant, then *svelte* is your word. Be careful of unintended connotations. Recently, I compared the joys of drafting to walking through a hemlock forest. The comparison came from my own satisfaction in being surrounded by hemlocks that have made, in the past hundred years, a revival in the Catskills. An editor, though, reminded me of many people's association of *hemlock* with poison. She was right, and the risk of a missed association wasn't worth it, so I changed it to the more commonly positive association of "evergreen forest."

A select verb can invigorate a sentence and your message's connotations, but not just any old verb will suffice. Choices for describing the manner of a vociferous character's speech, for example, include *harangue, babble, ramble, elucidate, gibber, expatiate*. Of course, *elucidate* stands out from the pack as being the kindest in connotation due in part to its root, the Latin *lucidus*, "bright." To elucidate is to "shed light" on a subject. *Expatiate* rightfully sounds the most neutral, as it means "to speak or write thoroughly." *Babble, ramble*, and *gibber* have similar negative connotations of the relative who will not cut to the chase so the rest of us can eat our dinner, but each word has a slightly different denotation. *Babble* is sheer nonsense, the sort that makes the most diplomatic among us bite our tongue in amazement that the speaker's jaw doesn't come unhinged from being overworked. *Ramble*, like the Rambler automobile of the 1950s, suggests a way of talking at once leisurely and digressive. To *gibber* can be to talk nonsensically, but it also can describe speech purposefully vague or pretentious.

Now, one person's view of a "rambling" speech may be another person's view of sheer "babble," while what one person considers to be a careful "elucidation" may be to another person nothing more than a "harangue." But you're the writer, and you're the one who gets to have fun playing with point of view, character, and purpose. Imagine you're writing a story about a woman named Elizabeth who is dying from an unknown cause. Your narrator is a man who purports to love her, and here is your first effort for him to describe her appearance:

> Her **frame covered** by **thin epidermis**, Elizabeth appeared unhealthy.

This description sounds almost comical in part because of the use of the formal word *epidermis*. *Frame* also sounds oddly neutral or suggestive of a building's structure, not a loved one's body. Maybe that's your intention. Maybe this character remains throughout the first part of the story emotionally detached and aloof from the reality that Elizabeth is dying. But maybe you were just having trouble choosing the right words. A rewrite might read as follows:

> Her **skeleton draped** by **translucent flesh**, Elizabeth might have disintegrated in the breeze.

This description is still a bit stiff, but more emotive (if not more affected) not only for the hyperbole that closes the sentence but also for the diction. It also implies the character's emotional attachment and creates for the reader a far more vivid and emotionally charged image of Elizabeth than does the first description. It would make an interesting story if at times the narrator's emotions seemed affected and disingenuous.

Economy matters too. Whereas my drafting buddy can spend words freely, my taskmaster budgets everything—especially the number of words I can use. At this stage her pruning shears and her gleaming smile come out. "Less is more," she parrots like the Mies van der Rohe of writing. I have numerous tricks for pruning, but a favorite is to discern the wicked whiches from the good whiches. The *which* in the following sentence can go without losing meaning:

> Ben works in the Zenith building, ~~which is~~ the tallest building in downtown Phoenix.

You often can cut a phrase to a word or two. Take the following first draft of a sentence from this very paragraph:

> **Drafting buddy's version:** I have any number of tricks to share for pruning, but one of my favorites is to discern the wicked whiches from the good whiches.

> **Taskmaster's version:** I have numerous tricks for pruning, but a favorite is to discern the wicked whiches from the good whiches.

Numerous replaces *any number of*, and *a favorite* butts out *one of my favorites*. The phrase *to share* is implied, so it can go. Revising saves me six words in one sentence. Multiply six by however many wordy sentences your first draft contains, and you realize that a

hefty thousand-word story or essay could become a lean seven hundred words.

The more careful the practice, the easier this part of the writing may become—if you can let go of delusion and control. Take these two sentences, for example, from a student's story that express the same basic idea:

1. Eleanor, who is a woman noted for her ability to be able to make rudely bold and demanding business executives soften with her small talk and to make really angry clients feel less angry, was a perfect candidate for the customer service desk at Bulworth Associates. (Forty-six words.)
2. Eleanor's warm soft-talking could melt the most brazen executive and defuse the most incensed client. No doubt, she was a perfect candidate for Bulworth Associates' customer service desk. (Twenty-eight words.)

Delusion would justify that the first sentence is thorough and substantive. Actually, it's long winded, redundant, and clunky—yet structurally typical of many first drafts. With a few revisions of word choice and sentence structure, the second sentence not only saves your readers' time; it also gives the idea more force and, thus, effect than the first version. The metaphors of *warm* and *melt* give you a more vivid sense of the power Eleanor's voice possesses and may even help you imagine how she'd sound when handling an ornery client. Breaking up the first sentence into two sentences and including the more colloquial *no doubt* also makes the voice less formal than the first. You'd be hard pressed to justify not revising that first sentence.

Yet—and this point is essential—clarity and economy are not incontestable aesthetic virtues (although Strunk and White zealots may argue otherwise). I relish, for reasons of philosophy and disposition, artful digressions, fanciful yet purposeful sentence structures, poetic language, and vivid images—all elements of writing that may test readers' patience. You have to decide, ultimately, whether revising a sentence for fewer words subtracts from the sentence's voice, music, and overall effect. But as in all cases, beware of pleading "poetic license" to justify poor writing (and laziness when revising).

Joe, a yoga teacher I know, takes his students through the same pose four different ways. He lets them feel the pose one way that, without discernment, might seem right. Then he shows them another way of coming into the pose that, through contrast, lets them experience how much better some simple adjustments can make experiencing the pose. Then he'll have them press into their left big toe mound, for instance, while stretching, say, a hip extensor and then shifting their right shoulder three inches to the left. Joe's refinements of a pose mirror how writers must approach part of their writing. Of course, spending this kind of energy on every move in yoga would make the practice tedious just as it would in writing. But refinement and discernment deepen your appreciation of details.

To revise your work is to respect your writing as well as your potential readers. It is to acknowledge the art of "getting it right," whether "it" be the tone, image, word choice, phrasing, or sentence structure. If you're unwilling to tend to your writing's details, you're treating your own writing too cheaply, as if it's expendable and forgettable. Recently, I waited on a plane before takeoff for over thirty minutes while the mechanics checked and double-checked the plane's wiring and engines. The man next to me complained. "Another delay! Don't these people know we have schedules to keep? They're just clueless." I understood his response. Delays are irritating, and before taking off on a flight I'd like to think I were in control when really I'm anything but. But to this flustered man I suggested that if we have to wait another thirty minutes to assure the plane flies right and safely, then I don't mind at all. He didn't respond and checked his watch. If you want your writing to get off the ground, if you want it to soar, and if you want your readers to come back to your writing, tend to the details. Revise.

$\mathcal{T}$AKE A BREATH:
A CONTEMPLATION ON WORDS AND SELF

INTENTION:
If you either are blocked about revising a piece of your writing or if you just need aid developing discernment, try this practice.

Vi in viveka (*discernment*) *means "to separate." Try to separate yourself from your writing. Come into a comfortable seated position of your choice. Let your spine grow long as you close your eyes. Draw in your breath, and then let it all out. With each soft inhalation, just appreciate what your self takes in from this world, and with each exhalation appreciate what this self releases.*

Then, with closed eyes centered between your eyebrows, imagine the words you're writing as floating into your body along thin fibers that connect the world and the words to your body. While in your body, they mix with your essence. The words you write come from your center, pivot on that calm point of your authentic self, and then, once on the page, are something more than even your true self. You take in these words, let them dance while you can, and then with each out-breath give them back to the world.

But even in such a beautiful process, these words aren't your self. You can imagine the words buzzing according to your self's charge, but they're still not the same as your self.

As you open your eyes and approach your writing that needs revising, consider how ephemeral, how malleable, these words are. If you rewrite directly onto a computer, all the better to see their ephemeral virtual quality. On the screen, a sentence's shape shifts like mercury, a phrase changed here, a few words dropped there. It's a wonderful process, and you're not in near as much control as your taskmaster likes to think you are. So be it.

CHAPTER TWENTY-TWO

Friendly Warnings
of Inauthenticity

My very first public reading initiated me in the temptations of inauthenticity. In my early twenties, I was just starting to publish my poetry and read some of it at open-mike events. Someone asked me if I would like to be one of three poets featured at a special reading. I was flattered. This seemed like big stuff. When I found out who the other two poets were, though, I froze. One was an older guy known for his slam-style poetry and the other was a young, sexy woman—both of them the most popular poets among the mostly youthful poetry scene because of their bold and clever sex-driven poems. Plus, they had snazzy names like Belle and Devo. I had no erotic poem, or hip name for that matter, to compare or compete. I was in my ascetic abstinence stage, then, and my sexiest poem explored the passion of making popcorn.

It was my first reading, and I feared coming off as the pathetic, sexless poet. I had two weeks before the reading to change that, and in two weeks I managed to write three erotic poems drawn from pure imagination. One was about a guy who, while having sex, can't stop comparing his girlfriend's navel to divine metaphors. The poems were clever but corny, to say the least, and latent with gratuitous references designed not only to titillate but also to make me look like a hot-blooded American male poet who could compete with the hottest poets in town.

The reading occurred at a quiet coffee shop located in a mostly conservative neighborhood and frequented mostly by sweater- and khaki-clad adults. The host introduced us, and the format upon which we agreed was for each of us to read one poem and continue to circulate in this manner. I went first and started with a poem about bridges in Texas. Belle and Devo followed with similar placid pieces. The latté-drinking couple at the table in front seemed pleased. Then, as I read one of the erotic pieces, the same couple suddenly looked as if they were watching a John Hughes film that had become a raunchy skin flick. When I finished, Belle pulled out and read a poem about faking an orgasm, complete with sound effects and gyrating hips. I read yet another erotic poem, and a few poems later, while we poets seemed engrossed in a linguistic ménage-à-trois, the coffee shop was nearly empty, and the proprietor threatened not to let the host return. Devo shook my hand and said he had a new respect for me. Belle said she should have married me instead of the drip she'd recently hitched. I went home feeling like a completely successful fraud. I made myself some popcorn and went to bed alone.

The heart of inauthenticity is not acting upon what you know at your core to be true. In most instances, only you will know if you're being inauthentic when you write, but we can heed a few "indicators" of inauthenticity. They're reminders for myself as much as they can be for you.

Much of inauthenticity has to do with trying to fit in. I know a writer who wanted to write a book about earth-related spirituality and religion. When I asked him what had inspired him to think of writing the book, I expected him to refer to something such as a lifelong love of nature or his interest in American Indian cultures, or of his passion to promote reverence for this planet. I was disappointed when he answered, "I read an article in a publishing journal that said that ecology and spirituality books are a hot sell." There's nothing wrong inherently with wanting to sell your books. Few writers want to publish a book that isn't going to sell copies and be read. But I suggest you find your subject first and let an appropriate angle to reach your desired audience follow rather than trying to find a large audience first and letting your subject follow accordingly. Notice, too, when you're writing or rewriting an essay or story or poem to fit in, to be trendy, to try to get your writing into a particular journal or magazine. Subscribe to and study such publications because you appreciate the quality of writing, not solely because a writer or writing teacher told you that you should be reading them. Submit your work to publications whose writing you respect.

Similarly, catch yourself if you're editing part of your work so as not to offend somebody. If it's essential to your story that your characters have sex, that they're addicted to heroin, or that they say "fuck" all of the time, let them. Your job is to present your characters as truthfully as possible. Sanitizing is not truthfulness or authenticity—regardless of what a parent might have told you. On the other hand, if you've lived in upstate New York most of your life and you're tired of your characters talking about the weather and church and carpentry, you don't have to create a crack-shooting sex fiend with a foul mouth just to be "gritty" or "realistic." Booker Prize–winner James Kelman's characters say "fuck" three times in a sentence because, as Kelman says, *fuck* to his Scottish characters is a comma. To Kelman, language is language is language, and distinctions such as standard language, dialect, colloquialisms, or vulgarities contribute to class inequities. When you have that kind of perspective, the *fucks* are fitting, not gratuitous.

Sometimes beginning writers, particularly younger ones, so want to thwart conventions that they equate authenticity with raw emotion. I know one young poet who, every time he reads a poem, yells and screams, repeating something like "What have you done to our planet, you bastards?!" Here is an example in which raw emotion in writing is dramatic, if not histrionic, but doesn't always lead to authenticity.

As I've written elsewhere in this book, to write authentically is to write from your own authority, and so many matters of writing without authenticity relate to denying your own authority and deferring to someone else's. Teachers, professors, and other writers can be seductive in their authority—the more charismatic, the more persuasive. I know of one college writing teacher whose colorful talks on the hazards of writing conventions and craft enchant his students. Appealing to the rebellious teenager in all of us, he likes to posit himself as an iconoclast—particularly when he slashes his students' writing. It's his way or no way, one of his former students once told me. This particular student said that for nearly two years she would write with the sole intention of pleasing her teacher. If she could please him, then she knew she would be a good writer. It's easy to fool ourselves into thinking so.

You can learn from such teachers, but if you find yourself following only every word that writer says despite your own thoughts, then you're giving your authority away. It's one thing to be a writing apprentice (an honorable yet underrated role in our country); it's another to be a lackey. An apprentice, while receptive and open, should be full of questions, tinged with curiosity and healthy skepticism, and willing, of course, to essay things. I've been fortunate to have teachers—in yoga and in writing—who aimed ultimately to wean me away from them and whose intention was to try to make me my own best teacher. So if you find yourself in a writing class in which the instructor is unbending in entertaining differing yet legitimate views about writing and seems hell bent on thrusting a singular agenda—namely on gathering his or her disciples—run. You don't have time to waste with egomaniacs. (The same loosely applies, incidentally, when seeking a yoga teacher.).

When you're in a writing group, ego dynamics can surface in even more complex ways. Check in with yourself when writing a story, poem, or essay that you know you're going to share with your writing group. The anticipation of having your piece read and critiqued can alter what and how you write. Say you're crafting a scene between your character Betty and her new coworker Alex. You're having one of those rare moments when you're completely absorbed in the scene, and the sexual tension between them is mounting subtly. Something else is happening, too, in the scene with language—you're playing with the jargon of their financial-consulting lingo and the language of lovers. Just when you think the scene is flowing, you remember Andrea. She's been publishing her stories steadily and recently has assumed queen-bee status in your writing group. She hates scenes or plots related to love or sex. Boring, she says. Andrea's always talking about "layering" and "contextualizing" with other subjects like history and physics. You don't really get what she's up to, but you feel you should. Soon you notice you're questioning Betty and Alex's relationship in your story. Maybe you should throw in some physics or history references somehow—the history of bending time with financial consulting?—to "layer" the story.

This compromising we do unknowingly. We substitute a professor's authority with another person's authority. If you genuinely want to write a story in which the characters may have an intimate relationship, or there may be tension that suggests they want to have sex but aren't sure about the whole love thing, then go for it. Make it as authentic as you can. At your next writing group meeting, if Andrea begins one of her "layering" sermons, hear her out. Maybe she'll say something that makes sense this time. But when she's finished and everyone else has finished commenting, you can do one of three things: First, concur and perhaps recognize some validity to some of the comments. Second, let Andrea and the rest of the group know that writers will never exhaust the complexities of relationships and that you intend to continue exploring how to render freshly these complexities. Or, if you think that comment will only goad Andrea into another hour's worth of lecturing, you can smile and genuinely thank everyone for his or her comments and move on. You don't have to take anyone's suggestions, and a reference to physics or history won't necessarily improve a story. Being in a writing group should help you gain fresh perspectives and insights into your writing that you otherwise may hold too closely. So welcome comments by trusted teachers and fellow writers without negating your own authenticity.

These are only a few suggestions—almost all of which come from my own wrestling with authenticity and in working with other writers and students. You have to be the one who checks in with yourself to know whether or not you're being authentic or whether you're putting up a front in your writing. Almost everything I've suggested in this chapter, if not in every other chapter, goes back to being clear about your intentions. A yogi obsessed mainly with trying to stretch out her hamstrings so she can perform intricate poses and make her students ooh and ahh is no more authentic in intention than the writer who seeks mainly to get his name in print so his friends can read with envy. Returning every day not only to the question of what you are writing for but also to smaller questions such as why you're including one scene in your story or why you're writing about a particular subject helps keep you authentic. Most writers don't suddenly become authentic in their intentions. It's an ongoing part of the journey.

CHAPTER TWENTY-THREE

For Writers Who Already Practice Yoga

Most of this book I've aimed toward writers with little or no experience with yoga. But I'm meeting more and more writers around the country who have been practicing yoga, yet aren't sure how their two passions—yoga and writing—can complement one another. So, I want to offer those of you who already practice yoga regularly a few more suggestions.

FLEXIBILITY AND MOVING TOWARD THE DIFFICULT

Be inventive and mentally flexible. If you've been practicing yoga for a while, you probably have a good-sized tool belt of yoga poses, breath work, and principles. So how do you use these *upaya*, these "skillful means"? Begin with creating your own "writing flow" of poses, breath work, visualization, and/or meditation that seems most compatible with your writing process. The general guidelines that follow later in this chapter can help you be creative. Learn what you need as a writer, and try out the tools to help you build a strong personal writing laboratory: your body-mind-imagination. For me, an embodied writing process, again, includes these elements in this order at least five times a week:

- **Setting a Twofold Writing Intention:**
  - What am I writing for?
  - a specific statement of my focus for a particular writing session
- **practicing yoga** for fifteen to sixty minutes to manifest that intention

- **writing** for at least three hours a session with frequent awareness of my breath, body, thoughts, and imagination (If three hours a session seems too long, you begin with where you're at: thirty minutes, sixty minutes).

This is the process that works for me. Although I work best with some regular flow of poses and breath work, I daily vary from this flow according to whatever ache, sensation, or mood surfaces. Sometimes, I surrender to the mat and stop pushing the flow to sense what pose naturally needs to follow.

Work with what challenges you in your writing. Acknowledge what's difficult in your writing, and dare to employ the yoga tools that help you work with (although not "fix") that challenge. I heard yogi Rodney Yee once say that he could distinguish beginners, intermediate students, and advanced students accordingly: Beginners, eager to learn anything, will try any and all poses and practices. Intermediate students, savvy to their own limitations, will practice only those poses that they can do well and will avoid the other ones. Advanced students, also aware of their limitations, deliberately practice those very poses that challenge them. If you've been writing and practicing yoga for a while, then move toward the difficult. It could be your most important habit to cultivate as a writer. You probably know your physical, emotional, spiritual, and creative limitations. (Don't we all? Don't remind me, you say.) When I told this to a group of writers in California, one woman rolled her eyes, smiled, and said, "You know, I've had enough difficulty in my life. I'm at a stage in which I don't think I need to move toward it because it moves toward me." I know what she means. Busted relationships, disappointing jobs, betrayed friendships, broken bones, and collapsed organs can be part and parcel of our daily difficulties, so why move toward it as if stepping onto the middle of a freeway? I'm suggesting we recognize and work with—rather than try to ignore and overcompensate for—the limitations of our creative writing and our writing life. I've had to work with the limitations of my erratic mind that loves to play, my delusions of grandeur and my pity parties (sometimes in the same day), as well as my proclivity for happy endings. The beauty of having a regular "advanced" yoga practice as a writer is that the repertoire you have available to work with those limitations grows so substantially that after a while you may not even recognize a challenge as a challenge but simply as a creative problem to work with.

Here are some ideas and general guidelines when considering how different poses affect the body-mind-imagination. I've had to simplify some of the explanations for the sake of space, but these guidelines I hope will be enough to prod you to test out for yourself how your breath, your body, your mind, can indeed be your muse.

STANDING POSES, BALANCING POSES, CONCENTRATION, AND PRESENCE

Standing poses are good for **concentration** and **presence**. By drawing attention downward and away from our heads, we can quiet the chatter. These poses remind us of our physical connection to the ground (and flighty writers I know beg for grounding), which in turn helps us remain present in this body and world. Since we have numerous nerve endings in the feet, these poses also naturally quicken other body parts and organs. Poses such as **MOUNTAIN POSE, EVEN-HEARTED MOUNTAIN POSE,** and **WARRIOR II POSE** aid diaphragmatic breathing, as well, which quiets the brain and the sympathetic nervous system. **EXTENDED SIDE-ANGLE POSE** (*utthita parsvakonāsana*) so stretches the torso that it also increases your breath capacity and aids the digestive system— boons to concentration. (Note: **ADAMANTINE/KNEELING POSE** (*vajrāsana*) also stimulates several important nerve and energy points in the feet and legs, which makes it an excellent pose to open and close a sequence for heightened **concentration**.)

STANDING BALANCE POSES aid **concentration**. If you want to develop a sequence for **concentration** before writing, try to include at least one balancing pose. With some standing poses' benefits, balancing poses can deepen your concentration because more parts of the brain are stimulated. Choose a balance pose such as **TREE POSE** (*vrksāsana*), **WARRIOR III POSE** (*viribridāsana III*), **EAGLE POSE** (*garudāsana*), or **HALF-MOON POSE** (*ardha chandrāsana*) with which you already are familiar and comfortable. (Note: These are not illustrated.) The more accustomed your body is to the pose, the more your fretful thoughts and hastened breath can relax while your brain remains stimulated.

BACK BENDS AND EMOTIONS

In the early morning and midafternoon, sometimes we need a jolt of energy. BACK BENDS, such as LOCUST POSE (shalabhāsana), COBRA POSE (bujanghāsana), UPWARD FACING DOG POSE (urdvha mukha svanāsana), or CAMEL POSE (ustrāsana)—not illustrated—generate intense energy and can be allies for **perseverance** and working with intense emotions such as **fear, passion,** or **anger.** They counter our feeling overly relaxed or drowsy by rousing our sympathetic nervous system, encouraging energizing thoracic breathing (that is, breathing in the chest area), stimulating beta brain wave activity, and preparing us for action. They also open our heart region and break down our emotional armor. So, while some students become a bit cranky, irritable, if not mad, during back bend sequences, they also prepare their bodies and imaginations for **compassion.** Of course, if you've been practicing yoga for a while, you know that they're best practiced not only with caution and after some warm-up but also in tandem with other kinds of poses, especially forward bends, which have a reverse effect on the brain, mind, and imagination.

ABDOMINALS AND PERSEVERANCE

Practices that work the **abdominal** (that is, stomach) muscles also help you develop long-term **perseverance.** Whereas back bends kick in quick energy, **abdominal** poses build a long-term reservoir of inner heat. **Leg lifts,** if executed safely with the back flat on the ground, increase blood oxygen. The SOARING LOCK (uddiyana-bandha) in which you lift your abdominals is one of the most efficient ways to generate long-term heat. It's also possibly the only hatha-yoga practice that stretches the diaphragm. SHINING SKULL CLEANSING BREATH (kappala-bhati-kriyā) not only stimulates the abdominal muscles and digestive organs but also rouses the

brain approximately three to seven times more quickly. These practices increase blood oxygen, steroids, glucose, and adrenaline in addition to toning our abdominal muscles, so sixty rounds of
SHINING SKULL BREATH followed by three minutes of the
SOARING LOCK before each writing session can shift your outlook
and stamina. Again, be cautious and know your body. If you have a
history of high blood pressure, avoid these types of practices. If you
have an ulcer or hernia, best to consult a holistic physician.

CONCENTRATION AND PERSEVERANCE SEQUENCE

After I set my twofold writing intention, I flow through my daily
morning sequence that I created for concentration and perseverance. It takes all of eight to ten minutes and usually sets me on
my way for three hours of sustained writing. I begin by sitting my hips
on my heels first with tops of the feet down as in ADAMANTINE/
KNEELING POSE and then hips on my heels with every toe rolled
under. I then include a SQUAT with SHINING SKULL CLEANS-
ING BREATH, MOUNTAIN POSE with SOARING LOCK, TREE
POSE, a STANDING FORWARD BEND; then WARRIOR II POSE,
EXTENDED SIDE-ANGLE POSE, and HALF-MOON POSE on
each side; another STANDING FORWARD BEND, DOWNWARD
FACING DOG, and back to KNEELING POSE followed by ALTER-
NATE NOSTRIL BREATHING. This skeletal flow gives my body-
mind-imagination a familiar sequence, from which I then deviate
according to what I know or intuit of my writing needs. This
sequence, a foundation in many of my Yoga as Muse workshops,
has helped numerous writers develop their own embodied writing
process.

FORWARD BENDS, INVERSIONS, AND IMAGERY

FORWARD BENDS, such as STANDING FORWARD BEND, DOWN-
WARD FACING DOG, and BACK EXTENSION POSE, stretch the
lower back and hamstrings as well as increase hip flexibility, so we

can sit—on our meditation cushions or at our desk—for longer periods of time without strain. They also calm the sympathetic nervous system as well as the autonomic nervous system. These poses,
mixed with back bends, help me work with intense emotions of
anger and fear, respectively, so they, too, become manageable muses
instead of hindrances.

I find forward bends especially stimulate my subtle imagination,
that embodied reservoir of fresh imagery and ideas. When I begin a
first draft or feel my writing lacking fertile imagery or ideas, I induce
a dreamy "theta brain" state of mind that stimulates my subtle
imagination. To do so, I flow through a series of poses that then finishes with BACK EXTENSION POSE for three to five minutes,
KNEE-TO-CHIN POSE (*janu sirsāsana*)—not illustrated—and then
move to SHOULDER STAND (*sarvangāsana*) for seven minutes,
practice three minutes of ALTERNATE NOSTRIL BREATHING
(*nādī-sodhana prānāyāma*), and finish with five to seven minutes in
LYING RELEASE/CORPSE POSE (*savāsana*). Twenty to thirty minutes of working with my muse in forward bends and SHOULDER
STAND usually grants me hours of richer writing.

While being cautious of your neck and cervical spine and
avoiding these poses altogether if you have high blood pressure,
consider these options, for instance, for the TAKE A BREATH exercise in Chapter 20:

Variation #3: REVERSED ATTITUDE GESTURE (vipari-
takarani mudrā). *See illustration in Appendix. You may place a blanket
underneath you for extra padding in this pose. To come into this pose
from resting on your back, press your hands, palms down, as well as the
forearms against the floor, and use your arms and your abdominals
(stomach muscles) to lift your legs, knees straight and feet together for
better control. Keeping your arms on the floor, bend your elbows, and
place your hands under your pelvis for support. Your thighs and legs can
be at an angle so that your feet come over your head until you get accustomed to this pose, or your legs and thighs can be vertical and perpendicular to the floor. This pose places considerable weight on the forearms, and
so you may find it too difficult, but it's a good preparation for shoulder
stand and is a pose honored in the Hatha-Yoga-Pradipika as one of the
most essential poses for maintaining the brain's vital energy. It also places*

less blood pressure in the neck and chest than the standard shoulder stand and in fact releases constrictions in the neck's vessels, which lets more blood flow to the brain.[1]

Variation #4: SHOULDER STAND (sarvangāsana). See illustration in Appendix. From lying on your back, roll your shoulder blades back toward one another, bend your knees, and, using the hands to support the pelvis, lift your hips overhead. Place your hands near your rear against your lower back and wrap your thumbs around your sides. Your body may be at a 140-degree angle or so at first. If your neck and chest are comfortable here, you can experiment with moving your hands farther toward your upper back as your torso gradually straightens. Remember to listen to what your body needs and not to what your will insists that you think you should do to achieve some ideal Form.

HUMMING AND HEARING

Humming or **chanting** rouses the brain, the throat, and our cells. The practice helps us hear with our inner ear, a vital trait for any writer who must spend hours talking to herself and those myriad voices and who also must tend to the cadences of her words, lines, and sentences. My mother sent me a photograph of her singing at church. Joy rippled through her body. In this way, she chants at the level she's comfortable. Whereas Mantra-Yoga is a far more intricate system in practice and principle—just try humming. Even singing a nonsense song is a start to help you hear how words vibrate in your body and in your readers' inner ears.

LETTING GO

Finally, let go of intentions. This book begins with and sustains a focus on setting an intention. The book's focus also has explored yoga in service of writing. Remember, though, the sweetness of practicing yoga is to practice yoga. Get to the mat just to see what happens or what doesn't happen. More than one student has told me she feels most at home or most herself when on the mat. Yoga teachers can lose sight of this unconditional practice just as writing teachers can forget the joy of writing to write, for more than one writer likewise has told me he feels most at home and most himself when on the page. So write to enjoy this crazy thing we do, that we still love despite the agony it sometimes brings. And you know, usually it's not writing itself that brings agony so much as our expectations of it or because of the sorrow-laden rooms it takes us to.

Yoga's principles and practices seem endless. I know that may sound hokey, but understanding yoga is like trying to understand India: The more I think I know, the more I realize I have to learn. But the more I study and the more I try things out for myself, the more I learn about my own writing process, my own crazy congress that tries to legislate my thoughts and actions and feelings, my own pernicious Heckler, and this wonderful ally that has been with me since I was a long-haired, towheaded boy climbing trees in Fort Worth: my imagination.

Don't stop with this book. Continue to explore for yourself how your practice feeds your creative process. Send me a note about what works for you and what you're discovering for your own process.

And be patient. Nothing so counters our American desire for transformation than our assumption that we can drive through and order bliss with our happy meal. Yoga is no panacea for writing woes. But if you're persistent, if you do in fact give yourself at least a five-week plan and try some of the practices and principles for at least fifteen consecutive writing sessions, you will notice some changes in your body-mind-imagination. Though yoga still won't make writing easier per se, it can make writing all the richer and you all the more resourceful on your path to write authentically.

CHAPTER TWENTY-FOUR

A Writers' *Sat-sanga*

Yoga, more than any writing workshop, has taught me the value of community. The more I practice yoga, the more I am able to open up and give—as well as to receive—from the heart. My teachers created for me an environment of support characterized by clear communication and compassion, free for the most part from words of egotistical cruelty, egotistical narcissism, or egotistical passive-aggression. Which is not to say that the yogis I know—teachers or students—don't have their ego issues. They do, of course. Within these yoga communities, I've known randy single mothers, flustered business executives, women and men who left their corporate jobs, young men and women fresh out of college seeking to deepen their soul's education. Tattooed girls and CPA men. Politically, we were liberal and conservative, green as well as red-white-and-blue capitalist. Yet, because each of us students shared the same intention (to transform how we lived in our bodies and in this world) and the same set of tools to manifest that intention (the principles and practices of yoga), we loosely could be called a community of like-hearted individuals—what in Sanskrit is called a *sat-sanga*.

Lately, I've been working to create an authentic writers' *sat-sanga*, a place where we writers can communicate with one another on a basis of clarity, truthfulness, and compassion. It is a place where we can gather on our journey, sit a spell, share our experiences, and receive some helpful advice and perspective on our work—our writing. It is a place not unlike the inns that welcomed sojourners centuries ago—a sanctuary of diverse camaraderie and conviviality. For now, this place is virtual and online—possibly the twenty-first century's answer to the pub or ashram. The idea stemmed from a group of writers who have attended my workshops and felt they needed ongoing support outside of the workshops. So, as an extension to the workshops, we've created through the Web site *www.centertopage.com* an online writers *sat-sanga* called YAM Writers Online. YAM stands for Yoga as Muse, but *yam* also is the seed syllable for the heart region, a reminder for where our intentions lie when we seek responses from and offer responses to one another regarding our work and our journey. Through the Web site and e-mail, we post work for comment to one another, share with one another our experiences with yoga and writing, offer suggestions for publishing, and in general remind one another that we're not alone on this journey. Because many of us live everywhere from the Catskill Mountains to the West Coast, the virtual *sat-sanga* suits our needs best for now.

You can create your own writers' *sat-sanga*. A virtual *sat-sanga* can begin as easily as exchanging e-mails with one another. You'll probably want to clarify some guidelines and some commitments to one another (explained later in this chapter). If you're going to meet face-to-face, so much the better, I think. Decide upon a regular time and place to meet. A common coffee shop or diner or bookstore (with a tolerant staff) or library room is usually the best route, because no one feels pressured to host the group at his or her house. One group I know of meets in a college classroom on Sunday afternoons when the building is virtually unoccupied. The regularity—once a week works best—also often increases each member's commitment level.

But then I'd advise you in a few areas. First, be clear with one another about the group's intention. Our group's intention is to offer one another support that is both truthful and compassionate. This means that when we genuinely feel that a person's writing is not working well to serve her own writing intention, it's our duty to respond tactfully yet truthfully. If some writers only want positive feedback and bristle at the thought of receiving or offering constructive criticism, then they're going to feel out of place. Your group's intention, however, may be just that: to offer one another positive feedback. That's fine as long as you're clear with one another. Another group of writers with whom I worked (and played) years ago met at a downtown club every Wednesday. We had the intention of supporting what was dynamic in each other's works so we eventually could collaborate with one another to create a performance reading event at the club. Consider, too, whether or not you wish to limit the writers to discussing works of a specific genre. Some writers work best in fiction groups versus poetry groups, whereas other writers feel completely at home in learning from and mixing genres. Just be clear.

Second, regardless of the format you choose, be clear about how to offer feedback. In the YAM group, we keep our comments focused on the writing's craft and its spirit, not on the writer's personality or on our own personal experiences (which can become narcissistic). We also aim to be as specific as possible, always sure to move far beyond "I like it" or "That's nice." Identify as specifically as possible two things: 1) *what* part of a piece of writing you're commenting on and 2) *how* the part works or doesn't work for the writing as a whole. For instance, if I say, "Your introduction is good," I've specified what I'm referring to (the introduction), but I haven't been specific as to how it works. I could say, "Your opening sentences' references to water and blood set the themes for what follows later in the story when Benny almost drowns in the river after his head cracks against the rock." Notice how this comment not only is more specific (and thereby helpful to a fellow writer); it's also more factual and less evaluative than simply saying something is "good." Other comments, however, may be more subjective in terms of how certain parts of a work pique your curiosity or make you feel as a reader. So, if a writer's story is rather bland until the third scene on page four, you might say, "The scene in which Albert meets this desperate punk-rock chick really hooked my interest in the story and in Albert. Before then, I didn't feel very connected to Albert. Maybe you could move this scene to appear earlier in the story," which is far more specific, helpful, and certainly more compassionate, if not more truthful to the story, than simply saying, "The first three pages are really boring." Thus your response as a reader will help writers figure out how their work potentially affects readers— one of the greatest values, of course, of writing groups and workshops.

Third, encourage risk in one another. A truly supportive *sat-sanga* lets us question the norm and try out new forms. If you notice a fellow writer always begins a story with the same type of interior monologue, then prompt her to imagine another way of beginning— a third-person observation, an ironic or omniscient description of a whole town, a dog's point of view. The dreariest part of being in a writers' group for too long is that everyone's aesthetic response becomes pat and predictable. A good writers' *sat-sanga* guards against complacency and mediocrity—either in writing or responding to writing.

Fourth, extend your *sat-sanga*'s services beyond the workshop model (which is helpful but limited). Invite one another to offer a fifteen-to-thirty-minute talk on a certain topic relevant to writers. Maybe each of you offers an introductory talk on an author's work. Maybe one of you offers a talk on what you view as "the state of fiction in the United States" or "the role of the writer in the twenty-first century." In other words, grant yourself and others permission to *think* about what it means to be a writer at this time in history. It need not be a forum to pontificate, but a place to explore ideas. A salon, in essence. Such was the spirit of what some of us created when we developed Dallas's first literary nonprofit organization, WordSpace, and such is the spirit of what James Navé of Taos, New Mexico, is creating with his Taos Creative Writing Salon. At these five-day events, Navé invites writers to offer workshops to other writers, but he also infuses the event with topical discussions about writing, the writing life, the writing scene. He also includes workshops by drummers, yogis, and painters so that writers are fed by people in other creative disciplines. The idea is for us to guard against being myopic as writers in looking at our work solely in terms of words, images, sentences, and scenes. Such myopia is like regarding yoga solely with reference to the poses.

Another way to extend your *sat-sanga*'s service is through generously sharing information. Writers want to know about new publications or old publications that they've never heard of but perhaps should read. As we each should keep abreast of what's happening in publishing and should be supporting small presses, we can in turn suggest to each other books and journals and magazines to read.

You may only need, though, a *sat-sanga* of two or three. One good writing friend, a writing mentor, coach, or teacher, can provide regular feedback and guidance. Some mentors and coaches also can ask the right questions—if not the tough questions—to help you move your project farther along. Be sure you cultivate a relationship with someone whom you trust. (The same dictate, incidentally, always followed when I sought a yoga teacher.) Know the person's background. Know his or her motives for working with you. Sense in the first or second session whether or not the relationship will work and if you each will get from the relationship what you need. Otherwise, you're wasting your time, and writers don't have time to waste.

A few final caveats about working with groups: Overly critical people can squelch your fire. Overly sympathetic people can fan your hot ego. Also, guard against depending too much upon your allies. Meeting with them and talking about your project can substitute for the actual, regular work that needs to be accomplished: writing.

Which is to say that most writers, like it or not, are happiest and most productive in a *sat-sanga* of one. It is in solitude, after all, when we can best listen to those crazy, multifarious voices, when we can best heed those random images and characters that call for our attention, when we can step across the threshold, out of the familiar house, and into the woods where, perhaps, after a long trek of faith in the dark, we'll find a clearing, we'll find the center of our life that then will guide us back home and to the page.

Appendix of Poses with Contraindications

Photographs by Mickey Pantano

FOUNDATION POSES

LYING RELEASE/CORPSE POSE *(savāsana)* Come onto your back, legs straight, palms up. For a variation that relives your lower back, either bend your knees and keep the soles of your feet on the ground or place a pillow beneath your knees. Induces deep relaxation and stimulates the imagination.

CHILD'S POSE From a kneeling position, bend forward bringing your forehead to the ground and your arms to the sides. To relieve your lower back, either place a pillow between your thighs and calves, or spread your knees wide apart, allowing your torso to rest between your knees. Good for resting between poses or between writing sessions. Also good for withdrawing and checking in with the imagination.

MOUNTAIN POSE *(tadāsana)* Stand with feet hip-width apart and with insteps parallel. Place weight in both feet and at your perineum. Lengthen your spine by spiraling the insides of your thighs back, tucking your tailbone down, and drawing your navel and lower ribcage back. Good for setting your intention before a writing session.

SEATED POSE OPTIONS

WRITER'S/FRIENDSHIP POSE *(maitrīyāsana)* Sit comfortably with your sitting bones toward the edge of the chair, feet planted on the ground, spine long, and shoulders relaxed. Assume a relaxed yet alert state of awareness.

ADAMANTINE POSE/KNEELING POSE *(vajrāsana)* Sit on your heels, not between them. Place a blanket between your calves and thighs for extra comfort. Stimulates the lower body to help quiet your thoughts.

EASY CROSS-LEGGED POSE *(sukhāsana)* Sit evenly on both sitting bones. Lengthen your spine by drawing back your navel and lower rib cage. Place one or two folded blankets underneath your buttocks to relieve lower back strain. Good for brief sitting.

ADEPT'S POSE *(siddhāsana)* **variation** Place your left heel beneath your perineum and your right heel in front of your left ankle. With your root center open and both knees on the ground, this pose can quiet your thoughts and help you concentrate.

LOTUS POSE *(padmāsana)* Holding your right shin, not your ankle, bend your right leg and place your right foot on your left thigh or at the left thigh crease. Then, do the same for your left leg, bringing your left foot as close to your right hip as possible without straining your knee. Practice this pose only if you've been practicing for a while under a trained teacher's supervision and if you know the pose will not strain your knees. This pose relieves the lower back from stress, grounds the lower body, and maintains the spine's length.

CHAPTER 1: EXPLORING YOUR INTENTIONS FOR WRITING

TAKE A BREATH:
SETTING YOUR TWOFOLD WRITER'S INTENTION

OBLATIONS GESTURE *(anjali mudrā)* in MOUNTAIN POSE *(tādāsana)* Stand with feet hip-width apart and with insteps parallel. Anchor weight in both feet and at your perineum. Bring your palms together at your heart, forearms resting near your chest. Press into your palms. Because this pose balances your energy and quiets your thoughts, it is ideal for setting your twofold writing intention.

CHAPTER 3: MUSTERING PERSEVERANCE

TAKE A BREATH: STOKE YOUR WRITER'S FIRE

The following sequence is ideal for efficiently generating inner heat, which can help you as a writer to develop self-discipline and perseverance.

SOARING LOCK POSE PREPARATION WITH TONGUE OUT *(uddīyāna-bandha)* Come into MOUNTAIN POSE *(tādāsana)* and bring your hands to your hips, chest open. On a long and forceful exhalation, stick out the tongue toward the chin, bend the knees, bring the hands toward the knees, fingers inside and arms straight.

SOARING LOCK POSE FRONT VIEW *(uddīyāna-bandha)* Then, with the last bit of breath exhaled, draw your abdominal wall in and up, creating a "lock" of energy that moderates your digestion system and inner heat.

SOARING LOCK POSE SIDE VIEW *(uddīyāna-bandha)*

FRIENDLY WARNING:
If you're pregnant or have ulcers, avoid drawing in and lifting the abdominal wall.

SOARING LOCK POSE WITH TONGUE IN *(uddīyāna-bandha)* Then, hold the breath, maintain the lock, and close the mouth. Holding the breath and keeping the lock, return to MOUNTAIN POSE *(tādāsana)*. After you release your stomach, slowly inhale fully, and repeat four more times.

CHAPTER 5: CREATING
AN AUTHENTIC VOICE

TAKE A BREATH:
STRIKE YOUR UNSTRUCK AUTHENTIC VOICE

OBLATIONS GESTURE *(anjali-mudra)* Bring your palms together at your heart, forearms resting on or near your rib cage.

SEATED EVEN-HEARTED POSE *(sama-hridayāsana variation)* In a comfortable seated position, spine lengthened, from **OBLATIONS GESTURE,** exhale and unfold your arms to the side, keeping your elbows bent, and facing your palms forward.

CHAPTER 6: PRACTICING PRESENCE

TAKE A BREATH:
LET YOUR IMAGINATION GET ON YOUR NERVES

STANDING FORWARD BEND *(uttanāsana)* From **MOUNTAIN POSE,** place weight in both heels. Spine lengthened, exhale and bend forward from your hips. With head and neck relaxed, press from the heels upward to your hips to relieve your lower back. This pose stretches the hamstrings, which relieves tension from sitting for long periods and also calms down the sympathetic nervous system—a plus for the imagination.

STANDING FORWARD BEND VARIATION *(uttanāsana)* To relieve lower back strain, bend your knees *while in* **MOUNTAIN POSE.** Keeping knees bent, bend forward from the hips and let your chest come toward your thighs. Fold your arms. You also can spread your legs farther than hip-width apart.

DOWNWARD FACING DOG POSE *(adho mukha svanāsana)* Bring your hands to the mat, below your shoulders, and place weight in the bottom knuckles of your hands (*not* in your wrists), middle fingers facing forward. Feet and hands typically are three to four feet apart with feet parallel and hip-width apart. Find the distance that stretches your hamstrings yet is not uncomfortable. On each exhalation, bring the heels closer to the mat. Because your heart is higher than your brain, this pose helps circulation in the upper body and can calm down the inner chatter while inducing imagery.

From **DOWNWARD FACING DOG,** bend your knees and come into **ADAMANTINE POSE/KNEELING POSE** *(vajrāsana)*. Sit *on* heels, not between them. Take a blanket between your calves and thighs for extra comfort. This pose can quiet your thoughts and help you concentrate. Then, move from here into **LYING RELEASE/CORPSE POSE** *(savāsana)*.

CHAPTER 8:
EMBODIED METAPHORS AND SYMBOLS

TAKE A BREATH #1:
MINE THE MOMENT FOR A METAPHOR

 ALTERNATE NOSTRIL BREATHING *(nāḍī sodhana prāṇāyāma)* preparation, close-up of hand Curl your middle and index fingers into your palm's thumb mound while extending the little finger, ring finger, and thumb.

ALTERNATE NOSTRIL BREATHING *(nāḍī shodhana prāṇāyāma)* Place the thumb tip on the outside of the right nostril and the ring and little finger tips on the outside of the left nostril. With eyes open or closed, close the right nostril and inhale fully and slowly through the left nostril. Close the left nostril, open the right nostril, and exhale completely through the right nostril. Inhale completely through the right nostril. Close the right nostril, open the left nostril, and exhale completely through the left nostril. Repeat four more times. This practice stimulates both of the brain's hemispheres and can induce alpha brain waves and possibly theta waves, aiding your concentration and imagination.

TAKE A BREATH #2: REIMAGINE A BODY

CAT POSE STRAIGHT BACK *(marjarāsana)* Come onto your hands and knees, bringing hands beneath your shoulders and knees beneath your hips. Let the tops of your feet rest on your mat or blanket. Straighten your back like a table as your heart melts toward the mat.

CAT POSE WITH ARCHED BACK *(marjarāsana)* Exhale and press into the base of your knuckles, not your wrists, as your upper back arches and your tailbone tucks between your legs. From these two poses, you can explore other variations such as turning from side to side, forming a curved "C" with your torso.

CHAPTER 14:
WRITING THE TRUTH

SOARING LOCK POSE PREPARATION WITH TONGUE OUT *(uddīyāna-bandha)* **close up** From **MOUNTAIN POSE,** take your hands to your hips and keep your heart open. Take a deep inhalation, and on each of your next two exhalations, extend your tongue out toward your chin as far as it will reach, direct your eyes upward, and from your feet and root center upward roar out an "AHH" as loud as you can, letting your grief or irritation or anger vibrate through your body, across the room, and off of the nearest mountain.

CHAPTER 15:
FACING FEAR

TAKE A BREATH:
LAUGH AT THE HECKLER AND
EMBODY CONFIDENCE

WARRIOR II POSE *(virabhadrāsana II)* Stand with feet approximately three to four feet apart, insteps parallel. Turn your right foot out ninety degrees and your left foot in about forty-five degrees. Your right hip will move slightly forward, but it should not be squared with your left hip. Exhale as you bend your right knee, bring your arms up, your right arm in front, left arm behind you. With spine vertical, drop your torso back slightly to assure you are not lunging forward. Anchor weight in both heels as well as in your perineum, and keep your chest open. Align the knee over the heel. Gaze stays just beyond the front middle finger. Repeat on the opposite side. If you feel pain in your back, hips, or legs, shorten your stance. This grounding pose roots your concentration and determination while also stretching the psoas muscle, a key muscle that, if stretched, can free your embodied will.

CHAPTER 16:
WRITING BASED ON YOUR SELF

TAKE A BREATH:
COMPASSION FOR THE INTEGRAL SELF

Useful especially if you are writing a memoir or are basing a narrator upon your-self when writing fiction or poetry, this sequence can offer fresh insight into how complex and seemingly contradictory is any self.

OFFERING MOUNTAIN POSE *(pushpa tādāsana)* side view From MOUNTAIN POSE with hands at your heart, inhale and bring your arms directly in front of you at shoulder height, palms facing forward. Refrain from extending the shoulders away from the shoulder joints.

EVEN-HEARTED MOUNTAIN POSE *(sama-hyridaya-tādāsana)* Exhale and glide each arm to each side, shoulder height. Curl your fingertips to your palms while you flex your thumbs toward your skull. Inhale completely into your chest region, and exhale as you turn your head to face your right thumb, blowing your breath through slightly parted lips from your heart to your right side. Inhale facing center, and exhale, repeating on the left side. Inhale facing center.

OPEN-HEARTED MOUNTAIN POSE *(hridaya-tādāsana)* Exhale completely as hands come behind you and clasp, if possible, arms straight or bent. Inhale completely into your chest region as you look up toward the ceiling, expanding your heart region.

OPEN-HEARTED STANDING FORWARD BEND *(hridaya-uttanāsana)*
Exhale completely and, with hands still clasped if possible, bend forward from the hips. Bring your hands toward the floor. Bend your knees if necessary.

AWKWARD CHAIR POSE *(utkatāsana)* With one full inhalation, release your hands, swoop them toward the floor, and lift them in front and beside you, bringing biceps toward your ears. Straighten arms at an angle and toward the ceiling with thumbs clasped and fingers pointing toward the ceiling. Keep the spine long in both directions by tucking your tailbone and drawing back your navel.

CHAPTER 18:
COMPASSION FOR YOUR CHARACTERS

CRAMPED HEART *(dukha-hridaya)* **side view** From a seated position, fold your arms and hold the opposite forearm. Arching your upper back, bring your chin toward your chest. As you concentrate on your heart region, notice what single word or image surfaces to describe how this position feels.

CRAMPED HEART *(dukha-hridaya)* **front view**

SEATED EVEN-HEARTED POSE *(hridayāsana* **variation)** In a comfortable seated position, spine lengthened, from **CRAMPED HEART POSITION,** exhale and lift your head as your arms unfold to the sides, keeping elbows bent, and facing palms forward.

CHAPTER 23:
FOR WRITERS WHO ALREADY PRACTICE YOGA

SIDE-ANGLE POSE *(utthita parsvokanāsana)* From WARRIOR II POSE, right foot forward, exhale and bring your right arm to the outside of your right foot and rest either your fingers or palms on the mat, depending upon your flexibility. Open your torso to the side by rotating the left hip and then the left chest and shoulder toward the ceiling. The left arm reaches diagonally overhead, the biceps touching the ear. Keep the knee aligned directly over the ankle. Look under your left arm and toward the ceiling if no tension surfaces in your neck and shoulders. Repeat on the other side. This grounding pose roots your concentration and creates space in your lungs for increased respiration—key for reducing a writer's fear and anxiety responses.

BACK EXTENSION POSE *(pasch-imāttanāsana)* From a seated position, bring your legs straight in front of you, feet touching. Lengthen your spine on an inhalation, and on an exhalation bend forward from your hips, not your chest. Keeping the spine straight, bring your chest toward your thighs. If able, either hold your big toes or the outsides of your feet or clasp your hands behind your feet. Close your eyes, and slow down.

BACK EXTENSION POSE VARIATION *(paschimāttanāsana)* From a seated position, bring your legs in front of you, feet touching. Bend your knees. Lengthen your spine on an inhalation, and on an exhalation bend forward from your hips, not your chest. Keeping the spine straight, bring your chest toward your thighs. Let your hands rest to the sides. Close your eyes, and slow down.

REVERSED ATTITUDE GESTURE *(viparīta-karanī mudrā)* You may place a blanket underneath you for extra padding in this pose. From resting on your back, press your hands, palms down, as well as the forearms against the floor, and use your arms and your abdominal (stomach) muscles to swing your legs up, knees straight and feet together for better control. Keeping your arms on the floor, bend your elbows, and place your hands under your pelvis for support. Your thighs and legs can be at an angle so that your feet come over your head until you get accustomed to this pose, or your legs and thighs can be vertical and perpendicular to the floor.

FRIENDLY WARNING:
If you have high blood pressure, glaucoma, detached retina, or are menstruating, either avoid this pose or see a holistic physician or qualified teacher before attempting this pose. If pregnant, avoid stressing your abdominal muscles when lifting or lowering your torso.

SHOULDER STAND POSE *(sarvangāsana)* From lying on your back, roll your shoulder blades back toward one another, bend your knees and, using the hands to support the pelvis, lift your hips overhead. Place your hands near your rear against your lower back and wrap your thumbs around your sides. Your body may be at a 140-degree angle or so at first. If your neck and chest are comfortable here, you can experiment with moving your hands farther toward your upper back as your torso gradually straightens. You should be able to breathe evenly, and you should feel no compression or pain in your neck area or cervical spine.

FRIENDLY WARNING:

If you have high blood pressure, glaucoma, detached retina, or are menstruating, either avoid this pose or see a holistic physician or qualified teacher before attempting this pose. If pregnant, avoid stressing your abdominal muscles when lifting or lowering your torso.

Glossary of Key Terms

This list provides definitions of terms related to yoga, writing, and neuroscience that are pertinent to this book.

Abhinivesha ("will to live"), a mode of clinging to certainties. Considered in the *Yoga-Sutra* as a primary cause of suffering and affliction, it's fueled by fear. It can hinder a writer from taking creative risks. Chapter 15.

Adamantine pose/kneeling pose (See *vajrāsana*)

Adept's pose (See *siddhāsana*)

Ahimsā ("without harm" "nonviolence"), the first ethical practice that Patanjali defines in the first of eight limbs of yoga; an all-encompassing practice that encourages yogis to think, speak, eat, and act without harm to others or to oneself; aids in a writer's capacity to render believable dialogue. Chapter 12.

Ajñā-cakra ("command center"), also called the third eye center, located roughly between the eyebrows and is activated by the pituitary and pineal glands. Responsible for our faculties of vision, imagination, and sensory knowledge, it's a vital area for writers to stimulate. Chapters 5 and 20 especially.

Alpha waves, brain waves that have 8–13 oscillations per second. Slower than beta waves, these waves are detected in people involved in creative activity, concentration, yoga, and meditation. Chapter 4 especially as well as Chapters 6, 9, and 18.

Alternate nostril breathing (See *Nādī-shodhana*)

Anāhata cakra ("unstruck center"), the heart center; vital for extending compassion to the self, others, and difficult characters. Chapters 5, 16, 17, and 18.

Anaphora, a sentence pattern in which a writer or speaker repeats the same word or words at the beginning of successive clauses or sentences. Chapter 11.

Anger (See *krodha*)

Anjali-mudrā ("oblations seal"), a hand gesture enacted by placing both hands, palms together, fingers up, at the heart. A common gesture of communicating the best in another person with the best in oneself. By bringing together left and right, it also signifies unifying all dualities. See Appendix. Chapter 16.

Antarā kumbhaka is suspension of breath after a full inhalation, useful for stimulating physical energy and brain activity. Chapter 11.

Antarā kumbhaka sama vrtti is suspension of the breath after the inhalation with even counts of inhalation, exhalation, and retention. Chapter 11.

Antar-jnana ("inner knowledge"), like *sahaja-jnana* ("inborn knowledge"), intuition. An essential faculty to cultivate for drafting, writing with truthfulness, and re-visioning. Chapters 13, 14.

Antar-trataka ("inner gazing"), a Hatha-Yoga method used to deepen concentration and contemplation.

Antithesis, a sentence pattern in which a writer poses a concept's opposing idea, usually in a grammatically parallel form. Chapter 11.

Arjuna (See *Bhagavad-Gita*)

Āsana, the term most commonly used for a yoga pose. It also translates to "situation" and "one's relationship to the earth." Patanjali defines it as that pose which is both alert and relaxed, strong and soft.

Avalokiteshvara ("One Who Hears the World's Cries"), an androgynous deity who sprouted a thousand arms and hands with eyes in the palms to reach out to all who suffer—a potent image for writers who wish to extend compassion to their subjects. Chapter 18.

Awkward chair pose (See *utkatāsana*)

Back extension pose (See *paschimāttanāsana*)

Bahya kumbhaka, suspending the breath after a full exhalation. By calming the sympathetic nervous system, this practice helps writers quiet the inner Heckler and deepen their ability to hear language's cadences. Chapter 11.

Beta waves, brain waves that have 13–36 waves per second—more than twice as fast as alpha waves. Chapter 4.

Bhagavad-Gita ("The Blessed One's Song"), a text that recounts the dialogue between Arjuna and Krishna on how Yoga aids in overcoming fear and doubt. Arjuna is the protagonist and warrior of *The Bhagavad-Gita*. In this context, the story elucidates the fear-ridden writer's plight. Chapter 15.

Bhakti yoga, devotional yoga characterized by chanting. Chapter 11.

Bhavana ("visualization"), an essential limb of Tantra-Yoga in which the practitioner develops the inner eye and shapes to the interior self by visualization

Bhaya ("fear"), one of a yogi's primary afflictions. In this context, we understand the nature of fear as it inhibits writers' creativity. Chapter 15.

Bhranti-darshana ("delusion"), a primary hindrance to yogis' ability to progress on their path, for the writer is attaching oneself to one's writing. Chapter 21.

Bija-mantra ("seed syllable"), a word with a sonic vibration that stimulates specific energy centers. OM, HAM, YAM, and RAM are seed syllables believed to stimulate the third eye, throat, heart, and stomach regions respectively. Chapter 10.

Cakra ("wheel"), a center of energy located in the subtle body and correlating loosely to centers in the physical body.

Cat pose (See *marjarāsana*)

Causal body (*ānandamaya-kosha*, bliss body), the innermost sheath believed to house our capacity for bliss or ecstasy. Chapter 9.

Causal imagination, the part of the imagination that houses imagery intimating union and bliss. Chapters 9.

Compassion, a writer's ability to perceive and to portray the self, others, difficult characters, or inanimate objects with respect for one's suffering, as well as with truthfulness and complexity.

Corpse pose (See *savāsana*)

Cramped heart position (See *dukha hridaya*)

Dharana ("concentration"), the sixth of Patanjali's eight-limb yoga system. Chapters 4 and 9.

Dhyana ("meditation"), the seventh of Patanjali's eight-limb system. In meditation, a writer's thoughts begin to cease distinguishing between self and the object of concentration. Chapter 11.

Doha, a Tantric poetic verse or song. Chapter 6.

Doubt (See *samshaya*)

Dukha ("suffering")

Dukha hridaya ("suffering heart"), a gesture in which the arms cross and the hands hold opposite forearms, and the chin comes to the chest. The upper back is rounded. This pose, in emotional gesture and physical sensation, counters **even-hearted pose** and **open-hearted mountain pose**. Chapter 18.

Dvesha-yoga ("yoga of hatred"), a rare practice drawn from a story in the *Bhagavata-Purana* and is based on the idea that one can learn to fear the divine by first hating the divine; from this intense near-feverish concentration, the practitioner ends up loving the divine. This practice gets a new twist for writers of satire in Chapter 19.

Easy cross-legged pose (See *sukhāsana*)

Ekagrata ("one-pointedness"), a practice of centering, for a sustained period, one's attention on a single concept or object. It is a writer's ideal state of body-mind-imagination when no external or internal distractions draw one away from the desk or page. Chapters 4, 9.

Epistrophe, a sentence pattern that repeats a word or words at the ends of successive clauses or sentences. Chapter 11.

Equal movement breath (See *sama-vrtti prānāyāma*)

Even-hearted pose (See *sama hridayāsana*)

Even-hearted mountain pose (See *sama-hyridaya-tādāsana*)

Faith (See *shraddhā*)

Fear (See *bhaya*)

Form for writers is the shape a piece of writing assumes. Ideally, it relates integrally to content, message, and intention. (See *rūpa*) Chapter 20.

Friendship pose (See *maitrīyāsana*)

Ganesha, an elephant-headed god who, among other attributes, signifies auspicious beginnings. Also the scribe of yoga, he can remind writers that they embody the ability to remove obstacles. Chapter 2.

Hatha-Yoga ("forceful yoga"), a term generally applied to all yoga practices and traditions in which the body is a vehicle of self-realization rather than something that should be negated or transcended.

Hatha-Yoga Pradipika ("Light on Forceful Yoga"), a seminal fourteenth-century yoga manual.

Hridaya tadāsana ("open-hearted mountain pose), a pose designed to stimulate the heart center and a writer's compassion. Appendix and Chapter 19.

Hypnagogic state, the state of mind and imagination in which a person, while awake, experiences intense imagery surfacing from memory or from the subtle imagination. It can be induced by calming the sympathetic nervous system, increasing cerebral blood flow, and slowing down the brain's waves to alpha and theta wave lengths. Chapters 7, 8, 9.

Ida-nādī ("comfort channel"), a channel of energy connected with the left nostril, the body's left side, the parasympathetic nervous system, and the right hemisphere. When stimulated, it can arouse the unconscious and imagination. Chapter 8.

Imagery, language that creates sensory impressions in a reader's imagination. It is a foundational trait of an embodied writing style—a way of writing that affects readers on a physiological as well as imaginative and emotional level. Chapter 6.

Intention, an act of aligning thoughts and will with body, imagination, and spirit. Chapter 1.

Intuition (See *anta-jnāna*)

Jāgrat ("waking reality"), daily consciousness and awareness. A yogi or a writer can practice being awake while dreaming (hence, lucid dreaming, which can lead to lucid writing). Chapters 8, 9.

Jālandhara-bandha ("throat lock"), a lock enacted by bringing the chin to the collarbone notch. Believed to help keep vital energy in the brain region, it also helps writers stimulate the throat or communication center to write with truthfulness. See Chapter 14.

Jīva-ātman, the individuated self, the personality that lives as a separate entity in this world. Chapter 16.

Jīvan-mukta, the self that achieves liberation while in this body and world. Chapter 16.

Jnāna-indriya, the "cognitive senses" believed to be essential for the yogi to harness for advanced practice. Similarly, writers can learn to heighten and harness their senses. Chapter 6.

Kaimura, described in the *Shiva-Sutras* as a "proclivity toward play." Chapter 7.

Kapāla-bhāti-kriya ("Shining skull cleansing"), a cleansing practice enacted by passively inhaling and forcefully exhaling. Its work on the abdominal muscles and the immediate rush of oxygenated blood to the brain makes it an essential practice for writers wanting concentration and perseverance. Chapter 3.

Karma ("action"), the belief that both a person's actions and a person's intention for acting will have moral consequences in the future or in a future life. Chapter 16.

Karunā, a Pali word meaning "active compassion." Chapters 16–18.

Kosha ("sheath"), our bodies' different layers. In most schools of yoga, it's believed that human beings have a physical, subtle (made up of three subsheaths), and causal body.

Krodha ("anger"), described in some ancient yoga texts as a primary gateway to mental, physical, and spiritual hell. In this context, it becomes a powerful force that can be converted into authentic writing. Chapter 19.

Lying release Pose/corpse pose (See *savāsana*)

Maitrīyāsana ("Friendship Pose"), also translated here as Writers Pose because it is a pose in which a yogi sits in a chair—a writer's most common "pose" or situation. See Appendix.

Manipura cakra ("treasure-city center"), the solar plexus, the center of energy located approximately in the upper pelvis, the stomach region, and below the rib cage. Associated with willfulness and action, it's a vital center for writers needing perseverance. Chapter 3.

Mantra, expressing a thought or an intention by sound. Chapters 10, 11, 14.

Marjarāsana ("Cat pose") is a foundational pose in which a yogi is on hands and knees, wrists beneath the shoulders and knees beneath the hips. Chapters 8, 17, Appendix.

Metaphor, a direct comparison of the familiar to the unfamiliar, the invisible to the visible, the physical to the metaphysical. Chapter 8.

Mountain pose (See *tadāsana*)

Mūla-bandha ("root lock"), a practice of sealing energy in the upper body by contracting the perineum. Its stimulation of the pudendal nerves is believed to help vital organs function properly. It can help writers concentrate and "root" their thoughts. See Chapter 4.

Mūlādhāra cakra ("root center"), a center of energy located generally near the perineum and when balanced can induce calmness, groundedness, and focus. Chapter 4.

Nādī shodhana ("Alternate Nostril Breathing"), a breath practice performed by inhaling and exhaling through one nostril at a time. See Chapter 8 on how it affects the brain and assists in metaphor making.

Nādī ("energy conduit"), not unlike an acupuncture meridian, a channel of energy. Some yoga texts claim we have seventy thousand *nadis* in our bodies that each contain vital energy. They are the tunnels through which *prana* travels within the body. By knowing how to stimulate certain *nadis*, writers can harness their energy. Chapter 8.

OM, the universe's essential sound. Pronounced "AUM," the first sound correlates to the lower part of the spine as well as to the waking world (*jagrat*); the second sound to the cervical spine and the dream world (*svapna*); the third sound to the third eye center and the sleeping world (*nidra*). When embodied together, the yogi experiences the fourth world (*turiya*), bliss, or joy-filled amazement (*vismaya*). See Chapter 14.

One-pointed concentration (see *ekagrata* and *dharana*)

Parallelism, a patterned sentence in which parts of speech, phrases, or clauses are grammatically the same. Chapter 11.

Parsvakonāsana ("Side-angle pose") Appendix.

Particularity, rendering a subject's attributes so uniquely as to make it at once believable and memorable. Chapter 6.

Paschimāttanāsana ("Back extension pose"), a seated forward bend. Appendix.

Patanjali, the author of *Yoga-Sutra* (circa probably 200 c.e. although some scholars have attributed them to 200 b.c.e.).

Physical body (*anna-maya-kosha*, "gross body"), the outermost layer of our body's organs, blood, bones, et cetera. See especially Chapters 6 and 17.

Physical imagination, that part of our imagination that receives and stores images and ideas from our cognitive senses; responsible in part for memory and the recollection of images. *Asanas* and other yoga tools help stimulate this imagination. Defined in Chapter 6.

Pingalā-nādi ("tawny current"), complementary to the *ida-nadi* as it is connected to the right nostril, the body's right side, the brain's left side, and the sympathetic nervous system. When stimulated, it heats the body and boosts adrenaline. Chapter 8.

Prāna ("life force"), that force which makes breath possible and which animates all life outside and inside of sentient beings. Chapters 4, 11.

Prānāyāma, harnessing the life force through breath work. Especially Chapters 4 and 11.

Pratyahara ("sensory withdrawal"), the active reduction of responding to sensory stimulation in order to heighten control of one's faculties. Helpful for writers who need to develop intuition for re-visioning. Chapter 20.

Proprioception, awareness of the body's proprioceptors, specialized receptors that receive signals related to tendons, muscles, and joints. This awareness increases writers' presence by helping them pay attention to their body's interior world. Chapter 6.

Pushing mountain pose, a standing pose. Chapter 16, Appendix.

Reversed attitude pose (See *viparīta-karanī mudrā*)

Rhythm, the patterns of repetition in a piece of writing. Repeated stressed syllables, sounds, grammatical forms, and words can create a piece of writing's rhythm. See Chapter 11 for more on its relationship to yoga and sentences.

Ritam ("universal truth"). Chapter 14.

Root lock (see *mula-bandha*)

Rūpa ("form") also translates to body, physical beauty, and the manifestation of the divine; thus, the term reminds yogis of a yoga pose's beautiful, if not divine quality. Chapter 20.

Sahaja-jnana ("inborn knowledge") (See *antarā-jnana*)

samādhi ("bliss"), the eighth of Patanjali's eight-limb yoga system characterized by the individuated self's complete union with one's realized self, which is part and parcel of all animate and sentient life in the universe. A Tantra view is that bliss is embodied by harnessing the energy and faculties of this physical body while living with joy in this physical world—not by negating this body or this world. Chapters 7, 9.

Sama hridayāsana (Even-hearted pose) Chapter 18, Appendix.

Sama hridaya-tādāsana (Even-hearted mountain pose) Chapter 16, Appendix.

Sama vrtti prānāyāma (Even-length breathing), a form of breath control in which one inhales and exhales the same length. Retention of breath for the same length after a full inhalation or exhalation can be added. Chapter 11.

Samprajnāta samādhi ("supported bliss"), the practice of concentrated gazing and meditation with a physical object. Chapter 9.

Samshaya ("doubt"), the state of having two conflicting drives. A primary obstacle to yogis and writers. Chapter 15.

Samskāra ("subtle impressions"), impressions made on our subconscious, our subtle body, and our subtle imagination. When left unconscious, they can dictate our thoughts and actions. Chapter 11.

Satire, writing that criticizes human behavior, figures, groups of people, or institutions; characterized by the intention to reveal truth and stylistically characterized by wit, irony, and clever use of language. Chapter 19.

Satya ("worldly truth"), the ability to speak and to act with certainty and yet without harm to others. (See "truthfulness") Chapter 14.

Satyagraha ("firm in one's truth"), Gandhi's practice of political resistance, distinguished from passive resistance. Chapter 14.

Savāsana ("lying release/corpse pose"), a supine pose in which one rests on one's back, palms up. Appendix.

Senses (See *jnana-indriya*)

Sensory withdrawal (See *pratyahara*)

Sensuousness, the quality of writing that stimulates readers' inner senses. Chapter 6.

Shimbava, the practice of gazing upward and between the eyebrows to help stimulate the third eye center. Chapter 20.

Shining skull cleansing breath (See *kapala-bhati kriya*)

Shiva-Sutra, a "revealed" text from the ninth century. An essential text for Kashmir Shaivism (a school of yoga), these seventy-seven aphorisms provide guidelines for reaching bliss in this body and world. Chapter 7.

Shoulder stand (See *sarvangāsana*)

Shraddhā, "faith" and "confidence," fully embodied. This essential trait helps writers counter fear and doubt. Chapter 15.

Siddhāsana ("adept's pose"), a seated pose. Appendix.

Side-angle pose (See *parsvakonāsana*)

Standing forward bend pose (See *Uttanāsana*)

Subtle body, a sheath of the human body composed of the vital breath body, emotional body, and intellectual body. One way to understand how energy, emotions, and intellect are "embodied" or directly influenced by, yet still distinct from, the physical body. Chapters 6 and 7.

Subtle imagination, part of the imagination that houses and releases random images from the unconscious body; often filters images with emotions. Chapters 6 and 7.

Suffering (See *dukha*)

Sukhāsana ("Easy Crossed-Legged Pose"), a seated pose good for brief sitting. See Appendix.

Svādhyāya ("moving into one's self"), self-study that involves both studying classic texts to understand the great teachings that precede one's path as well as studying the inner workings of one's own mind. This study applies to yogis as well as to writers. Chapter 5.

Svapna ("dream reality"), the state of dreaming while asleep or while awake. A vital state of awareness for writers wishing to access their unconscious consciously. Chapter 7.

Syntax is the word order of a sentence. Chapter 11.

Tādāsana ("mountain pose/standing pose"), a fundamental standing pose from which many other poses derive. Appendix.

Tantra-Yoga, a wide-reaching term that applies to diverse schools of philosophy including Buddhism, Shaktism, and Shaivism. What most Tantrikas share is a belief that the feminine principle plays a vital role in liberation, that the body is a vehicle for liberation in this world (not beyond this world), and that liberation is the province for everybody—not just the elite.

Tapas ("heat"), "self-discipline," the burning enthusiasm that helps one manifest an intention, "voluntary self-challenge." An essential quality for writers who wish to persevere. Chapter 3.

Third eye center (See *ājnā-cakra*)

Throat lock (See *Jālandhara-bandha*)

Truthfulness, that quality of writing that indisputably rings to the reader as right, honest, and real if not disconcerting. It typically addresses a subject's complexities. Chapter 14.

Uddīyāna bandha ("soaring lock"), an essential means to maintain vital energy in the torso and to stimulate physical energy in the body by drawing in and up the abdomen after a full exhalation. An effective tool for writers to cultivate perseverance. Appendix and Chapter 3.

Glossary of Key Terms

Ujjayī prāṇāyāma ("victorious breath"), a form of breath control enacted by contracting the glottis and creating a raspy-sounding breath along the back of the throat. Chapter 14.

Upanishads ("to sit near one's teacher"), a set of "revealed" texts that set forth the philosophy of the individuated self's relationship to the universe.

Upaya ("skillful means"), all of the tools and practices that yoga and other disciplines afford one for transformation.

Utkaṭāsana ("awkward chair pose"), a standing pose. Appendix.

Uttanāsana ("standing forward bend") Appendix.

Vāc ("voice"), the goddess of sacred speech. Applies to how the sounds that emanate from any voice and alphabet are divinely connected to the universe's primal sounds of creation. Chapter 5.

Vāc-maya-tapas ("disciplined speech"), the practice of refraining from unnecessary and wasteful talk. Chapter 3.

Vaikhari ("crude sound"), the basest level of audible sound. It is an essential yet superficial level of speech and communication. Chapter 12.

Vajrāsana ("adamantine/kneeling pose"), a seated pose. Appendix.

Vedanta, a far-reaching philosophy of nondualism that is reflected in the *Vedas* and especially in the *Upanishads.*

Victorious breath (See *"ujjayī prāṇāyāma)*

Vinyasa ("flow" "linking tool"), a way of connecting one situation to the next with mindful intention. Chapter 2.

Viparīta-karaṇī mudrā ("reversed attitude gesture"), an inverted pose. Appendix for variations.

Viribridāsana II ("warrior II pose"), a standing pose. Chapter 15 and Appendix.

Vishuddi cakra ("purity wheel"), the energy center located in the throat area; associated with truthfulness and clear communication. Chapter 14.

Vismaya, "joy-filled amazement" experienced when one can engage wakefulness, dreaming, and sleeping as one reality. Chapter 7.

Viveka ("discernment"), a critical faculty to help a yogi distinguish what elements of life help versus hinder one's progress; for writers, this analytical and clear-headed faculty is essential when revising to distinguish what parts of writing need to stay, be changed, or omitted. Chapter 21.

Warrior II (See *viribridāsana II)*

Writer's pose (See *maitrī yāsana)*

Yoga, derived from the root *yuj* meaning "to yoke, to harness," applies generally to endeavors aimed at harnessing the mind's fluctuations; extends in this book to endeavors, practices, and tools aimed also at harnessing intellect, emotion, and imagination.

Yoga-Sutra, a seminal text composed by Patanjali probably in 200 C.E.. Made up of 195 aphorisms, the text elucidates the different means of yoga to overcome mental afflictions and to reach bliss.

Endnotes

INTRODUCTION: Remember Your Body

1. Margaret Atwood, *Negotiating with the Dead:A Writer on Writing* (Cambridge University Press, 2002): xxiv.

CHAPTER ONE: Putting on the Robe:
Exploring Your Intentions for Writing

1. Bonnie Myotai Treace, Sensei, "Priest's Robe and Sound of a Bell: Gateless Gate, Case #16," Dharma Talk, Zen Mountain Monastery, Mt. Tremper, New York (7 July 2002).

2. Vanda Scaravelli, *Awakening the Spine* (HarperSanFrancisco, 1991): 106. Scaravelli, one of my teacher's teachers before she died a few years ago, wrote this remarkable book when she was in her eighties. I have much gratitude for Scaravelli's liberating and authentic approach to practicing yoga.

3. Jhumpa Lahiri, interview with Matthew Solan, *Poets & Writers* (Sept.–Oct. 2003): 37.

4. Sindiwe Magona, "Clawing at Stones," *The Spirit of Writing: Classic and Contemporary Essays Celebrating the Writing Life*, ed. Mark Robert Waldman (New York: Tarcher/Putnam, 2001).

5. Jean Bernstein, "How and Why," *The Essayist at Work: Profiles of Creative Nonfiction Writers*, ed. Lee Gutkind. (Portsmouth, NH: Heinemann, 1998): 215.

6. Ellen Gilchrist, "Like a Flower of Feathers or a Winged Branch," *The Essayist at Work: Profiles of Creative Nonfiction Writers*, Ed. Lee Gutkind (Portsmouth, NH: Heinemann, 1998): 110.

CHAPTER TWO: Schedules and Rituals to
Stretch Your Writing Time

1. This teaching of *vinyasa* is the heart of Krishnamacharya and his son Sri T.K.V. Desikachar's practice. Krishnamacharya was the direct teacher not only of his son, who has developed the *Viniyoga* of yoga, but also of the two earliest and most influential yogis in the West, B.K.S. Iyengar and Sri K. Pattabi Jois, who developed the physical *Ashtanga* Yoga system. Pattabi Jois in turn inspired David Life and Sharon Gannon to develop their innovative and spiritually grounded form of *vinyasa* called *Jivamukti Yoga*.

2. John Daido Loori, *The Eight Gates of Zen: Spiritual Training in an American Zen Monastery* (Mt. Tremper, NY: Dharma Communications, 1992): 172.

CHAPTER THREE: A Stoked Belly:
Mustering Perseverance to Keep Writing

1. Georg Feurstein, *The Yoga Tradition: Its History, Literature, Philosophy, and Practice* (Prescott, AZ: Hohm Press, 1998): 87–90, and Georg Feurstein, "Heating Up Your Practice," *Yoga International*, Jan. 2003: 28.

2. In this book I'm less interested in yoga's mystical or esoteric dimensions. I mention these energy centers and channels because after just a few years of deliberate practice, I began to experience ways to harness and direct my energy in ways that improved my clarity and my writing process. This book will share with you very practical ways to do likewise without feeling as if you're trying to levitate. Some yogis, I should note, dispute the idea that energy centers correlate to anything in our physical body. Shyam Sundar Goswami's *Layayoga: An Advanced Method of Concentration* (1980) is one such text. Although daunting, it's considered to be one of the most comprehensive texts on understanding the subtle body. For those of you, however, interested in one of the other, more comprehensive studies of these energy centers and channels and how they may correlate to the physical body's anatomy, I recommend you read Hiroshi Motoyama, *Theories of the Chakras: Bridge to Higher Consciousness* (Wheaton, IL: The Theosophical Publishing House, 1981). I'm particularly indebted to Motoyama's thorough empirical, scholarly, and personal insight. Readers also may find of value and interest the following studies:

- Arpita, "Physiological and Psychological Effects of Hatha Yoga: A Review of the Literature," *The Journal of The International Association of Yoga Therapists*, 1(1990): 1–28.
- Vinod D. Desmukh, "Neurophysiological interpretation of ida, pingala and sushumna," *Holistic Science and Human Values* 2 (1995): 68ff. Reprinted from *Neurology India*: 1991.

3. B.K.S. Iyengar, *Light on Yoga (Yoga Dipika)* (Harper Collins: India, 1999): 425.

CHAPTER FOUR: Inspiration and Joyful Concentration:
A Matter of Breath

1. Patanjali defines *dharana* as the sixth limb of yoga—an advanced state that leads to meditation and bliss, the seventh and eighth limbs respectively. Shyam Sundar Goswami elucidates the extensive practices of *dharana* common among some schools of yoga in his *Layayoga: An Advanced Method of Concentration* (London: Routledge & Kegan Paul, 1980).

2. B. K. Anand, G. S. Chhina, and B. Singh, "Some Aspects of EEG Studies in Yogis," *EEG and Clinical Neurophysiology* 13 (1961):452–456; B. Timmons, J. Salamy, J. Kamiya, and D. Girton, "Abdominal, Thoracic Respiratory Movements and Levels of Arousal," *Psychonomic Science* 27 (1972):173–5.

3. Ibid. See Herbert Benson, M.D., and William Proctor. *The Breakout Prin-*

ciple (New York: Scribner's, 2003) for recent research on how breath awareness releases nitric oxide, a key brain chemical that heightens creativity.

4. Swami Buddhananda, *Moola Bandha: The Master Key*. (Yoga Publications Trust: Bihar, India, 2000): 1.

CHAPTER FIVE: Dummies and Self-Study: Creating an Authentic Voice

1. Seamus Heaney, Introduction, *Beowulf: A New Verse Translation* (New York: W. W. Norton & Co., 2000): xxiii.

CHAPTER SIX: Practicing Presence: Ways to Heed and Harness Your Senses

1. Barbara Kingston, *The Poisonwood Bible* (New York: HarperPerennial, 1998): 13.

2. George Lakoff and Mark Johnson, *Philosophy in the Flesh: The Embodied Mind and its Challenge to Western Thought* (New York: Basic Books, 1999): 25, 26. George Lakoff and Mark Johnson make a compelling case for the ways our bodies influence how we construct ideas and concepts such as love, courage, and truth. Even our experience of color, they contend, our experience of blue phlox and of red poppies, doesn't come solely from any objective quality of a thing outside of human beings but comes from how human beings' physical circuitry interprets the ways light hits the surfaces of the outside world. "[C]olor is created jointly by our biology and the world," they write. "[T]he qualities of things as we can experience and comprehend them depend crucially on our neural makeup, our bodily interactions with them, and our purposes and interests. For real human beings, the only realism is an embodied realism."

3. Georg Feurstein, *The Shambhala Encyclopedia of Yoga* (Boston: Shambhala, 2000): 129.

4. Miranda Shaw, *Passionate Enlightenment: Women in Tantric Buddhism* (New York: Princeton University Press, 1994): 22.

5. Mircea Eliade, *Yoga: Immortality and Freedom* (New York: Princeton University Press, 1969): 204.

6. Ibid, 234–5.

CHAPTER SEVEN: Writing with Wonder and an Awakened Imagination

1. Swami Lakshmanjoo, *Shiva-Sutra: The Supreme Awakening* (Universal Shaiva Fellowship, 2002). The Kashmiri adept Vasugupta composed this text in the early ninth century. I am indebted to Swami Kahsmanjoo's commentaries on the *Shiva-Sutra*.

2. The play between waking and dreaming, the outer and inner, is the heart, too, of a practice called Tibetan Dream Yoga and Nidra Yoga (Sleep Yoga). These types of yoga include practices of lucid dreaming to heighten awareness about the nature of reality and self, to increase control of circumstances, and thereby to recognize the boundless possibilities of existence.

3. In more than one interview, Baker has noted that he doesn't fret about readers' wondering how much of his characters are "him." One novel he said is "87 percent myself." Another novel he said stemmed from remembering how,

when in fourth grade, he wished he could stop time so he could read the chalk-board while the teacher stood still. Then, he imagined, with time stopped, he could take off the teacher's clothes. From that boyhood fantasy, a novel was born.

4. Gladys Cardiff, "Combing," *To Frighten a Storm*, reprinted in *The Gift of Tongues*, ed. Sam Hamill (Port Townsend, WA, 1996): 41.

5. Green, Elmer and Alyce Green, *Beyond Biofeedback* (New York: Dela-court, 1977); K. C. Khare and S. K. Nigam, "A Study of Electroencephalogram in Meditators," *Indian Journal of Physiological Pharmacology* 44.2 (2000): 173–8.

CHAPTER EIGHT: Embodied Metaphors
and Symbols: The Brain's Yearning for Unity

1. George Lakoff and Mark Johnson. *Philosophy in the Flesh: The Embodied Mind and its Challenge to Western Thought* (New York: Basic Books, 1999).

2. Ibid. See especially Chapter Three, "The Embodied Mind," Chapter Four, "Primary Metaphor and Subjective Experience," and Chapter Five, "The Anatomy of Complex Metaphor."

3. This shift from a changing body to an altered worldview is precisely what author and Kundalini Yoga practitioner Terry Wolverton of Los Angeles de-scribed to me as having happened to her. Her whole outlook on life's possibilities and on other human beings has changed so subtly yet significantly that, of course, her writing's point of view has changed as well. My experience within two or three years of consistent yoga practice affecting my writing reflects Wolverton's.

4. Mitti Mohan, "Nostril Dominance (*Svara*) and Bilateral Volar Galvanic Skin Resistance," *International Journal of Yoga Therapy* 9 (1999): 33–40.

5. Annie Dillard, *Holy the Firm* (New York: Harper & Row, 1977): 17–18.

6. Henry David Thoreau, *Walden* (Penguin: New York, 1983): 354.

CHAPTER NINE: Bliss in a Toothbrush

1. Although different schools of yoga define *samādhi* differently and far more complexly than what I'm offering here, I'm of the view that bliss need not be overly mystified, lest it lead our thoughts away from the grandeur of this world; as writers we need ways to be at once in and out of this world.

2. Nicholson Baker, *The Mezzanine* (New York: Random House, 1986): 49–50.

3. Herbert Benson, M.D., of Harvard University reviews his own team's studies as well as those of other scientists in *The Breakout Principle* (New York: Scribner, 2003).

CHAPTER TEN: Tuning into Your Prose's Embodied Sounds

1. James Joyce, *A Portrait of the Artist as a Young Man* (New York: Viking Press 1969): 7.

2. William Faulkner, "The Bear," *Three Famous Short Novels* (New York: Vintage 1961): 194.

3. Suzanne Britt, "That Lean and Hungry Look," *Newsweek* (9 October 1978).

4. Annie Dillard, *Pilgrim at Tinker Creek* (New York: HarperCollins Perennial Classics, 1999): 79.

CHAPTER ELEVEN: The Pulse of a Sentence and the Yoga of Syntax

1. Seamus Heaney, "Introduction," *Beowulf* (New York: W. W. Norton & Co., 2000): xxiii.
2. George Lakoff and Mark Johnson, *Philosophy in the Flesh: The Embodied Mind and its Challenge to Western Thought* (New York: Basic Books, 1999): 13.
3. Don DeLillo, *The Body Artist* (New York: Simon & Schuster, 2001): 12.
4. Dianne Ackerman, *A Natural History of the Senses* (New York: Random House Vintage Books, 1990): 109.
5. Rick Moody, *Purple America* (Boston: Little, Brown & Co., 1997): 3, 7.
6. Maxine Kumin, "Morning Swim," *Our Ground Time Here Will Be Brief* (New York: Viking Books, 1981).
7. Annie Dillard, *Pilgrim at Tinker Creek* (New York: HarperCollins Perennial Classics, 1999): 3.

CHAPTER TWELVE: Straight from the Mouth: Artful Dialogue as Revelation

1. Jack Hitt, Act V, Episode 218, Dir. Ira Glass. *This American Life*, WBEZ, Chicago, 9 August 2002.
2. Ibid.
3. Charles Baxter, "The Cliff," *Harmony of the World* (Columbia, MO: University of Missouri Press, 1984).
4. John Cheever, "Reunion," *The Stories of John Cheever* (New York: Alfred A. Knopf, 1962).
5. Nathaniel Hawthorne, *The Scarlet Letter* (New York: Bantam, 1986).

CHAPTER THIRTEEN: The Art of Wandering in First Drafts

1. Kent Haruf, "To See Your Story Clearly, Start by Pulling the Wool Over Your Eyes," *Writers [on Writing]: Collected Essays from* The New York Times (New York: Henry Holt and Co., 2001): 87.

CHAPTER FOURTEEN: Dogs, Lovers, and Other Things That Bite: Writing the Truth

1. B.K.S. Iyengar, *Light on the Yoga Sutras of Patanjali* (New York: Harper-Collins, 1993): 142.
2. Ibid.
3. Roy J. Mathews, *The True Path: Western Science and the Quest for Yoga* (Cambridge, MA: Perseus Publishing, 2001): 47–49.
4. Ibid, 57–59. I am indebted to Mathews for his information and for his thorough argument of how the brain experiences truth as expressed in the Vedas and Upanishads.
5. Mohandas K. Gandhi, *Autobiography: The Story of My Experiments with Truth* (New York: Dover Publications, 1983): 284.

CHAPTER FIFTEEN:
The Inner Heckler Laughs Even at Sages: Facing Fear

1. I am indebted to Thomas Moore's interpretation of this myth in his book *Soul Mates: A Guide for Cultivating Depth and Sacredness in Everyday Life* (New York: Harper Perennial, 1994) in the context of the spirit and soul of relationships.

2. J. Mager, Vijayendra Pratap, Barbara Levitt, John Hanifin, George Brainard, "The Influence of Classical Yoga Practices on Plasma Cortisol Levels." ENDO 2003, Philadelphia, PA, June 2003. The Endocrine Society Web site: http://www.endo-society.org/pubrelations/pressreleases/archives/2003/yoga_endo.cfm (19 September 2003).

3. Andre Dubus, "Witness," *Meditations from a Movable Chair* (New York: Random House Vintage, 1999).

4. Stephen Mitchell, translator. *Bhagavad Gita* (New York: Harmony Books, 2000): 55.

CHAPTER SIXTEEN: You are Wide and Full of Contradictions:
Writing Based on Your Self

1. Nancy Maris, *Remembering the Bone House: An Erotics of Time and Space* (Boston: Beacon Press, 1995): xiii.

2. F. Scott Fitzgerald, *The Crack-Up*, ed. Malcolm Cowley (New York: New Directions Press, 1945).

3. Adrienne Rich, "Integrity," *A Wild Patience Has Taken Me This Far* (New York: Norton, 1981).

CHAPTER EIGHTEEN: Compassion for Your Characters—
the Good, the Bad, and the Downright Depraved

1. I am grateful to Joseph Chilton Pearce's description of the heart in relation to the HeartMath Institute's research in his book *The Biology of Transcendence: A Blueprint of the Human Spirit* (Rochester, Vermont: Park Street Press, 2002).

2. Rosellen Brown, "Characters' Weaknesses Build Fiction's Strengths," *Writers [on Writing]: Collected Essays from* The New York Times (Henry Holt and Co: New York, 2001).

CHAPTER NINETEEN: Converting Anger into Authentic Writing

1. "I'll Try Anything with a Detached Air of Superiority," *The Onion*, Vol. 38, No. 41, 2002 Rptd. in *The Best American Nonrequired Reading 2003* (Boston: Houghton Mifflin Co., 2003): 222, 223.

CHAPTER TWENTY: Eating Leaves and Other Ways to Re-Vision for Form

1. Paul Heilker, *The Essay: Theory and Pedagogy for an Active Form* (Urbana: NCTE, 1996): 169.

2. John Cheever, "Reunion," *The Stories of John Cheever* (New York: Alfred A. Knopf, 1962).

3. Gary Soto, *A Summer Life* (New York: Bantam Doubleday Dell Books, 1990).

CHAPTER TWENTY-THREE: For Writers Who Already Practice Yoga

1. See particularly Chapter Nine of H. David Coulter's exceptional text *The Anatomy of Hatha Yoga: A Manual for Students, Teachers, and Practitioners* (Pennsylvania: Body and Breath, 2001).

Acknowledgments

Numerous allies on my journey have heped me directly or indirectly to write this book. First, I am indebted to my first agent, Laureen Rowland, whose genuine enthusiasm, from our first conversation, helped make this book a reality. I'm blessed, too, for my editor. Lauren Marino of Gotham Books has proven to be an exception in every sense. Her refreshing honesty, editorial acumen, and vision of this book carried me through much of this trip. Thanks, too, to Hilary Terrell of Gotham Books for her contributions to this manuscript, for countless hours of selfless assistance, and for promptly replying to many queries. I also appreciate Wendy Kagan and Michael Belfiore for critiquing parts of this manuscript as well as my agent Linda Loewenthal for her patience and balanced perspective. I also appreciate Mickey Pantano's graceful touch with this book's photographs.

A teacher is no teacher without students, and I am grateful to the thousands of writing students, yoga students, and workshop participants of the last seventeen years without whom this book would be meaningless. Thanks also for those students who not only have contributed their examples to this book but who also have been the immediate source of inspiration for many of this book's ideas. The good people at Byrdcliffe Artists Colony and Earthdance Retreat Center as well as many friends at various stages of this book's progress gave me a room of my own during my travels. Thanks also to the work of Georg Feurstein and of the Yoga Research and Education Center whose scholarly integrity inspires me, and to Trish Feurstein of the YREC for assisting me in my research. I appreciate, too, neuroscientist Adam Zeman of the University of Edinburgh and scholar Fred Turner of The University of Texas at Dallas for responding to my pesky questions about the brain.

And thanks to my wife Cory for walking by my side without wavering and for reading with honesty many parts of this manuscript.